THE PAST IS A FUTURE COUNTRY

THE COMING CONSERVATIVE DEMOGRAPHIC REVOLUTION

Edward Dutton and
J.O.A. Rayner-Hilles

SOCIETAS
essays in political
& cultural criticism

imprint-academic.com

Copyright © Edward Dutton and J.O.A. Rayner-Hilles, 2022

The moral rights of the authors have been asserted.
No part of this publication may be reproduced in any form
without permission, except for the quotation of brief passages
in criticism and discussion.

Published in the UK by
Imprint Academic, PO Box 200, Exeter EX5 5YX, UK

Distributed in the USA by
Ingram Book Company,
One Ingram Blvd., La Vergne, TN 37086, USA

ISBN 9781788360753 Paperback

A CIP catalogue record for this book is available from the
British Library and US Library of Congress

The past is a foreign country;
They do things differently there.
   — L.P. Hartley, The Go-Between.

Come out of her, my people,
lest you take part in her sins,
lest you share in her plagues
         — Revelation, 18:3.

Contents

Acknowledgements		viii
Chapter 1.	**The Paradox of Left-Wing Hegemony in the Twenty-First Century**	**1**
	The End of the *Chatterley* Ban	1
	Who Breeds?	4
	What Will the Future Hold?	7
	The 1960s: The Tipping Point	9
	The New Tipping Point…	10
	The Rise and Fall of Civilizations	11
	The Retreat of a Fallen Civilization	13
	'It Couldn't Happen to Us'	15
	'Oh, Yes It Could…'	20
Chapter 2.	**The Psychology of Conservatives and Liberals**	**21**
	Free Bloody Birds	21
	Look Left, Look Right	22
	Why the Woke Are Not the 'New Conservatives'	25
	Individualists and Tribalists	28
	Not 'Business as Usual'	33
Chapter 3.	**Why Does Culture Always Seem to Move to the Left?**	**35**
	Proto-Protestantism and the Peasants Revolt of 1381	35
	Haidt's Moral Foundations	37
	Moral Foundations, Liberals, and Conservatives	40
	Moral Foundations and the Move to the Left	42
	Out-Group Loyalty and Intransigence	43
	Hijacking the Culture	44
	Intellectual Conformity and Intelligence	47
	Why Do Societies Move to the Right? The Case of Margaret Thatcher	48
	Related Models of Societal Cycles	52
	How Can Leftists Be Individualists?	57
	Understanding Group Selection	60

Chapter 4.	**The Weakening of Group Selection**	**63**
	Those Who Remain	63
	The Rise and Fall of Intelligence	65
	The Flynn Effect	68
	The Industrial Revolution and Its Consequences	70
	The Remaining Individualizers	74
	The Critique of Religion and Its Consequences	78
	The Death of the Individualizers	81
	The Consequences of Extreme Individualism	85
	Intelligence and Not Wanting Children	88
	Why Bad Ideas Come from the Middle Classes	90
	The Consequences of Collapsing Group Selection	92
Chapter 5.	**The Future Belongs to Those Who Turn Up**	**97**
	And That Much Never Can Be Obsolete	97
	The Heritability of Conservatism and Religiousness	98
	Who is Reproducing?	99
	From One Extreme to Another?	102
	Understanding Heritability	105
	The Advantage of the Right	106
	Why is this Happening?	108
	Why is Religiousness Associated with Fertility?	113
	Modelling and Reservations about Modelling	114
Chapter 6.	**Modelling the Future**	**119**
	A Waste Land?	119
	The Decline of American Intelligence	121
	The Rise of the Underclass	122
	The Death of Liberalism	125
	Generation Z's Rebellion	129
	Examining Our Data	130
	The Conservatism Promotion Effect	133
	The Low IQ Rebellion, Led by High IQ Autistics and Psychopaths	135

	American Politics as a Racial Game	136
	American Political Affiliation	139
	'It Don't Matter If You're Black or White'	142
	Why Non-Whites Might White-Align	148
	A Darker Left Throws the Woke to the Wolves	150
	Rising Liberalism Among Some Non-Whites	151
	The Nearer Term	154
	The Breakdown of the Education System	160
Chapter 7.	**The New Byzantiums**	**162**
	Most Things May Never Happen…	162
	Autumnal Societies and Intelligence	165
	How Roman Civilization Held On	166
	Our Classical Collapse	168
	The Right-Wing Backlash	171
	McCarthyism in Reverse	172
	Now is the Summer of Love Made Glorious Winter by Our Discontent	177
	The Concurrent Decline of Western Civilization	183
	Problems with the Classical Comparison	187
	The Late Bronze Age Collapse	189
Chapter 8.	**The Long Slide**	**193**
	Never Such Innocence	193
	A Scenario Road Map to the New Dark Age	195
	Environmental Catastrophe	196
	Economic Catastrophe: The Break-Up of Nations	199
	A Rural Renaissance?	203
	Calling in the Debts	204
	Paradise	209
References		**211**
About the Authors		242

Acknowledgements

We would like to thank Dr. Michael Woodley of Menie for reading through the manuscript and providing useful feedback. This book also draws upon parts of *At Our Wits' End: Why We're Becoming Less Intelligent and What It Means for the Future* by Edward Dutton and Michael Woodley of Menie (2018). We would like to thank Dr. Mike McCulloch for also reading through and providing insightful comments on this book. We are grateful to Dr. Gerhard Meisenberg for his comments on an early version of the manuscript and for his assistance with aspects of the data analysis. Similarly, we extend our thanks to Professor Heiner Rindermann for reading and providing his comments on the book and also to Mr. H.R. English for his helpful comments. Edward Dutton would like to thank Herr Emil Kirkegaard, as discussions with him on aspects of the manuscript have been very fruitful and he has forwarded much useful literature. Edward Dutton would also like to thank all of the drinkers at *The Jolly Heretic,* many of whose stimulating questions have helped him to develop his thinking with regard to aspects of the subject explored in this book. In particular, he would like to acknowledge Professor Paul Gottfried and Herr Froði Midjord, interviews with whom helped to clarify his thinking in a number of areas. J.O.A. Rayner-Hilles would like to express his gratitude to Mr. Lewis Low for locating several salient studies and assisting him in analysing the graphs. Finally, we would like to extend our gratitude to Dr. Sean Gabb for his role in bringing the two authors together.

Edward Dutton and J.O.A. Rayner-Hilles
August 2021

Chapter One

The Paradox of Left-Wing Hegemony in the Twenty-First Century

'Sexual intercourse began
In nineteen sixty-three
(which was rather late for me) —
Between the end of the 'Chatterley' ban
And the Beatles' first LP.'[1]

The End of the *Chatterley* Ban

In many of his verses, the celebrated English poet Philip Larkin (1922–1985) attempted to capture the dramatic changes in Western culture that had begun to crystallize by the 1960s. For this modest university librarian, who wrote a few lines every evening after work (Rossen, 1989, Ch. 1), it was as though an Old World was passing away and a New World was not merely being born but was living through the prime of its youth.

The Old World might reasonably have been called 'conservative' or 'right-wing'. It firmly believed in traditional religiousness, specifically Christianity and the kind of 'conservative' morality with which this was associated. Sexuality was something taboo and shameful; only to be explored within Christian marriage for the purposes of having children. Backed-up by Christian teaching, males and females had clear and distinct roles, ordained by God. There was an accepted social order and this was not only natural but desirable. It was believed that people were very much 'unequal' and that they, therefore, naturally divided into social classes in a hierarchy at the top of which sat the monarch and then God Himself who, of course, existed. In fact, recognizing that people were not

---

[1] 'Annus Mirabilis' (Larkin, 1974).

'equal' was clearly positive for society as a whole—because people would perform the roles of which they were the most capable—and that was far more important than how individuals might *feel*. If the best people were placed in the correct positions, then society would be more likely to triumph in the battle over resources, influence, and power with other societies. After all, the English were, essentially, an extended family who wished to ensure that they were the wealthiest and most successful of all families in the world. And their motivation for doing this was, in part, that they perceived themselves to be God's chosen people (Purchase, 2006, p. 101) and, thus, fully deserving of world dominance, which they pursued for the greater glory of God. There were variations, such as along social class lines, in the extent to which they conformed to the relatively puritanical lifestyle to which this gave rise. The morality of the 'lower orders' was, in fact, a matter for constant concern (McEnery, 2004, p. 72). However, this was broadly how England, and other Western countries, could be described. 'This happy breed of men, this little world, This precious stone set in the silver sea, Which serves it in the office of a wall, Or as a moat defensive to a house, Against the envy of less happier lands', as Shakespeare put it in *Richard II* (Act II, Scene I).

Around the time of World War I, this was the dominant way of thinking, though even by then it was beginning to be questioned. By 1963, it was beginning to fall apart as the culture turned to a 'liberal' and 'left-wing' way of seeing the world (Murray, 2012). This was characterized not only by a belief in the importance of 'equality', but also by an emphasis on personal freedom: on the right of the *individual* to live as he or she wished. Traditional religiousness, and the social order and system of morality which it upheld, began to be cast aside. The novel *Lady Chatterley's Lover* (Lawrence, 1960) by English writer D.H. Lawrence (1885-1930)—privately printed in 1928 and banned in Britain for being obscene—had been published in the UK in 1960, resulting in an obscenity trial in which a Church of England bishop had argued in its favour (Mews, 2012). In 1963, this same bishop—John A.T. Robinson (1919-1983), Bishop of Woolwich in southeast London—published a book, *Honest to God*, in which he seemed to deny almost every Christian doctrine, including the literal existence of the Almighty (Robinson, 1963). By the end of the 1960s, male homosexuality was legal in England, abortion had been decriminalized, and there were growing campaigns for the rights of women and for the rights of ethnic minorities (see Goodhart, 2017).

The taboo on sexuality heavily declined over time. It became increasingly acceptable to get divorced, and even to commit adultery and to have illegitimate children. By 1994, there were female priests in the Church of England (Saunders, 18th March 1994). By the early 2000s, the ban on gays in the British army had been overturned (Jones, 2019), the age of homosexual consent had been equalized with that of heterosexual consent at 16 (Kilkelly, 2017), and by 2016 women were allowed in military combat roles (*BBC News,* 8th July 2016). Then there was adoption by unmarried gay couples, which began in 2005 (Mulholland, 30th December 2005), gay marriage, legalized in Britain in 2013 (*BBC News,* 17th July 2013), and, most recently, a campaign for 'equality' for transsexuals, with the meaning of the word 'transphobia' still needing to be explained to newspaper readers in 2009 (Tozer, 19th May 2009). This process, more broadly, has actually been termed 'the Great Liberalisation' and it has paralleled public attitudes becoming increasingly accepting, across time, of these kinds of changes (Goodhart, 2017, p. 38).

The British *Social Attitudes Survey* records this liberalizing shift, even between 1983 and 2012, and it has been substantial. In 1983, 68% of Britons belonged to a specific religion; by 2012 this was down to 52%. Across the same period, the percentage of the population who identified as 'Anglican' halved from 40% to just 20%. In 1989, 70% of British people felt that 'people who want children ought to get married'. By 2012, this had declined to 42%. Indeed, in 1983, 28% of the population believed it was 'always or mostly wrong' to have sex outside of marriage. By 2012, this had fallen to just 11%. Sixty-four percent of British people, in 1989, felt that women should stay at home until their child started school, but this was a mere 33% by 2012. In 1983, 50% of the British population asserted that homosexual relationships were 'always wrong', rising to 64% by 1987 (Park et al., 2013), in the wake of increasing popular knowledge about the AIDS epidemic which was heavily impacting homosexuals (Vincent, 2016, p. 38). By 2012, only 22% of the population took the view that homosexuality was morally wrong. Opposition to gay couples being allowed to adopt children fell from 87% in 1983 to 52% in 2012 (Park et al., 2013).

Before long, we had created a culture that was so left-wing—and so liberal—that it would have been unthinkable even when Larkin wrote about what had happened by the end of the 1960s:

'When I see a couple of kids
And guess he's fucking her and she's
Taking pills or wearing a diaphragm,
I know this is paradise.'

But that Larkin poem—'High Windows' (Larkin, 1974)—hit upon something particularly intriguing; something which is key to this book. The young, liberal couple is having lots of sex, but they are not going to have children. After all, she's 'Taking pills or wearing a diaphragm'. Larkin continues, musing on how this world is the one that everyone 'old has dreamed of all their lives'. The conservative England of 'bonds and gestures' has been 'pushed aside', with young people left 'going down the long slide / To happiness, *endlessly...*'; to a world with *'No God, anymore...'*. This makes Larkin suddenly nostalgic for that lost England that *was* in touch with something eternal; where there was a different kind of 'happiness'.

Who Breeds?

But a shrinking minority of people *have* stayed in touch with that sense of the eternal. They hold to the values of the traditional England, including being 'conservative' (as currently defined) and being 'religious'. And those people—unlike those who are liberal and left-wing—have children. Many of them have *lots* of children. As we will see in more detail later, there is a substantial fertility advantage in Western countries to people who are on the political 'far right'; those who might be described as 'extreme conservatives'. This advantage exists even when you control for being religious, something which crosses over with being an 'extreme conservative' as we will show anon. And there also exists a substantial fertility advantage to simply being extremely religious (Fieder & Huber, 2018). As we will discuss in greater depth, both religiousness and political orientation are highly heritable. Differences in how religious you are, or in how right-wing you happen to be, are influenced, to a substantial extent, by your genes, something that has been discerned from studies of identical twins (Bradshaw & Ellison, 2008; Hatemi et al., 2014).

This fact is the fundamental paradox which our book aims to solve. Modern culture appears to move ever-leftwards—ever-more in the direction of individualizing values, the promotion of equality as a good in itself, scepticism about traditional religiosity and its morality, and self-actualization being the essence of the good life. Yet, at least since the 1960s, fertility has been associated with traditional religiousness and with being right-wing; the more right-wing, the greater the fertility advantage. Those who are high in fertility are strong in 'binding moral foundations'; that is, the belief that the group is more important than the individual. They do not perceive equality as a good in itself and they often believe that people are *not* equal. They believe in traditional religiousness and they are also ethnocentric, geared towards promoting their own ethnic group which they perceive, accurately based on analyses of genetic assay data, as an extended genetic family. Two random Englishmen are more closely related than a random Englishman and a random Frenchman, meaning that, in a war, it would sometimes make sense, in terms of promoting your evolutionary fitness (the direct and indirect maximization of the extent to which your genes are passed on), to lay down your life for your ethnic group (see Salter, 2007; Hamilton, 1996, 1964). They hold to the worldview of religiousness and national interest that was common a century ago. In that the heritability of these viewpoints is high as we will explore later, we would surely expect society to become ever-more right-wing, both due to genetics and due to the transmission of right-wing views within families.

Of course, it is not just religious people who tend to breed, although the other groups that breed do, to some extent, promote greater religiousness. Another group that tends to have large families is the less intelligent. In science, a correlation is a relationship between two variables. If one increases as the other increases, it's a positive correlation with 1 being an absolute positive correlation. The correlation is 'statistically significant' if we can be at least 95% certain, based on the sample size and strength of the correlation, that it is not a fluke. There is a weak but significant negative correlation, of -0.1, between fertility and IQ among white people, -0.16 among white women. Among black women in America, it is even stronger, at -0.27, all based on large samples (Meisenberg, 2010). Intelligence, which we will discuss in more detail anon, is defined as the ability to solve cognitive problems combined with how quickly you can solve them. The quicker you can solve the problem, and the harder it has to be before you're stumped, the more 'intelligent' you are. A key predictor of socio-economic status is intelligence. Your IQ ('Intelligence Quotient') is how well you score in IQ tests compared to others of your age. The scores are strongly associated with other measures of cognitive ability, such as academic attainment, as well as with concrete measures such as your reaction times — the quicker you react to stimuli, the quicker you solve problems — and brain size; the brain being a thinking muscle. IQ tests are 'culture fair' because groups that score poorly in them score the most poorly on the most 'culture fair' components of the test, which are actually the best measures of intelligence (Jensen, 1998). Furthermore, the notion of 'stereotype threat' — that groups stereotyped to do poorly on IQ tests perform badly on them due to the stress of some stereotype about them doing badly — has been comprehensively refuted. Some groups primed with the idea that they will do badly do better than expected, and there is clear publication bias, with theses that don't substantiate the thesis not being published (Ganley et al., 2013).

Intelligence is important in, and is prized in, all cultures, with negative correlates of intelligence, such as criminality, being disliked in all cultures (see Jensen, 1998). The negative correlation between fertility and intelligence in industrialized countries exists for a number of reasons, such as that intelligent people are more efficient users of contraception (Lynn,

2011, p. 67) and partly because intelligent people simply desire fewer or no children in these countries (Kanazawa, 2012, Ch. 12). But intelligence is also weakly negatively associated with being religious (Dutton, 2014) for reasons that remain a matter of debate (Dutton & Van der Linden, 2017).

Certain personality traits also predict fertility and these personality traits have been found to be approximately 0.5 heritable (Nettle, 2007, p. 232). It would seem to be the case that those who have a strong desire to nurture and to care for others; who are high in the personality trait 'Agreeableness' (altruism and empathy), would want to have children and they do (Jokela, 2012), and this trait, anyway, is associated with religiosity in all cultures for reasons we will explore later (Gebauer et al., 2014). Similarly, 'Neuroticism' (mental instability, anxiety, depression) is being selected against (Jokela, 2012) and religious people tend to be highly mentally stable (Dutton et al., 2018) for reasons we will also look at shortly, with the exception of converts and others who go through phases of intense religiosity before returning to being relatively irreligious (Hills et al., 2004). Likewise, autism—which is characterized by an obsession with systematizing and a lack of empathy—is negatively associated with religiousness (Dutton et al., 2018). This appears to be due to the autistic deficits in empathy or 'mentalizing' (Jack et al., 2016). Those who are high in empathy are obsessed with the external signals of internal states—the essence of empathy, reading the minds of others—to the extent that they find evidence of these in the world itself. Accordingly, for such people, there is a 'mind' behind the world. Schizophrenia partly involves 'hyper-mentalizing' ('hyper-empathy'), in which evidence of a mind is perceived everywhere (Badcock, 2003). Hence, schizophrenics tend to be hyper-religious, often having religious delusions (Koenig, 2012). But, crucially, autism means that you're introverted and lack social skills and you're irreligious, so it is negatively associated with fertility (Mullins et al., 2017).

The narrow trait of being extremely selfish and incentive-seeking is associated with fertility in women (Gutiérrez et al., 2013), possibly in part because having more children garners higher welfare payments in many welfare societies which the mothers can spend on themselves (Perkins, 2016). Those who are low in the personality trait 'Conscientiousness' (impulse control and rule following) actually have more children, simply for lack of fear and will, that would otherwise drive them to use contraception. And those who are high in the personality trait 'Extraversion' (feeling positive feelings strongly and taking risks in pursuit of them because you crave stimulation) also have more children, presumably because they are sexual risk takers (Jokela, 2012). Indeed, it has been found in Iceland that people who carry genes that are associated with Attention Deficit Hyper-Activity Disorder (ADHD), which manifests as poor impulse control, have elevated fertility compared to controls (Mullins et al., 2017). But, broadly, breeding patterns would predict increasing conservatism.

What Will the Future Hold?

So why are Western politics and culture becoming ever-more left-wing? Will these counter-current breeding forces ever reverse the trend, and if so, how and when?

We will argue that cultures will always tend to move leftwards because they are comprised of a balance of liberals and conservatives and these differ in terms of what are called 'Moral Foundations'. Conservatives are about equal in the five moral foundations, some of which are group-oriented — placing the good of the group above that of the individual — and some of which are individualist, placing the individual's good above that of the group. Liberals, by contrast, are high in individualizing foundations and *low* in group-binding foundations (Haidt, 2012). As a result, they will tend to hijack the culture and push it leftwards, because conservatives can empathize with liberals while liberals cannot empathize with conservatives. This will continue until an 'evolutionary mismatch' is reached, when people find themselves in an environment to which they are not evolved; something that creates unhappiness and dysphoria (Geher & Wedberg, 2019, p. 27). In this mismatch, most people's desires for binding foundations — such as in-group loyalty, order, and respect for the sacred — are not met, to the extent that it is intolerable. The result of this is often a 'conservative backlash', which will continue until too many people feel that their individualizing foundations — their concern with harm avoidance and equality — are not met. As we will see, these swings have occurred throughout political history.

However, we will show that while this backlash is likely to take place, the Western world is on the cusp of an even more fundamental shift. This shift is explicable in directly evolutionary terms. Until about 1800, we were under harsh conditions of Darwinian selection in which the child mortality rate was as high as 50% in the West (Volk & Atkinson, 2008). As such, we were very strongly adapted to our ecology, meaning that random mutation almost always made us less adapted to it. This meant that, every generation, the population was purged of those that had mutant genes — 'high mutational load' — and, thus, who had poor immune systems and could not fight off disease. We were also under an intense level of what is known as 'group selection'. This concept is controversial among some researchers, but we will demonstrate its veracity below. Group selection is the idea that there is a battle between groups — such as ethnic groups, which have been shown to be extended genetic families —

for resources (Salter, 2007). The groups which tend to triumph in this battle are those that are high in positive ethnocentrism (internal cooperation) and negative ethnocentrism (repelling the outsider) (Hammond & Axelrod, 2006). In other words, we were under selection to be optimally group-oriented; to be low in 'individualism'. We were also under selection to be religious. Religiosity is strongly genetic (Bradshaw & Ellison, 2008) and tends to promote binding foundations—acting in the interest of the group—as God's will (Sela et al., 2015). And we were under selection to be intelligent. This is because intelligence was associated with wealth (Jensen, 1998) and being wealthy meant that more of your children would survive due to the better living conditions you could provide for them. Thus, the wealthier 50% of the population had a fertility advantage of about 100% over the poorer 50%, based on English parish record data from the seventeenth century (Pound, 1972).

As we will see, and as has been laid out in depth in an earlier book co-authored by one of us, *At Our Wits' End: Why We're Becoming Less Intelligent and What It Means for the Future* (Dutton & Woodley of Menie, 2018), the results of this rising intelligence—noted in our becoming more literate and numerate across time and even our heads getting bigger to accommodate our larger brains—were, eventually, the breakthroughs of the Industrial Revolution. This changed everything by introducing inoculations against killer childhood diseases, other medical innovations, healthier living conditions, cheaper food, and much else. The consequence was that environmental harshness was heavily weakened, with child mortality collapsing from 50% in 1800 to 1% or less today (Volk & Atkinson, 2008). Group-selection pressure was also weakened, as groups no longer had to battle for scarce resources in order to feed their populations. Accordingly, the human population level exploded and mutation from the pre-Industrial 'norm'—intelligent, religious, genetically healthy, and group-oriented—ceased to be selected out. We will show that the result of this was not only more and more people who were high in mutational load, and thus physically and mentally ill, but more and more people who are 'individualists', as it is individualism that is, inherently, the deviation from what we were previously selecting for.

The result was also falling average intelligence, to the extent that—for reasons we will explore in more detail later—there is now a negative association between intelligence and fertility which exists for genetic reasons. We will also see that an individualistic worldview correlates with mental illness and other evidence of high mutational load. The *culture*, becoming more concerned with individualistic values of harm avoidance and equality, also changed in such a way as to reduce intelligence. The rise of feminism meant that the more intelligent women tended to delay childbearing and thus limit their fertility. The rise of contraception meant that low intelligence people, who tend not to think too much about the future, would get pregnant by accident. The rise of welfare, with council housing provided according to need and extra 'benefits' for each child, effectively encouraged low IQ people to have children (Lynn, 2011, p. 68). Indeed, at the time of writing, in the UK, if we divide between families where both parents are working (IQ of about 100), families where one parent is on welfare (IQ of around 90), families where both parents are on welfare (IQ of about 85 or less), and designated 'troubled households', that require interventions from the authorities and in which both parents are on welfare, only the 'troubled households' are breeding at above replacement fertility. Moreover, fertility increases the more welfare dependent the household is (Perkins, 2016, p. 159; Committee on Finance, 1996, p. 101). Based on twin studies, the heritability of IQ in adult samples is roughly 0.8 (Lynn, 2011, p. 101; Jensen, 1972, p. 294). So, in that IQ is overwhelmingly genetic, it is obvious what this will auger for the future. It will mean a huge growth in the 'underclass'. But the key point is that a genetic change led to a cultural change, which had further genetic consequences.

The 1960s: The Tipping Point

It has been found in experiments that once approximately 20% of a group deviate from the group norm, a 'tipping point' is reached and people start to migrate, on mass, over to what they see as the powerful and up-and-coming way of seeing the world (Centola et al., 2018). We will argue that something like this happened in the 1960s, as the country tipped from being centred around binding foundations to being centred around individualizing foundations. The consequence was an arms race of left-wing virtue-signalling where people who, a few hundred years earlier, might have competed to signal their religiosity and group-orientation, began to signal their focus on 'equality' and 'harm avoidance'. This was more extreme among more intelligent people—people with higher IQ, better at solving cognitive problems—because intelligence predicts absorbing the dominant ideology and persuading yourself that you believe it due to the social gains associated with so doing (Woodley of Menie & Dunkel, 2015). This pushed society in an ever-more left-wing direction.

This kind of thing had happened before, but it was limited by the fact that, partly for genetic reasons, people were more resistant to individualism, they were more group-oriented and they were more fearful of inter-group conflict, with weakly group-oriented groups likely to be invaded and subjugated (Hammond & Axelrod, 2006). In the absence of these pressures, runaway individualism ensued, up to a point where

'Woke' leftism became associated with fitness-reducing ideas; and especially with not having children. An example of this can be found in extreme environmentalists renouncing procreation for the good of the planet, something that was reached after an arms race of signalling ever-more commitment to the environment, beginning with less radical signalling, such as recycling and vegetarianism. And it has also inculcated the population with guilt simply for being white (Grzanka et al., 2019), subjected them to many of examples of extreme evolutionary mismatch (which tend to cause dysphoria and maladaptive behaviour, including childlessness), and inculcated them with a sense that life has no purpose and that breeding is pointless, as we will explore below.

The New Tipping Point…

The result of this is that breeding became associated not just with low intelligence but also with being, for genetic reasons, religious and right-wing and, thus, resistant to Woke ideology. Drawing upon a large dataset we will model how this is likely to develop. Among the more intelligent, breeding will become associated with conservatism and with being religious, both of which are highly genetic. One may easily see how the political right's lesser contribution to fertility, against the greater tumultuous growth of the underclass, might at least slow down the terminal decline of society regarding moral standards. Intelligence has in recent history been negatively associated with religiousness and conservatism (Dutton, 2014). Yet don't be deceived by these correlations: the patterns in the fertility trends of the West, as we will analyse further on in this book, show that here, the right will put an immense stopper in the cognitive-capital haemorrhaging process.

We will show that, among those who have relatively high intelligence, religiousness and conservatism are *crucial* predictors of fertility. This is because 'liberal' intelligent people almost completely fail to have children due to the compounding handicaps of both 'intelligence' and 'liberalism'. Conservatism however, especially of the religious persuasion, goes very far to ameliorate or compensate for the fertility penalties on IQ; you might say conservatism 'protects' IQ—it protects a large female brain from sterilizing her womb with leftist ideology. Thus, unbeknown to the world at large, intelligence is in the process of becoming increasingly *more* associated with conservatism and religiousness. All the while the authoritarian left has been dominating the culture and institutions of the elite, beneath the surface, the elite are becoming more conservative, and it's only a matter of a couple more generations or so before they and their descendants are all that remains of today's cognitive upper-strata.

The Rise and Fall of Civilizations

Nevertheless, against the overwhelming downward trends in breeding, rest assured that this spells a 'Coming Apart' of the West. Declining intelligence is associated with decline in all of the robust correlates of intelligence. Intelligence is correlated with trust, the ability to delay gratification, belief in democracy (due to the need for trust inherent in it and the delay of gratification involved), low dogmatism, low criminality, low corruption, with educational attainment, wealth and socio-economic status achieved, social skill, civic participation, open-mindedness (as this helps to solve cognitive problems), sexual restraint (as this involves future-orientation), genetic mental and physical health, life expectancy, and much else. Thus, declining intelligence would predict a decline in every aspect of 'civilization' (Lynn & Vanhanen, 2012) because it would predict a decline in the ability to deal with social and cognitive complexity, just as it does in individuals (Oesterdiekhoff & Vonderach, 2021). Indeed, one study found that a general factor—likely group average intelligence—explained 52% of the variance in various measures of cultural complexity (Murdock & Provost, 1973). National average IQs have been found to predict all aspects of national development; in other words of 'civilization'. They strongly correlate with other indicators of national-level cognitive ability, such as scores in international student assessments and the frequency of alleles associated with high educational attainment (Piffer, 2018). They have been heavily criticized, and they have been completely recalculated in order to take these criticisms into account. The new national IQs correlate with the old ones at 0.87 (see Lynn & Becker, 2019).

Indeed, we will see in later chapters that human history has been marked by the rise and fall of civilizations and that the pattern is very similar every time. Under harsh conditions, civilizations begin as warlike and extremely religious. These conditions select for intelligence. This is selected for because intelligence permits people to better solve the problems with which these harsh conditions confront them. Such conditions also select for group-orientation, because working together as part of a group means you are better able to survive and to defeat rival groups. Such a group starts to produce an excess of resources, such that more and more people can pursue something other than agriculture and the population can grow. It develops towns and sufficient resource-excess that a growing class of people need not do any physical labour; able to concentrate on more intellectual concerns. Eventually, such a group becomes so intelligent that it creates some kind of 'civilization', which reduces these harsh conditions, such as through innovations like drainage, clean water, and military innovation such that the society cannot be invaded. If it then becomes warmer, this will permit even more people to turn away from agriculture, and the population will be able to expand due to the easier conditions. It grows in size but it ceases to select so strongly for intelligence and group-orientation. Intelligent people in particular—the members of the higher social classes—seem to stop wanting children, and the society starts to question its religion and other traditions (Glubb, 1976), an indication of high intelligence and of low stress, with mortality salience tending to make people religious (Norenzayan & Shariff, 2008) due to religiosity being an evolved cognitive bias, these manifesting especially at times of stress (Yu, 2016).

Eventually, such a society becomes highly individualistic and materialistic and, whether it is in Athens, Rome, or Baghdad, you see the rise of feminism and women in positions of power. In declining Baghdad there were even female lawyers and imams, because the religion, which had promoted patriarchy as the will of God, was no longer so strongly believed in (Glubb, 1976, p. 16). You see immigration (because the society ceases to believe in its God-given superiority), tolerance of sexual deviance and sexual freedom (because religious prohibitions on this are ignored), nihilism, childlessness, low social trust, extremism and polarization, and tyranny, as 'democracy' is associated with intelligence (Lynn & Vanhanen, 2012). The heroes at this stage are always entertainers, rather than explorers or military men. Science is questioned and debased by faux-profound sophists, and eventually intelligence is too low to maintain the innovations earlier bequeathed by the more intelligent ancestors. The civilization collapses; no longer bright enough to deal with the problems nature throws at it. The result is the collapse of the population, the abandoning of the cities, and a return to a simpler life on the land, and to harsher conditions. Then the cycle begins all over again (Glubb, 1976).

We know that this cycle is significantly a matter of intelligence, as one correlate of intelligence is per capita major innovation; major innovations per million of population per year. These are produced by the 'smart fraction' of a population, so if these are decreasing then, in general, the population's average intelligence is also decreasing (Rindermann, 2018, p. 199) These innovations rise and fall across time in parallel with civilizations rising and falling (Dutton & Woodley of Menie, 2018; Huebner, 2005a/b). This is part of a broader pattern called the 'Malthusian Cycle' which we will discuss anon. With regard to per capita major innovations in Classical civilization, this can be seen in Figure 1.1, where it can be observed that these major innovations decline until the collapse occurs, usually dated to the Fall of Rome in the year 410.

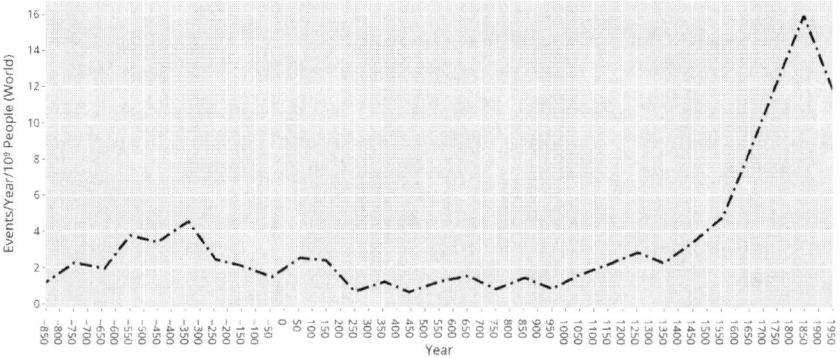

Figure 1.1. Rate of Major Innovations Per 10 million of World Population Across Time in the Ancient and Modern Worlds.

Everything that was once predicted to occur in a society of falling intelligence is now happening to the West. In 1938, English psychologist Raymond Cattell (1905–1998) set out what he thought would happen (Cattell, 1938). Cattell's shockingly prescient predictions included people spending longer at school (to try to compensate for slower learning), a fall in academic standards and thus grade inflation, a growing unemployable underclass, decreasing levels of major innovation, greater delinquency and a greater cultural focus on sex, growing political extremism (look at the rise of the Woke mobs), anti-democratic attitudes and general totalitarianism, reduced social cohesion, and increasing imitation of previous cultural achievements, as seen in the constant 'remakes' on television.

The Retreat of a Fallen Civilization

But all is not lost. The Roman Empire did not completely collapse. It *retreated,* to Byzantium. And we will explain how a small minority of conservative, intelligent people in the collapsing West will maintain Western civilization. By nothing more than ordinary push-pull economic migration a residual conservative-cognitive elite will 'break away' and 'escape' into citadel refuges, whilst the rest of the 'first world' dissolves back into the 'third world'. This broader idea of 'Coming Apart' from a purely class-based perspective has been explored by American political scientist Charles Murray (2012) in his book of the same name. But, here, we are able to build richer predictions on what sort of rupture is going to occur in the future, across all demographic markers, including class, politics, geographical location, intelligence, personality, and ethnicity.

Over the near term, we will show that Western people will flip to the right in a turbulent societal schism along political lines. A rising conservative elite will continue to drum up confidence, find its voice, and push back against its receding enemies on the opposing side. We'll see how a large sub-section of 'Generation Z' (those born at the end of the 1990s and later) has dramatically bucked the generational drift leftwards. Evidence of this trend (e.g. Kaufmann, 8th July 2020) has led some scholars, such as American political commentator, theologian, and classicist Steve Turley, to enthusiastically predict a 'Conservative Renaissance' whereby the forces of Wokeness will be vanquished and some kind of conservative utopia will be ushered in (e.g. Turley, 2019). This is, to some extent, wishful thinking. In his analysis of the rise and fall of civilizations, German philosopher Oswald Spengler (1880-1936) spoke of a 'Silver Age' that sometimes occurs during a decline; a mini-revival in civilization during a broader collapse, which may or may not be what Turley has in mind. But unless our predictions should all sound rather 'white-pilled', remember: the coming 'Silver Age' in politics is to coincide with a monumental collapse, not seen since the Bronze Age three thousand years ago. The world will drift into an over-population crisis of the very stupid and the very antisocial.

This book will be a story of exile and abandonment in that context, not triumph and rejuvenation. There will be a 'Great Escape', whereby intelligent, conservative people flee apocalyptic chaos to establish refuges of civilization in which they weather the storm of the Dark Age. Those exiled will be conservative, middle class, and white (defined very broadly), set against 'post-liberal' areas of mixed ethnic minorities, with some white admixture. Today, the Woke will continue to induce guilt in the white or otherwise 'privileged' middle-class population, but tomorrow the underclass will be the frightening majority of the Western population, and too vast in size, and offensive in character, to sustain further sympathy. Lower IQ whites, reluctant or unable to move due to the associations between low IQ and conservatism and between high IQ and migration, will simply merge into the majority non-white populations; dissolving away into extinction like the Neanderthals.

Conversely, escaping the chaos, we expect many of the higher IQ non-whites to ally and migrate with the higher IQ whites, where standard of living comes above ethnic allegiance. These will constitute the Byzantium-like refuges of civilization, as barbarian-anarchy mounts all around them, and that's what will survive of the 'Silver Age' collapse. Due to declining trust, greater genetic diversity (with genetic similarity predicting trust, as we will see) (Rushton, 2005), growing polarization, and lack of an external need to hold together in the face of a hostile group, nations will break up into smaller polities, as always happens in the winter of civilization. In the 200s, Britain was ruled by Rome and was, thus, united into one polity, with the exception of certain rebellious regions. In fact, for a brief period, Rome was ruled from Britain (Salway, 2001). By the 500s, England was a variety of separate Saxon kingdoms (Campbell, 1991).

But it gets worse. Our modelling indicates that, because those who lack a strong genetic desire to have children are being selected out by a Woke culture that dissuades them from having children, only those with a strong desire or habit to breed will be left. The result will be a huge spike in population just at the point where average intelligence is falling and in a context in which the low IQ majority will have very poor genetic mental and physical health. This association is in part due to the correlation between low intelligence and high mutational load (Banks et al., 2010). We were after all selected for intelligence and genetic health, meaning that the two are genetically related, and mutational load reduces brain functioning. Eventually, it will no longer be possible to feed or provide healthcare for these people. Most likely, a crisis will be set off by some kind of new virus which we simply lack the intelligence to cure and the resources to treat, as occurred in a limited way in India in April 2021 with regard to Covid-19 when there wasn't enough oxygen to treat patients (Dhar, 1st May 2021). The consequence of this will be a massive population collapse; mass death, in which, possibly, as much as 90% of the world population will die off over a relatively short period of time. This will be global, in a way that earlier collapses were not to the same extent, because of the globalized, interconnected nature of the modern world.

In this sense, we argue that in trying to understand where we are positioned now, we should not think of ourselves as akin to Romans in the fourth century—although, as we have seen, there is sound evidence from all kinds of markers of civilizational decline that we are at about that stage—but, rather, we should think of ourselves as like the Mycenaean Greeks, the Hittites, the New Kingdom Egyptians, the Assyrians, the Babylonians, and the Elamites, altogether circa 1200 BC, when the Late Bronze Age Collapse occurred, a collapse we will explore in greater depth below. It was followed by a Dark Age of about 800 years in which civilization only just held on (Cline, 2015).

'It Couldn't Happen to Us'

Despite the fact that every previous civilization has risen and fallen, and despite the evidence, which we will explore later, that we seem to be in the 'Winter' of this civilizational cycle, there are some people who insist that our civilization is 'unique' and that 'It'll never happen to us'.

It is possible that this belief may derive from the nature of the religion which has dominated our civilization: Christianity. Pagan religions tend to conceive of history as following a cyclical pattern, which is precisely what it appears to do when it comes to the rise and fall of civilizations. Christianity, in its traditional Augustinian form, understands time and history as linear; a constant progression starting from Genesis, moving through the Gospels, and culminating in an apocalyptic Judgement Day, followed by some kind of everlasting utopia after that. History, in other words, has a beginning and an end. There may have been some evolutionary benefits to holding this belief, and it may even have been, somehow, selected for. It may provide people with an incentive to strive and to not be fatalistic; a feeling that you are in control of your own destiny, and not subject to inevitable cycles about which you can do nothing at all (De Benoist, 2004). Possibly for this reason, there is often strong resistance to the idea that Western civilization could possibly collapse.

Justification for what appears to be a cognitive bias in favour of a linear understanding of history takes many forms. Firstly, people argue that a programme of eugenics could be developed in order to boost the intelligence of children. This could occur continuously, meaning that civilization could go on forever and we could colonize the solar system, the galaxy; perhaps even the entire universe. This seems witheringly unlikely. Society currently pursues individualistic, pro-equality values whereby anything that hints of 'eugenics' is regarded with horror. Accordingly, it appears most improbable that such a programme would ever be pursued. In order to pursue it, a society would have to be high in binding foundations, with a sense of its own eternal importance, just as it was in the nineteenth century, and even in the early twentieth century, when English scientist Sir Francis Galton (1822–1911) espoused just such a programme. He noted in 1865 that:

> 'One of the effects of civilization is to diminish the rigour of the application of the law of Natural Selection. It preserves weakly lives that would have perished in barbarous lands. The sickly children of a wealthy family have a better chance of living and rearing offspring than the stalwart children of a poor one.' (Galton, 1865, p. 325)

Galton's language is direct, but, in light of the strongly heritable character of intelligence, it is difficult to fault his reasoning: 'the weak members of civilized societies propagate their kind', he argued, leading, inevitably, to 'degeneration'. Galton summarized that:

> '…there is a steady check in an old civilisation upon the fertility of the abler classes: the improvident and unambitious are those who chiefly keep up the breed. So the race gradually deteriorates, becoming in each successive generation less fit for a high civilisation.' (Galton, 1869, p. 414)

By 1904, Galton was clear that everybody needed to understand the importance of this, and they needed to be, in effect, inculcated with 'eugenics' as a replacement religion, such that they were inspired to zealously pursue it:

> 'It must be introduced into the national conscience, like a new religion. It has, indeed, strong claims to become an orthodox religious, tenet of the future, for eugenics co-operate with the workings of nature by securing that humanity shall be represented by the fittest races. What nature does blindly, slowly, and ruthlessly, man may do providently, quickly, and kindly. As it lies within his power, so it becomes his duty to work in that direction.' (Galton, 1904)

Eugenics did, indeed, become extremely popular among the educated classes up until World War II. But, thereafter, due to the association with the Nazis, combined with growing individualism, it dramatically declined and is now taboo (Lynn, 2001). It is thus witheringly unlikely that such a policy will be pursued, such that the collapse of civilization is reversed.

Moreover, even if it could be pursued, it probably would not accomplish what it desires to. As people become more intelligent, the positive manifold between the different components of intelligence becomes weaker, meaning that highly intelligent people can be very bad at things that are weakly associated with intelligence; in other words, highly impractical (Blum & Holling, 2017). This has been found to be true of many scientific geniuses—innovators of widely recognized major breakthroughs—who, despite their brilliance, cannot cook or drive a car (Dutton & Charlton, 2015). As people become more intelligent, they become higher in Openness-Intellect—openness to new things and interest in ideas, this correlates with IQ at 0.3 (Nettle, 2007)—and, as we will argue below, lower in instinct, including, it seems, the instinct to have children (Dutton & Van der Linden, 2017), especially if they live in an evolutionary mismatch, being highly environmentally sensitive. In addition, very high intelligence is associated with autistic traits, including low empathy, poor social skill, becoming easily overwhelmed by stimuli, and anxiety (Karpinski et al., 2018). This seems to be because autistic traits —systematizing and taking in more information—allow you to solve problems better. However, this implies that there is, in effect, a limit to human intelligence. Beyond a certain level, intelligence becomes fitness-reducing, because, for reasons we will examine shortly, it stops you from breeding, causing civilization to collapse but humanity to continue. And this is good, because if this didn't happen, and we went on becoming more intelligent forever, then society would be full of anxious, impractical autistics with no social skills and no desire to breed, and humanity would die out. And, crucially, we are currently at a very elementary stage of gene therapy (in a society of rapidly declining IQ) where we can disable only single mutant genes (see Funk et al., 10th December 2020). Intelligence is massively polygenic—it involves thousands of genes working together—making it very difficult to know how any individual gene that gene-editing might target will impact the whole or what negative side effects there might be from interfering with any particular gene.

Yet another argument, even putting this problem aside, is that China is going to do this and, thus, civilization will continue there, forever. This fails to appreciate that China is now a society in decline. It is becoming ever decadent and Western, and there is now a negative correlation between intelligence and fertility in China. It has been estimated that Chinese IQ is likely to have fallen by 0.75 points between 1986 and 2000. There is also a growing negative relationship between years in education and fertility in China. In 1945 it was –0.17 whereas by 1990 it was –0.42 (Wang et al., 2016). Thus, even if China wanted to institute a 'eugenics' programme—which would not work anyway—it is losing both the intelligence and will to do so. So, it is most unlikely, anyway, that such a major innovation would come out of China even if it wasn't moving towards individualism and falling intelligence, which it is.

A further argument is that the elites are psychopathic individualists and that they will somehow maintain civilization for this reason. Psychopathic personality is characterized by a series of traits including superficial charm, lack of guilt or empathy, impulsivity, and grandiosity (Hare, 2011). Now, there is certainly some evidence that highly elite, ambitious people who rise to the very top do have some of these highly heritable traits. Indeed, an analysis of a sample of extremely eminent people found them to have been high both in sexual deviance and sexual promiscuity, as well as being high in subclinical psychopathology. This isn't as bizarre as it sounds because extreme success seems to be predicted by a combination of very high intelligence plus certain moderately psychopathic traits that mean that you are not rule-bound (allowing you to make original connections) and you don't care about upsetting people (which original ideas have a tendency of doing, especially in relation to vested interests) (Dutton & Charlton, 2015). This biographical analysis of eminent men, by British psychologist Felix Post (1913–2001), implicitly estimated that 10% of the male population were subclinical psychopaths, meaning they had psychopathic tendencies sufficiently strong to adversely impact relationships or careers. This he estimated to be true of 14% of eminent men, meaning subclinical psychopaths were overrepresented. Among eminent writers, subclinical psychopathology was 20%, while among eminent artists it was 25%. Among politicians it was just 11%, only slightly above the general male population. However, using the less severe measure of having 'potentially handicapping traits' of antisocial personality disorder, Post found that this was true of 52% of politicians, 50% of artists, and 70%

of writers. Post cautiously estimates that this level of psychopathology applies to 16% of the male population. Accordingly, it can be averred that moderate antisocial behaviour disorder is elevated among the highly eminent (Post, 1994). But, according to this argument, our individualist elites are going to use genetic technology to ensure they and their offspring are genetically healthy, and ever-more intelligent, and they will enslave the rest of us, controlling us with technology. Thus, civilization will not collapse, because this elite will maintain its intelligence and its genetic health.

Such arguments would appear to commit the 'furtive fallacy', which is when you assume that the world is controlled by a huge, evil conspiracy based on little or no evidence (Hackett Fischer, 1970). Moreover, the over-detection of agency behind events is a known cognitive bias, due to it benefiting us to assume an unknown sound is an animal (we avoid predation) but it costing us nothing if we get it wrong (Barrett, 2004). So, we should be very sceptical of such explanations. Indeed, we can respond that there is no evidence for this conspiracy theory whatsoever; though that is not to say that there are never 'conspiracies', nor that some 'conspiracy theories' are not correct (Ratner, 26th April 2018). Indeed, it has been argued that the term 'conspiracy theory' was popularized as a means of mocking those who highlighted evident government cover-ups (deHaven-Smith, 2013). For some Early Christians, the Roman Empire—or even the world itself—was a Satanic-conspiracy against them. The Roman Empire, the elite, was the chief agent of Satan, its sole purpose being to spread evil throughout the world (White, 1888, p. 680). As discussed earlier, there is a strong crossover between schizophrenia and religiosity and, indeed, people with schizophrenic traits are strongly prone to believing in wild conspiracy theories (Dagnall et al., 2015). Dogmatic conspiracy theorists tend to be of low socio-economic status, giving them a sense of powerlessness which is assuaged by the feeling that they have some gnosis about the nature of the world, which thus makes them important (Van Prooijen, 2017). Related to this, intelligence seems to be negatively associated with conspiratorial belief, in the narrow sense that people who are high in analytic thinking are less likely to believe in conspiracy theories (Swami et al., 2014). Intelligence is also associated with trust, because if you are low in intelligence you are more likely to get conned, so it's best to trust nobody (Carl & Billari, 2014).

But, anyway, which is more likely? Are we unique, unlike any other civilization, meaning we will not collapse due to a baseless conspiracy of highly intelligent psychopaths who are working together to create a super-race and enslave the rest of us; there somehow being some impenetrable border between 'us' and this 'elite'? Or, will we go the way of every other civilization, including Roman civilization? If we were going the way of Roman civilization then we would notice evidence of declining intelligence, collapsing traditional religiosity, feminism, multiculturalism, materialism, collapsing traditional moral standards, polarization, debasement of democracy, and a general coming apart of formerly large polities. In that this is actually what is happening, as we will see later, and there is solid evidence for it, it seems a much more plausible state of affairs. And while it was happening, we would expect people, due to decreasing intelligence (and thus decreasing logical abilities) and increasing schizophrenia (due to higher mutational load) to be arguing that there was a Satanic elite that was going to succeed in enslaving us all. But the elite, failing to breed sufficiently, would fall, as it always has done before. Indeed, it has been argued that civilizational collapse neatly explains Fermi's Paradox, whereby, statistically, we would expect there to be advanced alien life, yet there is no evidence of it. If civilizations always collapse before reaching sufficient intelligence and thus technological innovation to find other alien civilizations then Fermi's Paradox is no longer a paradox (see Sarraf et al., 2019).

A related argument is that 'the elite' will stop society collapsing, by changing the conditions that are causing dysgenics. But these have been known about for centuries, and this all-powerful elite surely knows what's happening, yet they have done nothing. Such people will exploit the collapse and ensure that they are insulated from the anarchy—like African despots—but they show no evidence of doing anything about actually preventing tomorrow's disorder from unfolding. Moreover, the elites will be becoming less intelligent as society does, and have long been doing so. Thus, they are decreasingly able to do anything about it and they are decreasingly long-term in their thinking.

'Oh, Yes It Could…'

So, it *could* happen to us. But to understand how it's going to happen, and why a conservative resurgence will be part of it, we have to understand the nature of 'liberalism' and 'conservatism' and in particular the psychology associated with these two perspectives. It is to this that we will turn in the next chapter.

Chapter Two

The Psychology of Conservatives and Liberals

'...I wonder if
Anyone looked at me, forty years back,
And thought, That'll be the life;
No God any more, or sweating in the dark

About hell and that, or having to hide
What you think of the priest. He
And his lot will all go down the long slide
Like free bloody birds.'[1]

Free Bloody Birds

As we have discussed, based on a large number of measures, there has been a noticeable tendency—across the twentieth and now twenty-first centuries—for public attitudes to move in a more left-wing direction. We understand 'left-wing'—though we will examine how it is defined in more detail below—to refer to primary concerns with 'equality' and 'caring' and thus the avoidance of harm. Using the term 'right-wing', we refer to ideologies that are less interested in these traits and are more focused on the importance of 'hierarchy' and 'group-loyalty'. There is much debate over precisely what is meant by 'right-wing' and left-wing' (see Bobbio, 2016). Sometimes, for example, a division is made between being economically left-wing, and thus favouring a strong welfare state and wealth redistribution, and being 'socially left-wing', meaning that you favour social change in the direction of social equality. Some people

---

[1] 'High Windows' (Larkin, 1974).

are socially conservative but favour left-wing economic policies creating an economic levelling effect, something noticeable with certain kinds of nationalism (see Mudde, 2000).

Look Left, Look Right

In fact, there are many ways in which groups that might be regarded as 'left-wing' and groups that might be perceived as 'right-wing' cross over. This may occur due to contradictory conservative drives. On the one hand, conservatives are concerned with hierarchy and group-loyalty. But this also means that they like structure and order, meaning they dislike change, and they may be loyal to whatever they are used to. For these reasons, during the breakdown of the Soviet Union in August 1991, there was a sense in which the three-day coup, in which USSR reforming leader Mikhail Gorbachev was briefly replaced with eight Communist hard-liners, was a 'conservative' or 'right-wing' coup (see Bonnell & Freidin, 2015). This coup can be argued to have been motivated by attachment to group, to structure and to authority, and even to sanctity, with the Soviet Union or Marxism as a *de facto* religion (Eliade, 1957), over individualist desires for a wealthier way of life, or for fairness in a system in which a small elite, at the head of the Communist Party, were extremely wealthy.

This naturally leads us to enquire, 'What is the psychological type that produces a "conservative" worldview in contrast to a "liberal" one?' American journalist Ambrose Bierce (1842–c.1914) quipped that a 'conservative' is 'a statesman who is enamored of existing evils, as distinguished from the Liberal, who wishes to replace them with others' (Bierce, 2010, p. 41). The second half of the twentieth century produced a great deal of theorizing about the psychological roots of conservatism, such as German philosopher Theodore Adorno's (1903–1969) much-debated concept of the conservative as the 'Authoritarian Personality' (Adorno et al., 1950). Certainly, authoritarianism has often been argued to be related to conservatism. Intolerance of dissent has been conceptualized as intolerance of ambiguity at the psychological level. Perhaps an exaggerated demand for cognitive consistency is an important element of conservative thinking because it prevents people from thinking 'outside the box' and coming up with creative solutions. Punitive attitudes have been presented as an element of conservatism, as have moral injunctions on desires and impulses, especially sexuality. Just-world belief has been related to conservatism, where the existing order is justified by claiming that it is 'natural'. In-group versus out-group thinking has been described as a conservative trait. Nationalism, at least when a group is dominant, is the most prominent example. Treating people as members of a group rather than treating them as individuals has also been considered to be 'conservative' (see Wilson, 2013).

This raises questions with regard to how to distinguish between 'conservative' and 'liberal'. If we go through the shopping list of traits that are associated with conservatism—preference for the familiar; rejection of new ideas and practices; moralism as strong inhibitory control on inappropriate behaviour; authoritarian intolerance of dissent; in-group-out-group thinking; 'dehumanizing' people by treating them as members of an identity group rather than as individuals and even just-world belief—then most of these traits are found on both the extreme left *and* the extreme right, a point articulated by German-British psychologist Hans Eysenck (1916-1997) who was himself subject to a mobbing by extreme left-wing activists, as well as experiencing problems with actual Nazis when he was young (Eysenck, 1954, 1981; Buchanan, 2010). Preference for the familiar can also be regarded as a left-wing trait. For some people, the familiar is traditional religion, Christian values, and being embedded in family, nation, and religion. For others, 'the familiar' is freedom from moral restraints, shaped by a popular culture that glorifies selfishness, and a consumerist value system that extols freedom to choose whatever lifestyle and beliefs about the world make you feel good. It might even be argued that many younger people today, born around the turn of the century, have never known anything else. So, what is familiar to you, personally, depends on your generation, family, and cultural influences when you grew up. Freedom to choose your beliefs about how the world works, reality be damned, is an important part of this 'traditional' value orientation, even if this value orientation has developed only during the last few decades.

What about 'moralism'? Advocacy for transsexuals, and taboos on use of the 'wrong' personal pronouns, always with demonization of those who don't care about these issues or who are opposed… all of this is 'moralism'. It might be averred that all of this is, in a sense, 'conservative' for those who have been brought up with this as anything like the 'norm'. The suppression of 'natural' impulses and desires—such as the desire to have sex with whomever you find attractive, whether married or not—could be regarded as the essence of morality. But this impulse could include the suppression of 'natural' aversions to gay sex, transsexuals, and so forth. It has been found that the salivary response to seeing two men kissing, even of men who insist they are not homophobic, is the same as their salivary response to seeing a bucket of writhing maggots (O'Handley et al., 2017). This is what they are being forced to suppress.

What of authoritarianism, intolerance of dissent, and punitive and unmerciful attitudes? Suspected Communists were fired from their jobs in the US during the 1950s and 1960s (Moberg, 2018), including political scientist James Flynn (1934–2020) whose work we will explore anon (see Dutton, 2021a), and anyone labelled a 'sexist' and especially a 'racist' gets fired or otherwise persecuted today (see Carl & Woodley of Menie, 2019). In-group–out-group thinking? For the 'far right' it is nation, race, religion, and culture. The far left is more sophisticated because they emphasize ideological correctness as a sign of group membership, sometimes with sectarian divisions, such as radical feminists—known as TERFS, 'Trans Exclusionary Radical Feminists'—against trans-activists (Flaherty, 29th August 2018). In this sense, the difference would seem to parallel a distinction between polytheism and monotheism which has been highlighted by French philosopher Alain de Benoist. Polytheistic religions are primarily about ritual adherence and shared ancestry whereas, for monotheistic religions, obedience to doctrine and law is key (de Benoist, 2004).

Treating people as group members rather than individuals? The left does precisely this, only in their case it is based on sex, sexual orientation, immigrant status, on religion, race, or nationality. The key difference is that many on the left champion—or they claim to champion—identity groups other than the one they themselves belong to, at least at the leftist extremes. Hence, the stereotype of the privately educated white female who signals how much she cares about poor blacks: the Champagne Socialist, like Britain's former deputy-leader of the Labour Party and former Acting Leader of the Opposition Harriet Harman (see Harman, 2017). This probably signifies a moralism that is more intense than that of other religions and ideologies, because it flaunts people's willingness to act against their own interests, at least on an apparent level. However, in reality, they could just be acting against the interests of their group, precisely because it advances their own *individual* interests, and we will see below that this is precisely what they are doing.

What about 'just-world belief'? The conservatives claim that we live in a just world because natural inequalities justify existing social inequalities, with Nature cast as a kind of harsh God. The far left believes in a Rousseauian Mother Nature[2] that has fairly given everyone the same intelligence and abilities, but that this natural utopia is subverted by evil people who invent differences in society and culture in order to advance their own selfish interests. All attempts by the right to ascribe the

---

[2] Swiss philosopher Jean-Jacques Rousseau (1712-1778) regarded Mother Nature as a goddess-like benevolent force which created a world of love and equality which could be, potentially, returned to (Bongie, 1998, p. 299).

differences they fabricate onto Nature are seen as the heretical promulgation of a false and evil god.

This being so, it could be argued that all of the psychological mechanisms that are described as 'conservative' by twentieth-century psychologists are fully present among modern day 'Social Justice Warriors'. Only on the surface are they different. For example, the inappropriate behaviours that are suppressed today are those related to supposedly inappropriate gender roles, including housewifery, not inappropriate sexual practices, such as homosexuality and the use of contraception. So, it must be emphasized that it is complicated to get to the essence of the difference between 'conservative' and 'liberal'. Many of the moderate Social Justice Warriors (SJWs) today would likely have been moderate nationalists, had they been raised in a broadly right-wing society. Their niche, and this is the niche of many people as we will see below, is to play for status by taking the system which, being relatively conservative, they quite like, and signalling their commitment to it. Similarly, a portion of those on the 'far right' today may simply be contrarians who, had they been raised in Nazi Germany, would be active in the socialist resistance. Indeed, some of them, such as American writer Jim Goad, are perfectly conscious of this (Goad, 2017). Being 'Alt-Right' is predicted, in part, by psychopathic personality traits, an element of which involves being attracted to and enjoying danger and simply taking pleasure in upsetting people. By contrast, signalling left-wing values is predicted by Machiavellianism (a desire for power) and Narcissism (part of which is a desire to be adored) (Moss & O'Connor, 2020). We might reasonably expect these associations to reverse, to a great extent, in a broadly conservative society in which power and adoration will come from signalling group-oriented values, an issue to which we will return below. In this sense, it might be argued, we have two kinds of conservatism: the 'old conservatism' of traditionalism and Christianity and the 'new conservatism' of 'Wokeness'. The Woke signal their commitment to this 'new conservatism' by incrementally making it more pronounced, just as the Puritans once did, competing to be ever-more puritanical in the Cromwellian era (McEnery, 2004, p. 64).

Why the Woke Are Not the 'New Conservatives'

There are three counter-arguments to this perspective. Firstly, it effectively means that everybody in society is, to some extent, 'conservative' and, as such, the 'conservative category' becomes essentially meaningless. People can only be understood as 'conservative' if some people can be regarded as 'liberal'. This raises the question of who is more intuitively 'conservative': fundamentalist Christian traditionalists or Social Justice Warriors? Such a question answers itself.

Secondly, it may be argued that these summaries represent the extremes of the left and right and that there may be a certain psychological type that is attracted to extremes, as we will explore in more detail later. Such people may be high in various personality disorders. For example, Borderline Personality Disorder, which is more common among females, is associated with a weak sense of self. Such people do not know who they are; they are fundamentally insecure due to a feeling that the world is chaotic and uncontrollable. This may be itself underpinned by autistic traits, whereby people who are low in 'empathy' (reading internal states from external signals) cannot predict the behaviour of other people, and become easily overwhelmed by stimuli, meaning that they feel that the world is chaotic and their place in it is unclear. This leads to chronic anxiety, and the need for a clear sense of self, which attracts them to black and white extremes, and a strong desire to control those around them, whom they fear will abandon or turn on them. Ultimately, they are overcome by self-doubt, leading to a breakdown and, often, a sudden migration to the opposite extreme (Fox, 2020).

But, putting these extremes aside, there are nevertheless certain factors that distinguish stable right-wing people from stable left-wing people, which brings us to the third counter-argument: there is evidence that some people, no matter what the circumstances, favour change, are motivated by a belief that life is unfair, and become very animated about what they perceive as harm, especially harm from those whom they regard as dominant, to those whom they regard as weak (Haidt, 2012). Even in a conservative society, they will be overwhelmed by such feelings — because they are so evolved to fight for individual interests — to the extent that they will not conform even though non-conformity may damage their social status. They will be power-hungry and desire praise, perhaps, but that power will have to be reached via revolutionary means and that praise must come from their comrades. They will be so jealous that they will be simply unable to temper this in order to attain status within mainstream society. If they have high intelligence, they will be organized, articulate, and may come to prominence. Indeed, there is research showing that the expanse of a leftist's 'moral circle' becomes stronger precisely in accordance with how far removed it is from his own in-group or his immediate society, whereas it is exactly the opposite among the right (Waytz et al., 2019). In other words, leftists identify with out-groups, presumably so that they can collaborate with them against their in-group in their own individual interests. It makes sense that this can be taken to extremes with the out-group being not just other social classes and other ethnic groups but also other species. This is the paradigm of morality you would expect of a leftist-insurgent, because it is conducive to making alliances with enemies and overthrowing the host society's elite such that you can take its place. Leftists, thus, are particularly prone to discounting their immediate kin and community (Waytz et al., 2019). In a conservative society, these feelings might even cause people, much as they might want power and prestige, to adopt a revolutionary and socially unacceptable way of getting power, causing them to be regarded as 'traitors'. British history is replete with examples of liberals identifying with out-groups; seeming to loathe their own group. Whig leader Charles James Fox (1749-1806) was gushing in his praise for French dictator Napoleon Bonaparte (1769-1821). Poet William Wordsworth (1770-1850) implied that he wanted Napoleon to invade Britain. In 1933, the Oxford Union voted by 275 votes to 153 that 'This House will under no circumstances fight for its King and country' (West, 19th June 2021). People of typical student age tend to be leftist, for reasons we will explore shortly.

It could be argued that leftists also morality signal this, as we will see below, for individualistic reasons; as a means of seeming beneficent, while actually leveraging power against the present rulers. Other people care about equality and harm too, but they also care about order and structure (meaning they tend to dislike change), loyalty to their group, and traditional religious ideas of holiness and taboo to a greater extent, allowing them to conform in a conservative society slightly more. However, in a liberal society, there will be some people who will feel so intensely group-oriented that they, likewise, will not conform, even if this is detrimental to their immediate socio-economic interests. These two types, as we will see below, appear to sit at opposite ends of a spectrum and they map onto being 'liberal' and 'conservative'.

Some people find chaos intolerable, they are easily disgusted by deviant behaviour, and they perceive goodness as synonymous with loyalty to the group. Others thrive on chaos, are not easily disgusted by deviant behaviour, and perceive goodness as related to promoting equality and reducing harm; issues that relate to the good of the individual. The 'traditional conservatives' represent the first type; the extreme 'Woke', who are so Woke that even the current elite regard them as a problem due to their destabilizing influence, embody the second type. Between these two types, there will always be an abundance of less extreme individualists aligned with either of these categories, who simply adopt and signal the current perspective, because they realize that doing so will aid them in attaining status; a phenomenon known as 'effortful control' (MacDonald, 2008).

Individualists and Tribalists

Consistent with the interpretation that there are fundamental differences between 'liberals' and 'conservatives', it has been found that when conservatives feel cheated of a reward they feel that they deserve, then this elevates their feelings of hostility to other ethnic groups. They are group-oriented, so cheating them is cheating their group and that is what they care about. When liberals feel cheated in the same way, it elevates their feelings of hostility to members of their own ethnic group. Liberals are 'individualists' who are in a constant competition with other members of their own ethnic group; conservatives are 'tribalists' who are in a constant competition with other ethnic groups (Amd, 2020).

In line with this, there are consistent personality differences between 'liberals' and 'conservatives'. 'Psychoticism'—a broad personality trait composed of low altruism, low empathy, low rule-following, and low impulse control, and thus a trait which makes you individualistic rather than group-oriented—strongly predicts being 'liberal' rather than 'conservative'. Infamously, a widely reported study was published in 2010 which incorrectly proclaimed that Psychoticism was associated with conservatism at 0.5 (Verhulst et al., 2010). However, it turned out that the authors had made a 'coding error' and that the real results were thus 'exactly reversed'. Psychoticism correlates with liberalism at 0.5 (Verhulst et al., 2016). This means that, no matter what they might signal about kindness and equality, liberals are, in general, less selfless and more selfish than conservatives, even though conservatives may have harsher attitudes to punishing offenders, for example, than liberals. In addition, evidence indicates that the more liberal one is, the more likely one is to use dehumanizing language about one's political opponents; in other words, to hate them and incite hatred of them (Landry et al., 2021). If liberals have more compassionate attitudes, it seems that this is because they care less about the good of the group and because they understand that signalling compassion can get them status because, as we will see in more detail below when we return to the 'Moral Foundations' model, conservatives also value equality and compassion, it's just that they value other foundations as well. The contradiction between signalling selflessness and actually being selfish is consistent with the evidence already noted (Ok et al., 2020) that liberals are high in Machiavellianism and Narcissism. They are motivated by an individualist desire for power and, related to this, by a desire to be adored.

Liberals are also higher in Neuroticism than conservatives; they are more mentally unstable (Kirkegaard, 2020; Verhulst et al., 2016). Neuroticism is an adaptation to a world that is regarded as dangerous, chaotic, and unstable; meaning you have to look after yourself first

(Rushton, 1995). Accordingly, a left-wing—individualist—outlook is, to some extent, an expression of mental instability. The world is a dangerous, evil, unpredictable place, so you need to focus on pure survival, including on attaining power over others. It could thus be argued that there is an inherent relationship between leftism and Neuroticism. If you feel negative feelings strongly then you have low self-esteem, you are envious, you perceive yourself as weak, unfairly treated, and under threat, and you identify with others whom you perceive as weak, such as women or ethnic minorities, meaning you promote their interests. Perceiving yourself as weak, you cannot risk overtly playing for status—by signalling your power—as you will fear being harmed. Thus, you must 'disguise' your attempts to attain status; only playing for it covertly. Virtue-signalling is a covert competitive strategy. It is less likely to provoke direct conflict than signalling bravery or toughness, as it will make you seem kind. This tactic has been noted to be more prominent among females than among males (Benenson, 2013). Furthermore, you perceive the world as 'unfair' and yourself as in danger from the powerful, so you become Machiavellian, such that you can control this dangerous world. However, the negative feelings never go away; you can never have enough power. You have a strong need to socially conform on the one hand, as you fear the consequences of not doing so, but you also have a strong need to make the world more 'fair' (for you) and under control, creating a fundamental tension.

This tension is expressed, for example, in the way in which left-wing Europeans tended to support 'lockdown' during the Covid-19 pandemic of 2020, but then became heavily involved in initially conservative-led protests against lockdown; because these were also protests against those in power whom leftists, due to strongly negative feelings, regarded as wicked people by virtue of having power. It might seem as though there is a contradiction between wanting to avoid 'harm' and committing extreme acts of violence against your political opponents, as seen with the group 'Antifa' (Ngo, 2020). However, this relationship makes sense and thus we should not be surprised at a study which has found that Left Wing Authoritarianism, when compared to Right Wing Authoritarianism, is not only associated with 'higher negative emotionality' but also 'powerfully predicts behavioural aggression and is strongly correlated with participation in political violence' (Costello et al., 2021). Being high in individualizing values is a reflection of being a person who is low in altruism and high in Neuroticism. So we would expect such people to be paranoid and to regard those who disagree with them as dangerous and wicked and needing to be dealt with accordingly. Again, we must emphasize that 'leftism' has a variety of motivations, one of which could be genuinely-felt extreme empathy for the feelings of others that overwhelms all other considerations. Indeed, it has been found that there is a clear distinction between 'authoritarian' and 'liberal' Political Correctness, with only the former being high in Machiavellianism and Narcissism (Moss & O'Connor, 2020). However, overall, as already stated, conservatives score higher in pro-social attitudes than do liberals (Verhulst et al., 2016). Indeed, it has been found that the biggest single predictor of supporting a very left-wing policy (specifically coercive redistribution) is 'Malicious Envy' (effect: 0.26). This was followed by 'Instrumental Harm' (harming innocent people for some 'greater good', 0.21), 'Self-interest' (0.19), 'Communal Fairness' (0.15), and 'Compassion' (0.04) (Lin & Bates, 2021).

The model, with reference to the relationship between leftism and Neuroticism, is consistent with the evidence that 'conservatives' feel more in control of their world, feel that the world is fair, and generally feel happier than liberals. They also feel that life has 'meaning', while liberals tend not to. Liberals struggle with a sense of constant despair (Schenkler et al., 2012) which would make sense of data that over 50% of female extreme liberals in America under the age of 30 have been diagnosed with depression (see Kirkegaard, 2020). Conservatives are also happier to debate with liberals than *vice versa*, presumably because liberals feel intensely negative feelings—to the point of feeling 'unsafe' and needing 'safe spaces' on university campuses where their ideas cannot be challenged (Doyle, 17th December 2020)—when challenged, in a way that conservatives do not (Wu & Resnick, 2021). This is because paranoia is an aspect of Neuroticism, meaning that liberals will fear conservatives far more than the other way round. Accordingly, liberals will push for power but even when they attain power their self-esteem will be sufficiently low, and their paranoia sufficiently high, that they will still feel that their enemies are the ones with the real power, leading to a revolution that never ends and to frequent outbreaks of revolutionary fervour. This can be seen in the way that the Woke mob, which is an enforcer of the dominant ideology, perceives itself as somehow anti-establishment, as seen in wealthy, influential, leftist comedians who perceive themselves as anti-establishment by mocking the kinds of views held by the poor (Doyle, 24th January 2019).

This way of thinking can be seen in China's Cultural Revolution which took place decades after the Communist Party had taken power (see Clark, 2008). This revolution was dominated by morally-crusading young people, something also consistent with the relationship between personality traits and political perspective. We tend to become increasingly Agreeable and Conscientious and decreasingly Neurotic as we age, with the exception of a blip in early adulthood when we become less Conscientious, less Agreeable, and more Neurotic (Soto et al., 2011). Quite why this occurs is unclear; it could help to break the bond between parent and child. But it helps to explain why 'young people' will often go through a phase of being left-wing; a phase which most of them grow out of. As English philosopher Roger Scruton (1944–2020) put it, leftism, especially an aversion to your own group, is 'a stage through which the adolescent mind normally passes' (Scruton, 2007). In terms of average personality, the liberal mind would appear to be 'adolescent' while the conservative one is 'adult'.

So, we can see why liberalism is associated with these personality traits. However, we would expect some variation depending on whether the dominant values system was 'Liberal' or 'Conservative'. If it were 'Conservative' then we would expect at least some Machiavellians and Narcissists, in pursuit of power or adoration, to signal their group-oriented values. Similarly, we would expect some Neurotics, fearing social ostracism, to, likewise, strongly signal their conservatism, consistent with evidence that Neuroticism is associated with extrinsic religiousness, with going to church, and otherwise publicly being religious, though it is negatively associated with intrinsic religiousness (Hills et al., 2004). This is why there are such obvious parallels between the strongly conservative and judgemental 'Church Ladies' of a century ago and Woke females of today. This is why they have been termed 'The New Church Ladies' (Goad, 2017). But, broadly, we can see why liberalism would generally be associated with Psychoticism, Machiavellianism, and Narcissism, as it is, by its nature, low in group-orientation.

There will be individual variance in the group with regard to the extent of these concerns, leading to an approximate divide between altruists and individualists, with individualists having a strong incentive to indicate, to an exaggerated degree, that they are actually extraordinarily altruistic. This means that, ironically, the most selfish, individualistic people will likely be those that will want to make it known just how much more altruistic they are than the next man, as well as how much they are victims of other peoples' malevolence (Ok et al., 2020)—who might ironically be the real altruists; there's no logical sense in appealing for economic compensation or a status-reducing apology from an alleged assailant if he is truly selfish; but it makes perfect sense for a sociopath to manipulate the good will of an altruist. You can identify these people by the extreme lengths to which they will go to signal their altruism and victimhood, and the stark absence of any Darwinian basis in terms of benefiting the ethnic group—the extended genetic family—to which they belong. It has been widely found that exaggeration is generally a means of over-compensating for insecurity about the issue that is exaggerated. Thus, people who lack a sense of self-worth will stress their own importance (see Fox, 2020), something which, as we will see below, is often true of individualists. A professor of theology raised in a 'modest' household is far more likely to have the title on his cheque book changed from 'Mr.' to 'Professor' than is a professor of theology whose parents were academics themselves. Psychologically, the reason for this difference is obvious.

We would expect societies to oscillate between periods of group and individualist values. As we will discuss in more detail below, we can conceive of a process of 'group selection' in which different groups battle it out with each other for resources, and the most adaptive group triumphs. The groups which tend to win, as we will see, are those that are highest in these altruistic, group-oriented values. It's also logical, in conditions of peril and inter-group conflict, that any individualists are vigorously suppressed by other members of the group, as and when the entire group is under threat. In periods of relative peace, however, there can be more slack for those who are not at the top of the hierarchy—those in the middle—to play for status, for themselves, for their kin, and strategically for their wider social class; these are the people who are genetically similar to them, with socio-economic differences having been shown to be highly heritable (Clark, 2014) and significantly genetically influenced (Trzaskowski et al., 2014), based on twin studies, where even average blood type differs along social class lines (Beardmore & Karimi-Booshehri, 1983).

Accordingly, traits that are highly adaptive in evolutionary terms—such as religiousness or a desire for large families—will, during these periods, be associated with more 'individualist' values of harm avoidance and equality, as subordinates or subalterns will want to signal their virtue with these values. People will be generally more concerned about increasing their relative place in the social hierarchy or preserving their place, if they're at the top, and they will cunningly use even lower status people than themselves as allies, if not pawns and instruments, in that power struggle, to scare and intimidate those of higher status into ceding some power and socio-economic status to them, in exchange for calling off their mob. All the people who are adept at this game will, to some extent, move up into the ruling class, and then there may be a period of equilibrium, and further concern about group values.

Regardless, due to the way in which group-oriented people tend to survive, there is evidence that we have been under selection for conservative values—group-oriented-values—for many thousands of years, with selection pressures intensifying during colder periods, because this elevates inter-group conflict, and group-oriented groups tend to prevail in this competition, all else being equal (see Hertler et al., 2021).

Not 'Business as Usual'

Another major reason why the moral paradigm is so different for the left today is because being 'leftist' is now negatively associated with evolutionarily adaptive traits—such as mental and physical health—and, indeed, negatively associated with fertility (Kirkegaard, 2020). This change has taken place due to the breakdown in the intensity of Darwinian selection discussed above. This has created a very easy and predictable environment in which basic needs are always met and there is little need to worry about the future. The result has been a huge build-up of individualists, with there no longer being strong selection pressure against them, and this has led to runaway individualism, where individualism—in its desire to attain status, often through signalling virtue and other desirable traits—veers into fitness-damaging ideas, with no real selection pressures to stop it doing this. As a consequence, we have a group—generally in the middle of society—who combine adaptive traits, such as a desire for power, with pathological desires to be destructive, not only to their group but also to themselves, such as anti-natalism and nihilism, as we will explore in more detail below.

Being genetically relatively similar, these people find each other, as there is a large body of evidence that people are attracted to those who are genetically similar to each other as partners and friends, as noted above (Rushton, 2005). They will work together to attain status via advocating 'liberal values' which they also combine with assorted fitness-reducing ideas, most obviously anti-natalism and being irreligious. They will then spread these ideas to others. Anti-natalism, like extreme liberalism more generally, has been found to be associated with Machiavellianism and also with suffering from depression. Indeed, depression mediates (causes) the relationship between anti-natalism and Machiavellianism (Schönegger, 2021). The current 'conservatives' are the only ones who are resistant to them, despite the control the Woke now exert over pretty much every aspect of society. Thus, perhaps for the first time in history, the usual system has been turned on its head. Previously, in a period of relatively weak inter-group conflict, middle-class 'liberals'—who would combine individualistic foundations with adaptive desires, such as Protestant high fertility—would virtue-signal their way to the top, with their individualism being only weakly suppressed due to weakened pressure to be united in the face of the enemy. But, now, in a time of weak inter-group conflict it is actually *conservatism* which is associated with fertility. These remnant conservatives can additionally be conceived of as, in some respects, the remnant pre-industrial population, who are genetically evolved to be resistant to anything fitness-reducing. But the key point is that we can see how, within a pack, there will always be individualists and collectivists. It may even be that a small number of individualists are necessary in order to come up with new ideas, as innovation has been found to be associated with low empathy, meaning you do not care about offending vested interests, as we will explore in greater depth later (see Dutton & Charlton, 2015).

Now, we have previously highlighted the way in which this increasing left-wing dominance is superficially extremely strange because, as we will explore in more detail anon, since at least the middle of the twentieth century, fertility has been significantly predicted by being conservative, especially very conservative (including being religious) and the heritability of both political viewpoints and of religiousness is relatively high. We argue that there are two key processes which help to explain the tendency for society to move in a leftward direction. The second of these relates very specifically to our own Industrial Revolution-centred society, which is unique in human history. The first of these, which we will now explore, constitutes a more general pattern in human history.

Chapter Three

Why Does Culture Always Seem to Move to the Left?

'Now, helpless in the hollow of
An unarmorial age, a trough
Of smoke in slow suspended skeins
Above their scrap of history,
Only an attitude remains'[1]

Proto-Protestantism and the Peasants Revolt of 1381

The more general process whereby, in certain key respects, society appears to move leftwards can be observed even in pre-industrial societies and it is this upon which we will focus in this chapter. It is why, when in 1956 Philip Larkin mused on a Medieval tomb in Chichester Cathedral on which the Earl and Countess of Arundel had been carved as life-size effigies, lying side-by-side in death, that tomb seemed so fantastically out-of-date. History always seems to move leftwards. There is now a thoroughly 'unarmorial age' in which nobody, any longer, displays their coat armour and those who do have the 'hint of the absurd', as Larkin describes the faithful dog carved beneath the couple's feet. The nobleman to whose monument Larkin responded in verse was Richard Fitzalan, 10th Earl of Arundel (c.1313–1376). Richard Arundel lived through the beginnings of the Proto-Reformation. In fact, his younger son, Archbishop of Canterbury Thomas Arundel (1353–1414), was a major

---

[1] 'An Arundel Tomb' (Larkin, 1964).

figure in trying to stamp it out (Aston, 1967). We might highlight this period as an example of the dynamics of the leftward drift of culture.

In the late fourteenth century, England witnessed the stirrings of the Reformation; a period that is sometimes referred to as the 'Proto-Reformation' (e.g. Scruton, 2014). Theologians, such as John Wycliffe (c.1320–1384), espoused much of what would later be regarded as Lutheran or Protestant doctrine. Wycliffe, and his followers, who were known as the Lollards, wanted the Bible translated into English so that ordinary people could read it. They criticized the power and wealth of the Roman Catholic Church, espousing a return to the 'equality of all believers' which they perceived to be present in the Early Church. In line with what he regarded as Early Church teaching, Wycliffe averred that the Church should renounce all its property, and that everybody should embrace a kind of holy poverty; supposedly in line with the teaching of Christ. He argued that the only purpose of the monasteries was to make money, and thus all the monasteries—which were, indeed, extremely wealthy—should be dissolved. Wycliffe highlighted corruption within the Church and he drew attention to the way in which a lot of clergy simply joined it in order to become rich. He condemned the Pope as the Anti-Christ. Clergyman and layman supporters of Wycliffe spread his views to the English population; views which many peasants happily adopted because they seemed to religiously justify the destruction of a system in which the peasants were oppressed. The Lollards not only criticized the Church but also the entire unequal hierarchical social system as being diametrically opposed to the teachings of Jesus (see Lahey, 2008).

The eventual result—albeit sparked by the imposition of a poll tax—was a widespread rebellion which came very close to toppling the English government; the Peasants' Revolt of 1381. During this uprising, London was taken by a furious mob and the Archbishop of Canterbury, Simon Sudbury (c.1316–1381), was murdered; dragged from his London palace to Tower Hill, where he was beheaded by the bloodthirsty rebels (Justice, 1996). As stated, part of the reason for this was that the government had imposed a poll tax, specifically in order to fix runaway wages that had been caused by a massive labour shortage. This shortage had been precipitated by the Black Death which had ravaged the country 30 years before, killing 40% of the population, but about 80% of the large labouring class of serfs and free labourers (Dodds, 2008). The commissioners, who collected this poll tax, also sparked fury by the offensive methods which they employed to prevent people from fraudulently avoiding the tax. In one case, in Kent, this included royal sergeant-at-arms John Legge supposedly personally checking the vaginas of girls who claimed to be under the age of 15 in order to measure their pubic hair length; as only if they were under the age of 15 were they exempt from the tax. The mob executed Legge at the beginning of the uprising (Barker, 2014, p. 139). However, it is widely accepted that the rebellion's fervour was inspired by Wycliffe's teachings. And Wycliffe's Proto-Reformation did not happen in isolation. During the same period, there was a great deal of original artistic expression, which questioned accepted norms, and even lampooned the Church as corrupt, exemplified in Geoffrey Chaucer's (c.1343–1400) *Canterbury Tales* (Jones et al., 2004).

One interpretation of this would be that society had been moving in an increasingly left-wing direction for many decades. This may have been partly because faith in the entire social system had been shaken by the cataclysm of the Black Death, accelerating changes that had already been occurring (see Ziegler, 1969). At first, this resulted in what many people would regard as positive developments; greater freedom to critique those in power, leading to a period of artistic and philosophical innovation. But, eventually, England started to see the breakdown of hierarchy and order and, ultimately, a form of intensely violent, anarchic *de facto* rule by a fanatically religious, left-oriented, morally self-righteous mob. The gradual result was what, in modern parlance, we might call a 'right-wing backlash'. The Peasants' Revolt was quelled, and there was a heavy clampdown on Proto-Protestantism, and a strong revival of the 'traditionalist' Catholic Church. A law was passed in 1401 making Lollard heresy punishable by being burned at the stake; heresy not previously having been a capital crime in England (Coffey, 2014, p. 78). It became heresy, in 1408, to even translate the Bible into English, partly due to concerns about equality-promoting passages, and it became an offence to preach if you were not licensed by the Church. Wycliffe's works were banned in 1415 and his books were burnt. In 1428, Wycliffe's body was exhumed and he was posthumously burnt as a heretic (Lahey, 2008). For a long time after the Peasants' Revolt, a kind of Catholic traditionalism held sway in England. Indeed, it did so through the Renaissance until the Reformation, where it could be argued that the process, of moving leftwards, began all over again. The Anabaptists, and other extreme reformers of the time, could be thought of as constituting the 'extreme left' within the Reformation (see Harbison, 2013, p. 68).

Haidt's Moral Foundations

So why does this movement towards the left always seem to take place eventually? There are two interrelated ways of answering this question. The first relates to the Moral Foundations approach to understanding political differences that has been proposed by American psychologist

Jonathan Haidt (2012) and to which we referred in the last chapter. We will now look at it in more detail.

Haidt avers that there are five moral foundations, although in developments of his model he has extended these to six and even more. He argues that political differences between people can be substantially explained by the importance which they accord to each of these moral foundations. To put it another way, humans approach the world with these foundations, but they differ with regard to how strongly they feel each of them matters. Haidt argues that these foundations are, in many ways, fundamental to all humans, as a result of our evolution as a highly social pack animal. Haidt's original moral foundations were:

(1) *Care*. This taps into how much you need to cherish and protect others. Those who score low in this are tolerant of *Harm*. Clearly, as a highly pro-social species, we have to care deeply about other members of our group, create strong social bonds with them, and wish to assist them, if only because they might, as a consequence, assist us in the future.

(2) *Fairness*. This relates to the importance of justice or proportionality, according to a set of shared rules. It has been proposed that, as pack animals, humans have two vital inclinations. The first is the desire to climb the hierarchy and achieve high social status within it. This was particularly important in our evolutionary past; especially for males, because we often lived in polygamous social structures, where more dominant high-status males had greater access to females by virtue of their political power, and low status males were left involuntary celibates as a result (Betzig, 1986). But also, as far as monogamy was the norm, it made sense from the female side, with her kin, to select male partners of the highest socio-economic status, because for her and her offspring, they would be more likely to survive if the male invested time and resources in them, and he would be better able to do this if he were of high socio-economic status (see Buss, 1989). Consistent with this, it has been shown that, until the Industrial Revolution, there was a strong association between how many surviving children you had, and how wealthy you were; the richer half of the European population had about between 40% and double the completed fertility of the poorer half (Clark, 2007; Pound, 1972). And as already stated, in polygamous tribes—from which all modern humans descend—the fertility of a male was strongly associated with his place in the societal hierarchy, with most males having no wives and no children (see Dutton & Woodley of Menie, 2018, pp. 34-39; Lynn, 2011, p. 36).

But, on the other hand, computer models have shown that groups that are highly internally cooperative are more likely to triumph in the battle for resources with other groups (Hammond & Axelrod, 2006). This need for everyone to get along and feel valued militates in favour of instincts for fairness and even for a desire for relative equality, such that everyone feels appreciated. However, in such a cooperative group, where everyone contributes what they can, it must be ensured that 'free-riders' do not exploit and sponge off the group, for obvious reasons. So, we would expect ourselves to be very concerned about dishonesty and cheating. This brings us to the next foundation.

(3) *Loyalty to the in-group*. This taps into, in essence, how group-oriented a person is. To what extent are they prepared to suppress their individual desires in favour of the good of their group? In this regard, Haidt specifically refers to groups underpinned by genetic kinship, such as 'family' and tribe'. In our pre-history, these were, of course, the groups in which we operated and, as discussed, groups whose members were internally cooperative, prepared to be self-sacrificial for the group, were more likely to survive. Such groups would need to strongly monitor 'cheaters', 'traitors', and selfish people in general, who would be potentially disloyal to the group for their own personal gain, or who would be parasitic upon it.

(4) *Authority*. This foundation relates to a person's preparedness to submit to tradition, authority, and hierarchy. This would have been crucial in our evolutionary past of frequent warfare with other groups, because the group that was high in this trait would likely have been better organized, more efficient, and less likely to fission under pressure; making that group more likely to survive.

(5) *Sanctity or Purity*. At a very basic level, this refers to a sense of abhorrence towards things which are commonly regarded as repellent in some way, such as certain foods, people, or actions. At the evolutionary level, we would be adapted to experience a disgust response in the face of anything that was bad for our genetic interests, or for the genetic interests of our group. Conversely, certain things are regarded, by those high in disgust sensitivity, as strongly 'sacred' and 'pure' and, thus, absolutely not to be defiled. For many of its adherents, sacred places must be kept extremely pure for this reason, hence the need to remove your shoes when you enter a mosque or temple, or the ban on menstruating women entering certain Russian Orthodox churches (Fienup-Riordan, 1990, p. 113). Most religions are very concerned with purity, with even baptism being a symbolic washing away of the infant's 'Original Sin'. Indeed, it has been shown that deeply religious people tend to be very high in disgust sensitivity, even feeling a sense of disgust towards those who question their religion (Ritter & Preston, 2011). Inasmuch as religiousness is adaptive, as we will explore below, such a response to those who might undermine it would make a great deal of sense.

Broadly, these differences reflect two sets of instincts. Humans are pack animals, meaning that they must defeat other packs. This leads to instincts to act for the good of the pack: obedience to hierarchy and self-sacrifice for the group. But animals also want to protect their own interests and thus to avoid harm and to have at least as much as everyone else, if not more. They want to climb to the top of the pack, as this permits greater access to resources and, under harsh conditions of selection, means you are more likely to pass on your genes. So, these are individualist concerns. In a pack, they cannot afford to appear selfish, so subordinates or subalterns will play for status by signalling what cooperative people they are; how concerned they are about the harm and fairness moral foundations.

Moral Foundations, Liberals, and Conservatives

Now, Haidt marshals a great deal of experimental and survey evidence for a relatively clear left–right difference in terms of these Moral Foundations, based on a large-scale survey of over 11,000 people. The five factors appear to divide into two higher-order clusters: *Individualizers* and those who are *Binding*, as previously noted. Individualizers are strongly focused on 'Care' and 'Fairness', but they have relatively little interest in 'Authority', 'Loyalty', and 'Sanctity.' Binders are more focused on 'Loyalty', 'Authority', and 'Sanctity' and are less concerned about 'Care' and 'Fairness'. Of course, there will be all kinds of individual variance in the strength of these foundations, but, overall, this was the clustering that was found. However, the relationship between these two clusters and a person's political perspective is slightly more complex. Haidt and his colleagues found that, based on an American sample and across a number of studies, people who identified as 'Liberal' (which more than ever means 'left-wing') scored high in 'Care' and 'Fairness' and low in the other moral foundations. However, people who identified as 'Conservative' scored about equally in all of the Moral Foundations (Graham et al., 2009).

It should be emphasized that Haidt's method factors-down a large amount of data into a predictive model. This is useful to the extent that it permits us to make correct predictions and, even with some caution, make sense of the world. But reality is slightly more complex. For example, overall, conservatives are higher in a general disgust factor than liberals. But this disgust factor is composed of multiple kinds of disgust, such as sexual disgust, disease-disgust, moral disgust, and so on. Although liberals are lower than conservatives in general disgust, they appear to be higher on certain subcategories of disgust. It has been found that scoring high in Moral Disgust predicts particularly high scores on Fairness. By contrast, scoring high in Sexual Disgust *is* associated with conservatism (Leeuwen et al., 2017). This means that it is quite possible for a portion of those who score very high in Fairness to feel an intense sense of disgust towards those whom they regard as immoral, even though their more general sense of disgust is low. This would potentially help to explain why some extreme liberals appear to intensely dislike some conservatives, claiming to feel 'unsafe' or personally threatened in response to conservatives' presence on the same social media platforms or in the same higher education institutions.

For example, in 2015, Yale University sent an email to students and staff requesting that they refrain from wearing costumes that other students might find offensive. A Yale academic, Erika Christakis, wrote a carefully worded email arguing that the university should consider whether it really should attempt to control student behaviour in this way. The response to her email was a letter, signed by hundreds of students, calling on the academic to resign and claiming that the presence on campus of someone with opinions such as hers—in other words, someone not totally in agreement with them—made them feel 'unsafe' (Leaders, 14th November 2014). Dogged by the controversy and student protests, Christakis eventually resigned her position (Friedersdorf, 26th May 2016). It may similarly be that, though liberals score lower than conservatives on in-group loyalty overall, they may score higher on loyalty to certain kinds of in-group, such as those where in-group membership is based around collective self-interest and protection, such as trade unions, political parties, guilds, activist groups—all of which come with a telling set of 'shared moral values'. However, overall, we would expect liberals to be less self-sacrificial for any group of which they were a part, than would be conservatives.

Overall, liberals would be more individualistic than conservatives. And there is sound evidence for this. The tension between the 'left' and the 'right' can, to a certain extent, be understood as a competition between different genotypes, between people who differ for genetic reasons. Some of these genotypes want to boost individual-level fitness (sometimes at the expense of the group), and some of which want to boost group fitness (sometimes at the expense of the individual, such as in times of conflict). As a result, there is a consistent difference in average personality, something which is approximately 50% genetic, between conservatives and liberals. Psychologists generally agree that there are five key personality traits. These are known as the 'Big 5', and we have met most of them already. These traits are Openness (involving openness to new experiences), Conscientiousness (rule-following and impulse control), Extraversion (feeling positive feelings strongly and thus risk-taking in pursuit of them), Agreeableness (altruism and empathy), and Neuroticism (feeling negative feelings strongly, including anxiety and depression) (Nettle, 2007). They can be remembered using the acronym 'OCEAN'. Being group-oriented, right-wing people are high in Agreeableness (allowing you to get on with people), high in Conscientiousness (permitting you to control your impulses, avoid fights, and follow group rules), and low in Neuroticism, meaning they do not feel negative feelings strongly. This is important because negative feelings, with the exception of social anxiety, will cause social discord, and the group will be less able to function if it is full of depressed people, who will spread their depression to others (Joiner, 1994). Liberals are the opposite. They are low in Agreeableness, low in Conscientiousness, and high in Neuroticism (Verhulst et al., 2016; Kirkegaard, 2020). This means that they are out for the good of themselves, over the good of the group.

Moral Foundations and the Move to the Left

Now, returning to Haidt's findings, what does this mean in everyday terms? It means that conservatives can sympathize with liberals, as they have something in common with liberals. They can understand the concerns of liberals, because they also share these concerns, albeit to a lesser extent than do liberals. Conservatives, like liberals, *do* think about 'Fairness' and 'Care'; they just happen to think that other foundations are equally important. But this means that the average liberal (there will always be individual exceptions of course) cannot sympathize with the average conservative at all. The liberal inhabits a very different moral universe, in which the conservative's concerns simply don't matter. 'Why does the conservative care about Loyalty, Authority and Sanctity?', the liberal asks himself. 'These things aren't important; all that matters is Care and Fairness. Nothing else is relevant. How can the conservative be so mean; so hard-hearted? How can he regard some people as superior to others? He has such horrible values!' Here, even our shorthand use of the word 'he' could betoken, to a contemporary left-winger, insensitivity to women—but were we to change it to 'he or she' then we would still be accused of not being 'inclusive' to 'non-binary' people. Not even linguistic convenience can take priority over their equalitarian values, and hypersensitivity to perceived harm.

The consequence of this is that it is very easy for the liberal to regard conservatives—who are so much less concerned than her about what she regards as 'the only moral questions that matter'—as immoral, cold, elitist, and heartless: as, essentially, psychopathic people. However, the truth, as measured by Haidt, is that the conservative *can* and *does* sympathize with the liberal. So, he might regard the liberal as misguided, emotionally immature even, but not necessarily as morally bad, because the conservative can understand the liberal's moral concerns. Indeed, there is evidence that liberals and conservatives both caricature each other's concerns in their understanding of each other and both regard each other as immoral because of this. However, liberals do so to a much greater extent; liberals perceive conservatives as more immoral and more morally reprehensible than conservatives perceive liberals as being (Graham et al., 2012). And, following the research explored above on different kinds of disgust, liberals may, as a consequence, find conservatives, in a sense, viscerally repellent, in a way that is not reciprocated. Conservatives may be disgusted by the liberal, if he engages in a sexual act which the conservative is revolted by, but he will not find the liberal inherently disgusting because of the liberal's moral concerns. This difference is congruous with the finding that liberal–conservative sympathy works one way: conservatives can sympathize with liberals but not the other way around. In addition, it has been shown that liberals tend to be more dogmatic—certain and unwavering in their views—with regard to liberal dogmas, than are conservatives with regard to conservative dogmas (Conway et al., 2015). In other words, liberals are more likely to dismiss empirical evidence which questions their dogmas, and to stick to their dogmas, than are conservatives. They are more dogmatic. This may be partly because they create coalitions based around shared dogmas, where conservatives seem to create them based around shared tribal membership (Kaufmann, 2019).

Out-Group Loyalty and Intransigence

This group–individual dynamic in political psychology is further complicated by the reality that some individuals—at least in multicultural societies—will want to boost the fitness of a *different group*, be that an ethnicity, a nation, a religion, or whatever else, external, and perhaps hostile, to the main group. And inasmuch as that external group is in competition with the main in-group in a given locale, it is usually in their interests to sabotage that same dominant group's fitness, in order to boost the fitness of their own group. Such individuals, in the strictly group-selected definition of conservatism that we have thus far been talking about, are right-wing—they possess a right-wing psychology or personality. But to the degree that they are hostile to a society's dominant in-group identity and its institutions, they are more likely to align themselves with the political left of that society, despite natural incompatibility on certain social issues, mostly to do with sexuality and family. It might seem strange that such 'foreign-right' groups occupying the left-wing polity can be embraced by the 'true' left, that is, the psychologically-individualist left. Do they not also lack the same binding values to sympathize with these external group's traditionalist institutions? Apparently, until a given foreign-right group takes over as the new dominant group in a society, such conflicts can usually remain dormant. Indeed, the left-wing personality is inclined to apply their individualistic sympathies of fairness and harm avoidance towards allied foreign-right groups, by reducing these groups to a collection of individuals like them; advancing the narrative that each *individual* is picked on because of their 'identity'. Thereby, minority group membership paradoxically becomes an expression of individualism.

This paradox can be seen in Britain in the way in which some Muslims have become heavily involved in the Labour Party, with the current leader of the Labour Party in the Scottish Parliament, Anas Sarwar, being a Muslim whose family hail from Pakistan (Rodger & Grant, 4th May 2021) and the current Mayor of London, Sadiq Khan, also being Muslim (Mian, 4th May 2016). However, Muslim influence has also led to tensions in the Labour Party due to the traditionalist and group-oriented values of many Muslims. There has been a moral panic over anti-Semitism in the Labour Party, driven by a combination of traditional Muslim anti-Semitism and by whites identifying with the supposedly oppressed Palestinians over the supposedly imperialist Israelis (Holden, 4th May 2016). Evidence of homophobia in the Labour Party, implicitly Islamic in origin, has also been publicly highlighted (Leonard, 3rd April 2018).

Hijacking the Culture

The expected result of these findings is that those who are 'liberal' will be able to hijack the 'culture' and, up to a point, push it in an increasingly left-wing direction, even if those who are 'conservative' constitute the majority of the population. Based on the research we have discussed, this process will occur because the conservative will sympathize with the liberal, and thus give ground to him, in a way that will not be reciprocated. Thus, the liberal can effectively take advantage of the conservative's desire for Fairness and Care—even if it is much lower than the liberal's—and create a society focused very strongly around these Moral Foundations, riding roughshod over the other foundations that are of concern to the conservative. In addition, the liberal will be more dogmatic—more fervent—about his foundations than the conservative will be about his. In a sense, the liberal will feel the rightness of his cause more strongly, which would potentially mean that he would be better able to win conservatives round to his viewpoint by employing emotional means. These would include, due to the liberal's putative strong sense of moral disgust, casting conservatives who, despite these pressures, continue to disagree with him as simply inherently evil and dangerous, such would the liberal's sense of revulsion be for the conservative. Thus, we can begin to see how someone like John Wycliffe did not simply regard the Pope as misled or in error, but actually as something like the Anti-Christ.

Recall that conservatives tend to be high on both *Individualizing* and *Binding* moral foundations. This means that they can be swayed based on appeals to fairness and harm reduction. But it doesn't work in reverse. Liberals will seldom be swayed by appeals to group authority, purity, or in-group loyalty. This kind of asymmetry creates a dynamic that Lebanese statistician Nassim Taleb (2018, Ch. 2) has referred to as the minority rule. Non-democratic societal institutions are affected by the minority rule above all, when they're universalist; when they are predicated on an environment of universal social harmony and mutual good-will. If an impartial and apolitical executive on a board of management of any societal organization should appoint its successor based on competence alone, and without discrimination on any other basis, then that leaves it vulnerable to the inevitable event that executives, who are ideologically or tribally motivated, get appointed. These new executives would subsequently appoint only those of their own persuasion. Thus, an irreversible political transformation of human capital would swiftly overcome this formerly-universalist societal organization. Once captured and transformed, the organization can only thereafter evolve slowly over time, as each succeeding generation in executive leadership may be marginally, but never radically, different from the predecessors that appointed them. A politicized organization will never revert back to an apolitical one by itself, voluntarily, but a glacial evolution of executive leadership from the right back to the universalist-centre, and further leftwards, can occur by the aforementioned asymmetry in moral empathy.

This can be observed in the way in which the left have managed to capture universities in Western countries, with academics now being overwhelmingly left-wing (Carl, 2017). It can also be observed in the way that academics who refuse to suppress empirical knowledge that might undermine dogmas of 'equality' and 'harm avoidance', such as on issues such as racial differences in intelligence, are fired and otherwise driven out of universities, that is, 'cancelled'. This came to particular prominence in 2019 when political scientist Noah Carl was fired by St Edmund's College, Cambridge, due to the nature of his peer-reviewed, academic research, which it was felt might upset people:

> '...the panel also noted that the way in which Dr Carl has conducted himself with regard to his publications and the ideas he has expressed have had a detrimental effect on the atmosphere within the college, with feelings

of hurt, betrayal, anger and disbelief that the college could be associated with such views.' (Adams, 1st May 2019)

Many other examples of this ongoing persecution of academics who place empirical truth above individualizing moral foundations have been explored (Carl & Woodley of Menie, 2019).

Another way in which a universalist institution can be hijacked is through its customer base. An institution, a news media organization for example, might set out to target everyone, regardless of any group identity that they may belong to. However, certain groups may make more exacting demands than others on the nature of the institution's service or product. For a news outlet, it might be that a particular kind of reader demands a certain perspective be entertained or that certain language be used. If an institution is serious about placating all of its customers, then the most demanding group of customers will exert the greatest amount of influence over the nature of the organization. A turning point can be reached when such a particular group makes a demand on the organization that is necessarily incompatible with another group's demands. At this point the organization must forgo its universalism and make a choice as to which group or groups it must specialize to. Some people want their historical dramas to be realistic. Some people want them to be a means of rewriting the past in order to create a sense of racial unity in 'the now' or, perhaps, they just want to make traditionalists and those who prize objective truth (which traditionalists see as 'sacred') above 'equality' feel disgusted in order to exert power over them. The liberal group is more zealous and intransigent so, eventually, they triumph, and English sixteenth-century queen Anne Boleyn (c.1500–1536) is played by a black actress, as occurred in 2021 (*RT*, 30th October 2020) and she and Jane Seymour (c.1508–1537), Anne's successor as Henry VIII's queen, are sexually attracted to each other and passionately kiss (Lester, 2nd June 2021).

The mercy of free-market capitalism is that it allows a multiplicity of organizations to specialize in diverse profitable niches that the economy has to offer, thereby guaranteeing, in our example, that not *every* newspaper gets directed at a left-wing audience. In an alternative political economy, however, such as the public or charities sector, it must be kept in mind that no such balancing mechanism exists. Indeed, non-capitalist institutions are renowned for their rejection of entrepreneurship and experimentation, and for aggressively pursuing industry-wide standardization and general conformity with sister or partner organizations. Again, this can be seen in what has happened in the university sector in the UK, where all the most prestigious institutions were long-ago taken over by liberals (Carl, 2017). It can also be seen in the heavy leftist bias in institutions such as the BBC (Aitken, 2020).

The end result of a process where societal institutions are widely taken over and controlled by an intransigent minority is that people become increasingly inculcated, from the top down, with the viewpoints and demands of a domineering minority. Taleb (2018) proposes that an intransigent minority needs only to be about 3-5% of the population in general, for institutions to start taking an interest in their needs and how they may be accommodated. However, there may be another stage beyond this in the population-level concentration of the intransigent minority: a 'tipping point', where at once there is a mass movement towards political takeover and cultural supremacy of the intransigent minority. At that point, the population as a whole widely regards the group's societal agenda as the up-and-coming and soon-to-be-triumphant cultural paradigm. As discussed earlier, experiments have shown that once a 'critical mass' in a group of approximately 20% espouse a certain counter-cultural perspective, the rest of the group seem to relatively quickly adopt it (Centola et al., 2018).

Intellectual Conformity and Intelligence

Now, once this happens, a new process takes off which entrenches the 'liberal' perspective even further. Intelligence is associated with analytic thinking and being repelled by extreme points of view; perceiving greater intellectual nuance (Jensen, 1998). However, it also appears to be associated with intellectual conformity. It has been shown that people who are more intelligent are better at noticing what the dominant worldview is, better at realizing the social benefits of conforming to that dominant worldview, and better at forcing themselves to believe it, through coming up with superficially convincing arguments for so-doing. This, of course, better permits them to attain social status. Thus, there is evidence that if the dominant worldview is liberalism, then intelligent people will be more likely to force themselves, through effortful control, to adopt that view. Less intelligent people would be less able to successfully execute this strategy, partly because intelligence predicts the inability to realize one's own bias (West et al., 2012). This model, whereby intelligence predicts conformity to the dominant worldview, is known as the Cultural Mediation Hypothesis (Woodley of Menie & Dunkel, 2015). Consistent with this, it has been found that, where a society is broadly conservative, intelligence is associated with conservatism (Dutton, 2013a).

This sets off an arms race whereby intelligent people, whom we would expect to occupy relatively high socio-economic positions, will signal their conformity, their individualistic morality (in the case of a liberal dispensation), but also their intelligence, by very slightly questioning the current dominant worldview in order to push it in a slightly more liberal direction. They will not critique it to a pronounced extent, because that would indicate non-conformity, but they must critique it slightly in order to showcase their intelligence and liberalism and thus attain social status (Dutton & Van der Linden, 2015). In that these views will be held by those of high social status, the 'Trickle Effect' (Simmel, 1957)—whereby people tend to imitate those of high social status in order to attain status themselves—would predict that more and more people would start to adopt a liberal way of thinking. Only the least intelligent would fail to do so, possibly combined with those who have outlier high intelligence as this has been shown to be associated with autistic traits and thus with an obsession with the truth and with systematizing (Karpinski et al., 2018), a relationship we will explore in more detail below.[2] Accordingly, societies move leftwards and, once they start doing so, they can be pushed vary far to the left, due to these related factors.

Why Do Societies Move to the Right?
The Case of Margaret Thatcher

So, we can begin to understand why societies tend to move leftwards. But this cannot go on indefinitely. This is because, following Haidt, humans are evolved to be concerned about all five Moral Foundations. A society which only focuses on two of these foundations will increasingly bring about an evolutionary mismatch in which the population finds itself in an environment that is decreasingly like the one to which it is evolved. If a society pays no attention to authority and structure, then there will be a growing sense of disarray and disorder. If a society focuses on equality and fairness, then basic human desires—such as to ascend the social hierarchy or look after one's kin, over one's non-kin—will have to be repressed. If a society pays no attention to disgust sensitivity, then more and more people will be burdened with a permanent feeling of disgust, all the time. The social turmoil that this situation will gradually bring about,

---

[2] In addition, in that intelligence is associated with future-orientation, we might even expect the very intelligent to perceive, well ahead, that society is moving in a new direction and to accept persecution in the present for a substantial social status pay-off in the future. Intelligent risk-takers might be especially prone to this course of action (see Dutton & Van der Linden, 2015). Accordingly, these highly intelligent people would be the leaders of the growing dissident faction that would eventually create a tipping point (Centola et al., 2018).

alone, will slowly cause people to become extremely unhappy and to be aware, dimly at first, that others feel the same way.

In the case of an ideological advancement from the political left, there will of course be another intransigent minority, stubbornly resistant to these views; the traditionally religious and the very right-wing. Such people, going against the new ascendant cultural programming, would therein be the way they are for genetic, not cultural, reasons. This would be especially the case if they were directly exposed to left-wing culture, and not insulated by a counter-culture; compare a staunch Republican who lives in San Francisco versus rural Texas for example. But, even so, there would be people raised in a strongly leftist environment who would be, for genetic reasons, strongly oriented towards binding moral foundations and, indeed, towards perspectives associated with these such as religiosity, nationalism, and ethnocentrism. These kinds of people would be 'right-wing', in essence, no matter what the culture of the group told them they should be.

Besides these *overtly* resistant people, you would also expect there to be a *covert* non-intransigent minority, perhaps only moderately conservative and religious. Unlike their further-right counterparts, they would indeed compromise their natural political affiliation and points of view, at least as publicly expressed, in order to fit in with the new regnant left ideology and, perhaps, to thus maximize their ability to attain socioeconomic status. However, they may not actually, consciously or otherwise, shift to any significant degree in their private beliefs and behaviours, including, perhaps, in their fertility; their desire to have children, in part, to perpetuate their ethnic group; their extended genetic family (see Salter, 2007). This would be the difference between a politician like Enoch Powell (1912–1997), who was prepared to openly discuss racial differences and the full consequences of mass immigration (Shepherd, 1996, p. 365), and the more pragmatic Margaret Thatcher (1925–2013). In 2004, at a dinner in London, Margaret Thatcher told psychologist Richard Lynn, himself cancelled by a British university in 2019 for his scholarly research on race (Carl & Woodley of Menie, 2019), that Lynn's research on race differences in intelligence was 'very interesting but too incendiary for her to cite' (Lynn, 2020, p. 337).

Eventually, something will 'break'. A member of the elite will see an opportunity to ascend to the very top by espousing a conservative backlash, perhaps. Or a dissident conservative group, such as a group of retired generals, will become so popular that, in the chaos that has been created by extreme liberalism, they will be able to take control. Or, in democracies, people will elect a right-wing government, and this government will eventually attain sufficient power and confidence to take on the liberals, who will still control many societal institutions, and roundly defeat them. It could be argued that this is what happened in the case of Margaret Thatcher. By the late 1970s, a long period of leftist hegemony had rendered Britain the 'Sick Man of Europe'; a country in decline, dominated by strikes, social disorder, and also by the promotion of social liberalism (Casey, 2002, p. 1). The British people elected Mrs. Thatcher's Conservatives in 1979, but her government was neither sufficiently powerful nor sufficiently confident to take on the Trade Unions—these being a huge power in the land that could hold the government to ransom. As a result of winning the Falklands War in 1982 and then winning a landslide victory in the General Election of 1983, it was clear that the public were generally behind Mrs Thatcher's government. This gave the government the confidence to take on the Trade Unions and force them to surrender. With this accomplished, Mrs. Thatcher had the power to push Britain in a much more conservative direction (see Jenkins, 2006).

But, again, this does not last forever. There are two key reasons why conservative systems will tend to turn back to the left. The first is that, being very high in in-group loyalty, in some manifestations, the conservative society will expand the interests of their group, frequently through warfare and the invasion of other groups' territories. This is precisely what Argentine military dictator General Leopoldo Galtieri (1926–2003) did in 1982 when he invaded the Falklands, which, though being relatively close to Argentina, is a British territory. Mrs. Thatcher's government, of course, took the Falklands back. By the end of 1983, the Argentine military junta had fallen and Argentina had a Social Democrat president in the person of Raul Alfonsin (1927–2009). It could be argued that an extreme conservative tilt like this also creates an evolutionary mismatch, because it involves insufficient concern about Care, resulting in people looking to leaders that will create a society that is more caring and, also, who have a different worldview, as it is the 'conservative' worldview that appears to have brought about difficulties. Even a moderate swing towards conservatism could result in an evolutionary mismatch. After a long period of conservative government, a lot of people might begin to increasingly feel that there was now insufficient concern about Care, at least if those who led the government were very high in binding foundations, such as Margaret Thatcher, and we might expect the more pronounced conservatives to be particularly politically active in pushing their agenda. In other words, unlike mainstream conservatives, they would be high in binding values and low in individualizing values.

We have noted, however, that most conservatives are roughly equal in the strength of their Moral Foundations, raising the question of how a conservative government could ultimately lead to a left-wing backlash. One possibility is that once the 'evolutionary match' was achieved by a conservative government, society would be too lacking in 'Care' and 'Fairness' for the highly liberal minority within the population and, for the reasons outlined above, the liberals would be able to persuade non-liberals round to their point of view more easily than the other way around. They would also be more intensely unhappy about living in a conservative society than conservatives would be about living in a liberal society, providing them with a far stronger set of motivations. They would take control from beneath, and push the culture in a more liberal direction until people were persuaded, for example, to elect a left-wing government, which could then begin to take full control of the society, until a right-wing backlash took place. We looked earlier at how Margaret Thatcher led a conservative backlash. It could be argued that Tony Blair's New Labour landslide of 1997 — in which the Conservatives, who had been in power under Mrs. Thatcher (Prime Minister 1979-1990), and then the more moderate John Major, who led Britain from 1990 to 1997, for almost 18 years, were routed — followed roughly the process we have outlined for a left-wing reaction. While the Conservatives were in power, there was a long, liberal 'March Through the Institutions' with the left gradually becoming ever-more influential in the education system, the media, and other organs of power (Gabb, 2007) until, by 1993, there was a sense in which John Major's government was 'in office, but not in power', a phrase used in his own Chancellor of the Exchequer, Norman Lamont's, resignation speech (Seymour-Ure, 2008, p. 53).

The public reaction to the death of Diana, Princess of Wales (1961-1997) in autumn 1997, just after the election of New Labour, is often seen as symbolic of this move towards a more 'compassionate, sharing, caring Britain' (Hey, 2002, p. 73); a Britain where people cry in public; the British 'stiff upper lip' being rather less stiff than it used to be. The Blair government promoted individualistic ideas to a pronounced degree, desiring to open Britain up to the world; to dilute the sense of the British as a group. They deliberately allowed very high levels of non-white immigration in order to permanently change the country such that it was, without question, multicultural; to 'rub the right's nose in diversity' as Andrew Neather, a New Labour speech writer, put it (Kaufmann, 2019, p. 50).

So, based on the above discussion, it appears that politics is cyclical. It may appear, during a period of powerful conservative government or cultural hegemony, that society will always be like this and, from the liberal perspective, a sense of despondency might set in, that this is going to go on forever. The same feelings might envelop a conservative during a period of powerful liberal government or liberal cultural hegemony and, of course, it is possible to have a conservative government during a period of liberal cultural hegemony, and vice versa, though it is likely to be a relatively weak government, unable to make radical changes. However, it appears that human societies operate in cycles of liberalism and conservatism. Any cyclical system, of course, is unlikely to be without its 'humps and bumps'. Thus, we might expect that there would be mini-cycles of liberalism and conservatism within a broadly liberal period; cycles within cycles. In looking at the way in which the 1980s was 'conservative' in many European countries, and especially in Britain, it might be argued that this was a mini-cycle within a broader liberal trend that has enveloped Western societies, at least since World War II. However, our argument in this book is not simply that any current liberal hegemony will eventually give way to a period of conservatism within a broadly liberal trend. Our argument is that the entire liberal direction of Western societies, a macro-cycle which has been broadly followed for around a century or so, is going to dramatically reverse. But before we turn to that, we must look at the second explanation for how increasing genetic selection for traditional religiousness and conservatism can nevertheless result in an increasingly culturally liberal society.

Related Models of Societal Cycles

There are, it should be noted, other models which attempt to make sense of the way in which societies appear to move in political cycles. One of these is the 'hierarchy of needs' model. Once a certain level of material comfort is secured, people stop being concerned about this and they move on to the next level of the 'hierarchy of needs', which may simply be a desire for power and status (see Cinar, 2018, p. 41). If you are struggling for food, after all, you are not too concerned about strangers respecting your unusual lifestyle choices. The result is increasing social discord until the society is relatively impoverished, conflict also causing people to be exhausted and less ambitious. Another of these is the structural-demographical model presented by Russian demographer Peter Turchin (2016), which focuses strongly on making sense of cycles of peace and conflict in societies. According to Turchin, there are a number of key forces which interact in order to create cycles of peace or conflict in societies.

The first cause of conflict is simply an *excess of labour*. During an economic boom, a country will be attractive to immigrants, for example, leading to a huge pool of labour to choose from, which carries over when economic conditions subsequently become less favourable. This leads to declining labour prices and thus the relative impoverishment of those who must sell their labour; though it creates favourable economic conditions for the elite, who have access to cheap labour. This gives rise to resentful working- and lower middle-class people, who are angry about increasing economic polarization. Such people will be distrustful of the elite who govern them, and will be open to radical movements that help to foment conflict in society. There is, of course, debate over how these 'class' terms are defined. British social psychologist Michael Argyle (1925–2002) (Argyle, 1994) argued that the 'working class' is defined by physical labour, and the lower middle class as 'white-collar workers' or policemen. The 'middle class' is composed of 'lower professionals' such as teachers and accountants, and 'higher professionals' such as academics, doctors, and lawyers; the latter constituting the 'upper middle class'. The 'upper class' are, or were, the leaders in these various professions, as well as the old landed aristocracy, those who earned a sufficiently high income in rent that they need not work, and those in high positions of societal or political power; parliamentarians, bishops, military generals, and so on. Differences in class 'culture', such as speech codes, tend to map onto these divisions (see Fox, 2004). That being said, a century of globalization and big finance has largely unseated this more traditional conception of the upper-class elite, whose power has been decaying (Naím, 2014), as the very rich are now largely composed of an assortment of individuals from across the globe, who derive their income from offshore trust funds, and who sometimes reside abroad for tax purposes and in order to maintain a luxury lifestyle. Commonly referred to as 'plutocrats' or 'globalists', they mostly exert their influence through various species of international and transnational organization, from which most modern regulation, standardization, and investment will originate.

The second key factor is *intra-elite competition*. According to Turchin, favourable economic conditions for the elites results in increasing numbers of elite aspirants; a positive worldview whereby more and more people think they can join the elite or are even encouraged to believe that they can do so. The result is an over-educated society, in which there are too many qualified people for the number of elite positions available. In effect, a larger and larger proportion of society believe they are entitled to elite positions but, as the number of elite positions is limited, the result is conflict within the elite, as one-time markers of elite status become devalued, due to too many people possessing them. An example of this can be seen with the university degree. In England, at the time of writing, approximately 50% of 18-year-olds go to university. In the 1960s, around 5% did so (Chowdry et al., 2010). This change has occurred as more and more professions have required degrees rather than traditional apprenticeships or guild membership, as teaching and nursing colleges have been incorporated into universities, and have then required degrees rather than mere certificates, and as there has been a government-driven expansion of higher education. As this devalues the undergraduate degree, there has been an expansion of postgraduate education, once the preserve of a tiny intellectual elite (Williams, 2016). Clearly, this process devalues the qualifications as sureties of elite status, as elite places are limited, even if taking into account expansion in the number of universities and thus of university lecturers. For example, there were roughly 650 Members of Parliament in 1960. For this 'super-elite' to have kept track with the expansion of higher education, there would now have to be 6,500 MPs. And there would then be fierce intra-elite competition between these individually relatively powerless legislators.

In essence, elite over-production creates a large number of entitled people—who think it is their right to be part of the 'real' elite—who are profoundly resentful that they are not really part of the elite. This leads to intense conflict among the elite class, which can be expected to destabilize the entire society. One method that appears to have been successfully used among those with humanities degrees—which now lead to elite positions even less than do STEM degrees which were formerly associated with the inferior status of 'redbrick' universities (Williams, 2016, p. 95)—is virtue-signalling (symbolically indicating your virtue), especially with regard to identity politics issues, with the dictum 'diversity, inclusivity, equity'. Some of them have made a lucrative business of persuading universities and companies that their services are required to make these organizations much more virtuous, such as via being their 'Diversity Officer', an increasingly executive position found on a solid chip corporate board, which some have described as an expendable 'non-job' (de Castella, 23rd February 2011).

Another method is to try to drive out of any given elite institution anyone who differs from you, such as in their worldview. As intra-elite competition intensifies, we would expect competing members of the elite —in fierce competition for genuine elite positions—to engage in evermore Machiavellian attempts to attain these positions. This could potentially result in the elite, or aspirant elite, dividing into two or more competing factions that mutually despise and distrust each other; in UK politics, for example, there are multiple left-wing parties competing with each other: Labour, the Liberal Democrats, the Green Party, the Scottish National Party, Alba, Plaid Cymru, Sinn Féin, the Social Democratic and Labour Party, and the Alliance Party of Northern Ireland—and that's just the parties who hold seats in the UK parliament at the time of writing. All of these parties espouse broadly the same virtue-signalling 'Woke' morality of today's left, but each with its own subtly different emphases on issues, such as environmentalism, wealth inequality, or devolution.

Conversely, the centuries-old party of traditional conservatism in the UK, the Conservative Party, continues to successfully fend off all of its right-wing competitors in parliamentary elections, precisely because of the loyal and traditionalist mindset of most of its voters and members. The only other right-wing party in parliament is Northern Ireland's Democratic Unionist Party.

As we will explore below, we might actually expect these rival elites to be genetically distinct from each other, because we tend to cooperate with people who are more genetically similar to ourselves, and especially with people who are psychologically more genetically similar to ourselves, as opposed to physically more genetically similar. These are people who are similar in intelligence, personality, and other broader psychological traits, such as religiosity (Rushton, 2005). For these reasons, increased genetic diversity will result in decreased trust. It may be argued that some groups practise cousin marriage as a means of elevating in-group trust and positive ethnocentrism (Dutton, 2019a). This intense intra-elite competition would, partly, make sense of why left-wing academics are increasingly intolerant of right-wing academics and why they do all that they can to drive them out of academia (see Kotkin, 2020). Elite over-production leads to intra-elite warfare and that war is won, according to computer models, by those who are high in in-group cooperation and out-group hostility (Hammond & Axelrod, 2006). In a time of war, or of intense competition, we would expect the mere 'competitor' to morph into the 'enemy' such that we are more inclined to dispatch him.

We noted earlier that liberals and conservatives react differently when they feel that a deserved reward has been unfairly frustrated. Conservatives become more negatively ethnocentric, turning on other ethnic groups, whereas liberals turn on members of their own ethnic group. It could be argued that Woke-ideology reflects this. Bitter liberal graduates, who cannot find elite positions, turn on their own people, castigating them as 'racist' and 'transphobic' as a means of shaking the system that has cheated them and so possibly gaining status in the resultant turmoil. Conservative graduates, in the same position, are inclined to purify the group of the foreigners and individualists with whom they are competing, remaining loyal to their own people overall. However, this reaction of resentment will be more likely among left-wing people because, overall, they feel negative feelings more strongly than do right-wing people (see Kirkegaard, 2020).

The next factor is *state fragility*. This develops during a financial crisis, for example. It reduces the power of the government, and causes the government to appear to lack legitimacy. And the government's power will be rendered even more fragile by an *international environment* whereby a nation's competitors may wish to undermine the enemy by assisting a rival elite group within a foreign country. Turchin argues that these factors all existed in the 1920s and 1930s, leading to crisis and war in many Western countries. The elites dealt with this by attempting to bring about a more equal society, by limiting the excess of labour (such as by stopping immigration), by better regulating the economy, and by practising protectionist economics. The result was that, between about 1930 and 1970, real wages grew in Western countries. But, according to Turchin, such policies do not make countries, or the elites, rich. So, they eventually abandoned this paradigm in order to stimulate economic growth, and the process begins all over again (Turchin, 2016).

Turchin's model is sociological in nature and it is axiomatic in science that the sign of a successful sociological model is that it can be reduced down to the next level of analysis, this being individual-level psychology in this case; this is termed 'consilience' (Wilson, 1998). Thus, the processes that Turchin highlights should be reducible down to the individual level. We would suggest that this is quite possible. In effect, Turchin notes the way in which societies oscillate between periods of individualism and periods of collectivism. Periods of individualism appear to generate wealth, and certain kinds of confidence, but they also involve a reduction in social binding. It has been found that as people become individualistic, they concomitantly become more concerned with harm avoidance, whereas as they become more collectivist, they become more concerned with in-group loyalty (Yilmaz et al., 2016). In this sense, it could be argued that the cycles highlighted by Turchin are actually underpinned by the psychological process that we have outlined.

Moreover, it would appear that notions of 'fairness' and 'equality' are often the engine behind elite over-production. It is assumed that people are all of roughly equal capabilities, despite the very strong evidence of consistent differences in intelligence between people, which have been shown to robustly predict socio-economic status, at approximately 0.5 (Jensen, 1998). It is assumed that people can reach their full potential if only they are educated more, and so opportunities are provided such that this can occur. Accordingly, it is the value of 'Fairness' which helps to elevate intra-elite competition. We might also ask where an excess of unskilled labour comes from. Currently, at least, it mostly comes from immigration, the permitting of which reflects treating all people equally, regardless of their nationality, rather than being loyal to the in-group. So, it could be argued that it is indeed left-wing individualizing values that result in the eventual societal instability that Turchin highlights.

How Can Leftists Be Individualists?

It might be responded that it appears counter-intuitive to imply that left-wing people are 'individualists'. But we have already seen that the personality traits associated with being 'liberal' are individualist; such people are concerned with what is good for them or the groups with which they happen to identify for psychological reasons, with assisting them assuaging their sense of unhappiness. In effect, they are asserting that they are 'different'—an individualist trait—but they allegedly want to be treated the same as everybody else, and they want transferred to them the allegedly same amount of resources, which they purport others as having. A vegetarian who comes to a dinner party and necessitates a separate meal being cooked to accommodate her ('caring' and 'fair') lifestyle choice is being an individualist. A person concerned with the group would eat the roast beef along with everybody else, and be grateful to have been invited to the dinner party at all. It is no contradiction, however, that conservatism should be associated with being group-oriented while extreme conservatism—or being 'Alt-Right'—should be associated with being psychopathic; as psychopathology is a very specific set of traits beyond mere low Agreeableness and low Conscientiousness, including thriving on the danger of being a dissident, as noted earlier. Canadian sociologist Eric Kaufmann (2019) has noted that we might also expect people to feel a sense of guilt when they dissent in an extreme way from the dominant group morality. Those who are high in psychopathic traits, however, will be lacking in guilt.

Indeed, if we explore what we might call the 'Church of Multiculturalism' more broadly, then its individualistic dimensions are extremely clear. We will look soon at the specific ways in which multiculturalism parallels religion, but it is sufficient to state here that multiculturalism places the rights of the individual over the group. Language is constantly policed for 'offence' to 'excluded groups'; implying an overt concern with harm avoidance (see Ellis, 2004). The 'feelings' of individuals, or of groups of individuals, who are not part of the in-group are more important than those of the in-group. Thus, its counter-argument to the view that large-scale immigration might be bad for group cohesion is that this fails to take into account the feelings of immigrants, and it fails to treat them equally. Similarly, the counter-argument to the assertion that sex is biological and immutable is that telling a trans-woman (male-to-female transsexual) that he or she is not a woman hurts his or her feelings and singles him or her out as being unable to be treated equally. In this sense, objective truth—which could be regarded as a component of hierarchy and order—is less important than the 'feelings' of the individual. For this reason, we should not be surprised that there are contradictions in multiculturalism.

Contradictions are unproblematic for people who are unconcerned with truth. Indeed, British psychologist Simon Baron-Cohen (2002) has argued that we should conceive of a spectrum between what he calls the 'extreme male brain' at one end, and the 'extreme female brain' at the other, based on data about the ways in which males and females think differently, on average. The extreme female brain is deeply concerned with how people feel and with everyone getting along. It is high in empathy, but it is low in systematizing, being 'system-blind'. The extreme male brain, conversely, is primarily concerned with systematizing as well as with competition, hierarchy, and order, and it is low in empathy. In this sense, Baron-Cohen argues, the extreme male brain is autistic, with autism being characterized by an obsession with systematizing combined with a lack of empathy. So, following Baron-Cohen, we can argue that the left-wing individualist mind is low in systematizing.[3] Other issues are much more important than 'facts' and 'truth'. In pronounced cases, the individualist can happily believe one thing in one set of circumstances and something else in another, if doing so seems to assist that which the individualist regards as important.

It is dogma today that race and sex are 'social constructs' because to suppose the opposite case, that they are 'biological', means statistical race and sex differences in social status might be partly a result of innate psychological characteristics. This is an uncomfortable notion for agreeable people generally, because they do not wish to unduly hurt the feelings of those who might be described as not well endowed, but it is absolutely psychologically intolerable, for those with the radically equalitarian mindset, for whom low social status is the origin of all suffering in this world. Yet it is also a dogma today, in flat contradiction to the first dogma stated above, that if a member of a 'privileged race' (a white person) attempts to pass themselves off as black, as in the case of American black rights activist Rachel Dolezal (see Dolezal, 2017), then race is a fixed biological construct, because if it were merely a social construct, then it would make it difficult to aid the social interests of the seemingly powerless out-group with whom the leftist feels empathy, because they would no longer be a distinct out-group. Race also becomes biological when recognizing it as such helps non-white races, for whom

---

[3] That's excluding 'libertarian individualists', who generally occupy the centre right and are extremely high in systematizing and in a desire for personal freedom, and who are low in all of the moral foundations (Iyer et al., 2012).

there is a lack of organ donors in Western countries or who are genetically more susceptible to certain diseases (see Dutton, 2020).

And when it comes to sex, the level of paradoxical ontological duality rises to absurd levels. Though in perfect symmetry to the transracial taboo, it frustrates a certain renegade faction of feminism that a member of the privileged sex (a male) should pass themselves off as a female, because, again, it existentially threatens the existence of the powerless out-group, nevertheless these feminists are ironically classed as transphobic, and the overriding dogma here is that sex differences are biological when they're self-evidently not, and not biological when established science would suggest that they are. Here 'biology' is reduced to an empty theological assertion of what is supposedly objectively real; it has nothing to do with actually investigating life in the natural world.

We are increasingly seeing a trend among the Woke left, ready and willing to sacrifice not just large swathes of the life sciences, but even the scientific method itself, under the umbrella accusation that it's a conspiratorial factory of sexist and racist ideas. And indeed, inasmuch as psychologically predisposed as the modern left are to judging the natural world itself as sexist, racist, and altogether deeply unfair and unequal, with noticeable biases for less offensive species such as bonobos and dolphins, they would be correct. By their standards of rigid equality and utopian harm avoidance: science, nature, reality, truth, and so on really is racist and sexist and all the rest, and must be denied and supplanted at all costs. On this basis, it could be argued that those postmodernists among the far-left seeking to do just this are actually the most logically consistent and rational among their political faction. It is those who believe the same set of dogmas, but still identify themselves as 'scientists', or as people who 'love science', and as holding beliefs backed by an established body of research and evidence, that commit the ultimate act of inconsistency.

With regard to those who virtue-signal to elevate their status and who realize that, in a broadly leftist society, this is how they gain the status they desperately desire: what they believe can change—and contradict itself—in order to help elevate their status in any given set of circumstances. This is because they are extreme individualists and, for them, status is more important than structure and order, which is fundamental to fostering a successful, cooperative group. If society were deeply religious, these people would signal their religiousness in the most extreme way possible, but it is 'multiculturalist', so this is what they signal.

Those with binding values, by contrast, are so focused on the good of their group that their lack of concern about harm extends even to themselves, and they may sacrifice themselves for the group accordingly. They will be low in individualistic traits, such as Narcissism and Machiavellianism, meaning that they will behave in pro-social ways without drawing attention to this fact. They will give money to charities concerned with harm or fairness, and they will do so anonymously. They have only a limited desire to climb the group hierarchy. What matters for them is the good of the group as a whole. These are the kinds of people who would lay down their lives for their group in times of war. They are more focused on selection at the *group level*.

Understanding Group Selection

We have used the term *group selection* a number of times, briefly defined. However, before we move on to the next chapter we need to be quite clear what it means and we need to defend it from its detractors. According to American biologist Edward O. Wilson, in some respects, human society might be more usefully compared to termites than to a group of highly advanced chimpanzees. This comparison works because, like termites, humans, especially modern humans, live in intensely social societies in which there are extremely clearly marked divisions of labour and where the benefits to cooperation can clearly be seen at the cultural group level; as opposed to being strictly limited based on relative degrees of relatedness. In addition, human societies—like termite colonies—regularly compete with one another, meaning that they are subject to a very high level of 'group selection'. If there is competition between individuals then you have 'individual selection'. But you can also pass on your genes indirectly. You can do this via 'kin selection', such as when a spinster aunt, who has no children of her own, invests her resources in her nieces and nephews, each of which carries 25% of her genes. It has been shown that ethnic groups and races can in certain circumstances be modelled as if they were extended kinship groups. As Australian political scientist Frank Salter (2007) has shown, it is possible to calculate the amount of damage inflicted on a group's genetic interests based on how many outsiders are permitted to enter that group's territory and the level of genetic difference between the two groups. On average, random members of an ethnic group are related as first cousins in opposition to other populations. This encourages humans to be hostile to invading outsiders and easily triggered to engage in self-sacrificial behaviour in order to protect their ethnic group. Salter calculates, for example, how many members of a different ethnicity must invade a group's territory for it to be the equivalent of each member losing a child; in other words, he computes 'genetic interests'. For instance, if 10,000 Danes migrated to England, this would amount to the English people losing 140 children, due to the extent to which the English and Danes would integrate and fewer English genes would be passed on. If this were 10,000 Bantus, however, who are far more genetically distant from the English than the Danes, then the English would lose the genetic equivalent of approximately 11,000 children. So, you can pass on your genes indirectly, if there is competition between ethnic groups, by investing in that group. Culture, as a very diffuse 'extended phenotype' is also critical to understanding group selection in human populations, as human groups vary much more among themselves in terms of cultural diversity than in terms of genetic diversity. This means that when acting on human groups, it is 'culture' that gives selection something to act on, even when the cultural groups are largely identical to one another in terms of their genetic profiles (Richerson et al., 2016).

This is what is meant by group selection or cultural group selection. Most researchers who work in this area don't think exclusively in terms of group selection however, as they recognize that selection can also act at different levels of biological organization, including at the individual level. Furthermore, these levels can be antagonistic, such that individuals whose behaviours harm the group can be favoured in terms of fitness under certain circumstances. Multi-level selection is the term given to this process of selection acting across different levels of biological organization, sometimes even in opposing directions (Wilson, 2002). Doing so is a means of indirectly passing on your genes.

Some researchers remain sceptical of the concept of group selection, but their arguments can be easily refuted. It has been argued that human groups were too small to develop group selection. This is inaccurate with regard to pre-agricultural groups, as there is abundant evidence of intense, violent warfare between such groups and genocide enacted by them (Allen & Jones, 2016). The argument falls apart especially once we developed agriculture, which involved an enormous escalation in intergroup conflict, war, and genocide; with more technically advanced groups tending to wipe out or otherwise expand at the expense of less advanced neighbours (Cochran & Harpending, 2009; Kiernan, 2008). Some researchers dislike the model for emotional reasons, referring to the 'false allure of group selection' and presenting manifestly fallacious arguments against it, such that it deviates from the random mutation model of evolution (so what? It is bound to, because that refers to individual level selection) or that humans cannot possibly be selected to damage their individual interests (if so, how can we explain self-sacrificial behaviour?) (see Pinker, 18th June 2012).

There do not appear to be any logical arguments against group selection. It seems to be a concept that 'certain people' viscerally dislike for ideological reasons. So, with the concept of group selection clear in our minds, we can now turn to the second reason for the rise of liberalism and why there will be a strong reaction against it.

Chapter Four

The Weakening of Group Selection

'Hard times create strong men,
strong men create good times,
good times create weak men,
and weak men create hard times.'[1]

Those Who Remain

Now we turn to the second, and more fundamental, explanation regarding why, since at least the 1960s, Western societies have moved in a more liberal and more irreligious direction, despite fertility being predicted by extreme conservatism and religiousness. This relates to evolutionary changes in the population with regard to the intensity of group selection and thus of individualism.

As we have already observed, intense conditions of group selection create people who are strongly ethnocentric; they are high in positive and negative ethnocentrism (Hammond & Axelrod, 2006). This means that they are internally strongly cooperative; high in Agreeableness (altruism and empathy) and Conscientiousness (rule-following and impulse control) and low in mental instability (low in 'Neuroticism'), a trait which is characterized by feeling negative feelings strongly, with the exception of certain socially-useful negative feelings such as social anxiety (Fernandes et al., 2018). A group will be less cooperative if lots of people are prone to be jealous, angry, and resentful, or anxious and depressed, because these traits result in social withdrawal and sometimes even paranoia (Moritz et al., 2017). For a group to thrive in such circumstances, it must monitor and remove such selfish, antisocial, free-riding, or parasitic individuals, meaning that those kinds of people will tend to be selected out through

---

1   G. Michael Hopf, *Those Who Remain*.

social selection. In other words, such an ecology selects for a 'slow Life History Strategy' (LHS), also known more narrowly as a *K* strategy. A fast LHS, a so-called r-strategy, develops in an easy yet unstable ecology. This instability, where you could be wiped out at any moment, means you have to breed as quickly and copiously as possible, so you invest most of your energy in copulation. Think of crabs. They have numerous offspring per litter. These crabs are born practically as adults and the mother invests almost nothing in each individual crab. To the extent that you select for anything, you select for evidence of healthy genes, with physical attractiveness tending to be evidence of this.

As the ecology becomes harsher and more predictable, then its carrying capacity for the species is reached, and so members of the species start to compete with each other. In this harsh ecology, if they have lots of offspring who are not adapted to the environment then they could all just die. In addition, the environment is predictable, allowing you to plan for the future. So, you invest less energy in copulation and more energy in a smaller number of offspring, with a smaller number of partners. You transfer your energy over to nurture. You will be better at nurture if you are more Agreeable and less Neurotic, and you will be better at planning for the predictable future, and solving the problems of a harsh ecology, if you are more Conscientious and more intelligent. Also, in a harsh ecology, you are more likely to survive as part of a group, so group-selection pressure intensifies. Life also slows down, as it is competitively beneficial to have a longer childhood, in which you can learn all of the complex information necessary to successfully compete and survive in your harsh ecology (Rushton, 1995).

A number of factors have conspired to relax the strength of group selection over the last few hundred years, meaning that fast Life History strategists are selected out to a decreasing extent. Most importantly, since the 'Maunder Minimum' in the late seventeenth century, the climate has generally become considerably warmer. This has meant that food is less unpredictably scarce, and the price of food, and especially of grain, has stabilized (see Hackett Fischer, 1996; Zhang et al., 2011). This would mean that the selection pressure to be strongly cooperative with the in-group would be less intense. In a warmer a climate, with more abundant food, antisocial individualists would be better able to survive without intensely cooperating with the group. If they didn't have many friends to help them out in times of want, they could still survive, because these times of want would be less intense than was previously the case. And what would be true of the individual was true of the group as a whole. Due to the fact that conditions were easier, the result was a decrease in inter-group conflict, with groups ultimately fighting each other for land and thus the ability to produce food in an extremely cold climate in which it was difficult to produce sufficient food to feed the group. This decline in intergroup conflict—and the growing prevalence of intergroup peace —meant that there was less pressure on groups to be high in binding values; in positive and negative ethnocentrism. Accordingly, it was increasingly easier for individualists to pass on their genes and there was decreasing social pressure for individualists to force themselves to conform. From the Maunder Minimum onwards, the climate continued to become warmer, though with humps and bumps, through the eighteenth, nineteenth, and twentieth centuries, further heightening this process (Zhang et al., 2011). Consistent with this fall in the intensity of group selection, per capita war fatalities in Europe have been declining for over a century, even in spite of the massive death tolls of the two World Wars (Hertler et al., 2020).

The Rise and Fall of Intelligence

This warming would also have an impact on the average intelligence of the population. As already briefly noted, there was strong selection pressure for intelligence under harsh Darwinian conditions, and those that were more intelligent were able to sustain higher numbers of surviving offspring due to the relationship between intelligence and the ability to solve complex problems presented by a harsh and competitive environment, and also to accrue wealth. Under pre-industrial conditions, there was extremely intense selection for wealth. In England, for example, in the seventeenth century, the completed fertility (number of surviving children) of the richer 50% of the population was roughly double that of the completed fertility of the poorer 50% of the population based on parish registers (Pound, 1972) and about 40% higher based on wills, which tended to only be left by the wealthier 60% of the population (Clark, 2007).

Due to the robust connection between intelligence and wealth, this elevated the intelligence of the population every generation, as those at the bottom died out, and a necessary system of social descent filled the positions they vacated. For various reasons, such as the development of contraception (with higher IQ predicting more efficient use of contraception), this association has now been reversed (Dutton & Woodley of Menie, 2018), an issue to which we will return later. However, socio-economic status is about 70% heritable across generations in societies as different as India and Sweden (Clark, 2014). Accordingly, though people do move up and down the social hierarchy, there is a significant degree to which socio-economic status is genetic.

Until about 1800, we were becoming more intelligent, as noted above. This can be seen by looking at the behaviour of a number of robust correlates of intelligence, as previously explored in *At Our Wits' End: Why We're Becoming Less Intelligent and What It Means for the Future* (Dutton & Woodley of Menie, 2018). Levels of per capita major innovations were increasing, the size of the head (and thus brain) was increasing, literacy and numeracy were increasing despite living standards remaining relatively static, levels of violence were decreasing, and genes, from ancient genomes, indirectly associated with intelligence, were increasing. Intelligence allowed people to become rich, and wealth allowed you to provide better conditions for your children; so intelligence was selected for, and became more strongly correlated with other fitness-enhancing traits. Changes in per capita major innovation across time can be seen in Figure 4.1.

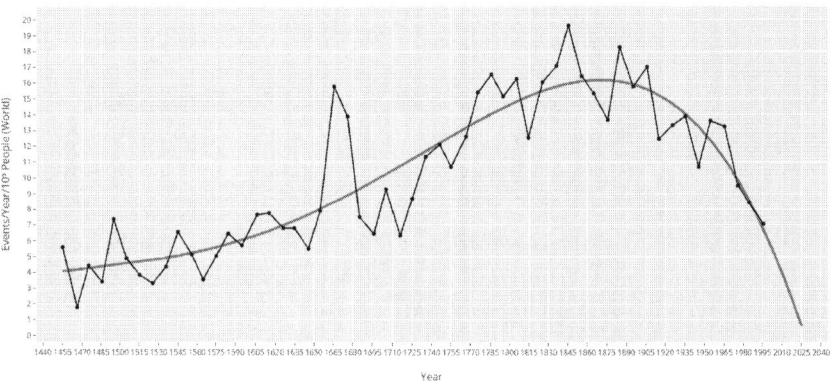

Figure 4.1. Per capita major innovations across time, 1450–2004.

Now, however, there is a large body of evidence that demonstrates that we are becoming less intelligent and becoming less intelligent for genetic reasons. Between the 1880s and the year 2000, reaction times—how quickly you respond to stimuli—have become longer, consistent with an IQ decline of roughly 10 points (Dutton & Woodley of Menie, 2018). You may have heard of a phenomenon called the Flynn Effect, where IQ scores increased in Western countries across the twentieth century. Its discovery is attributed to James Flynn, whom we met earlier. But we will see below that the Flynn Effect is an illusion, in the sense that it does not betoken a rise in 'general intelligence'. Rather, it reflects an increase in mental abilities that are very weakly associated with general intelligence, albeit abilities which, to some extent, aid you in solving problems (Rindermann & Becker, 2018). Data from Iceland indicates that over the past three generations there has been a decline in the percentage of the population carrying alleles associated with very high educational attainment, and thus with high IQ (Kong et al., 2017).

Colour hue-discrimination—another correlate of IQ, due to cognitive problems being easier to solve if you have a subtler understanding of the variables involved—has got worse across time (Woodley of Menie & Fernandes, 2015). The use of extremely difficult words in representative texts—with words being thinking tools which allow you to think in a more complex way—has declined since the Victorian era (Woodley of Menie et al., 2015). Currently, there is generally a negative 0.1 correlation between IQ score and fertility (Reeve et al., 2018).

If we examine the scientific genius, he is a person with outlier high IQ who is widely recognized as having made a hugely important contribution to his area of science; having made a crucial breakthrough. His high intelligence is combined with certain other psychological traits. Whereas the normal academic is high in Conscientiousness and Agreeableness, the genius is moderately low in these, meaning he has autistic traits. This means he can 'think outside the box', allowing him to generate highly original ideas, and he either doesn't care about offending people or he is too low in empathy to understand what might offend people. New ideas, especially radical breakthroughs, always offend against vested interests, but the genius won't care about this, so he'll have no qualms about presenting his breakthrough. His autistic traits of being obsessive, utterly focused on making sense of the world, and over-sensitivity to stimuli (meaning he'll take in more information and notice very subtle differences) mean he will not be deterred by setbacks, allowing him to work on his complex problem until he solves it (see Dutton & Charlton, 2015). We will return to the issue of genius anon, but key to our discussion here is that the extent of genius allows us to guage society's average intelligence level. Per capita levels of genius and per capita major innovation reached a peak in about 1870 and have now returned to the same level that they were in 1600. This can be seen in Figure 4.1. This intelligence decline will become highly relevant later, when we look at the kind of society with which we will be faced, in the coming decades.

It might be argued that this decline in 'recognized important innovations' has occurred because we have already picked all of the 'low-hanging fruit'. But this misunderstands how problem-solving works. Problem-solving involves making connections between pieces of already available information, so that, when it comes to solving problems, there is no such thing as 'low-hanging fruit'. When inventions, which we are now used to, were first innovated, they were regarded as extraordinary breakthroughs; geniuses having made connections which nobody had yet been sufficiently intelligent to make. It might also be averred that, though intelligence is declining, the population is rising, meaning any intelligence decline is more than offset by a rise in the absolute numbers of highly intelligent people. However, it has been shown that our intelligence decline is so rapid that this is simply not the case (Woodley & Figueredo, 2013).

It has also been suggested that the IQ decline, and indeed evidence of increasing mental disorders, is not due to genetic changes but rather due to pollution of various kinds, including endocrine disruptors (Demeneix, 2014). It can be countered that a path analysis has tested these two possibilities and found that the neurotoxin hypothesis did not explain any of the variance in intelligence across time while a genetic hypothesis explained some of it (Woodley of Menie et al., 2018). Moreover, there is direct evidence proving that the intelligence decline is partly genetically mediated, as discussed above.

The Flynn Effect

It should also be noted that the Flynn Effect—the secular rise in IQ scores across the twentieth century in Western countries—is entirely consistent with this model, as its putative discoverer (see Lynn, 2013), American political scientist James Flynn, himself conceded (Flynn & Shayer, 2018). Intelligence can be conceived of as rather like a pyramid. At the base of the pyramid there are numerous 'specialized abilities' that are only very weakly associated with intelligence, such as the ability to tie your shoe laces or catch a ball. Moving up, there are often considered the three main forms of intelligence, which are more strongly associated with how smart you are: mathematical, verbal, and spatial intelligence. People vary on how highly they score on tests of these. Some people are more verbally-tilted, while others are more mathematically-tilted. But, in general, those who score high on one kind of intelligence score high on them all, so we can conceive of a factor which underpins all of them. This is 'general intelligence', known as g, which is at the pinnacle of the intelligence pyramid. In general, when we speak of someone as being 'intelligent' we mean that they have high 'general intelligence', or g. Some people argue that there are 'multiple intelligences', including 'emotional intelligence' (Gardner, 1983), but this weakly correlates with 'intelligence' as normally defined (Kaufmann et al., 2011). Indeed, one very occasionally meets people who have high verbal intelligence but are not especially high in 'general intelligence': think of stereotypical postmodern social scientists.

The documented rise in IQ scores has been found to have been on intelligence abilities at the base of the intelligence pyramid, and, in particular, on the subtest 'similarities'—the ability to make associations. This ability is only a very weak measure of intelligence, but due to the fact that it has increased extremely rapidly, and due to the imperfect nature of IQ tests as means of measuring intelligence, certain personality traits, such as impulse control, can also elevate your ability to solve problems — this has shown up on the IQ tests as an overall IQ rise. Flynn has argued that this occurred because we are an increasingly science-oriented society that increasingly teaches people to think in an analytic way; it makes them don 'scientific spectacles' (Flynn, 2012, p. 15). This process has pushed these intelligence abilities to their phenotypic maximum, overwhelming an underlying decline in actual intelligence.

Once the phenotypic maximum in intelligence is reached, then declining IQ would show up even on the IQ tests, and this is what began to happen in the West with cohorts born around the year 1980, according to some studies (see Dutton et al., 2016). This new trend is being widely referred to as the Negative Flynn Effect, connoting a phenotypic decline in IQ, and there is some evidence that this decline is actually driven by g; on the most genetic parts of the IQ test, as we would expect (Dutton et al., 2016). So, there is no inconsistency between intelligence decline and the Flynn Effect. Indeed, it may be that a hypothetical 'Negative Flynn Effect' comes about, leading to accelerated reduction in IQ for environmental reasons. As people, such as teachers, become less intelligent for genetic reasons, they will be less able to push the IQ of their pupils to its phenotypic maximum, meaning that the pupils' IQ will fall for both genetic and environmental reasons.

In summation, the warming of the environment with surplus production of food and universal welfare has relaxed selection pressures on intelligence. The decline in inter-group conflict has also reduced the selection pressure for group intelligence, where more intelligent groups triumph; due to superior planning, better weapons, and better management of resources. This has in turn virtually extinguished the number of extant geniuses in the Western population, and, in any case, reduced the need to be tolerant of the antisocial genius personality type in public research and higher education institutions, types who would otherwise produce these innovations. Thus, the level of per capita major innovation has dropped off to pre-industrial levels, indeed to the same levels that we saw in 1600, as can be observed in Figure 4.1.

Inasmuch as intelligence, overall, tends to be associated with pro-social behaviour and group-oriented values, these changes also predict the rise in individualism. So, with the traditional elite of the Victorian era failing to achieve above replacement fertility, those who were from the middle of that society have moved up to take their place, and now their descendants occupy those elite positions; a rank below them replaces the middle class, and so on, and a new underclass, which didn't exist in the Victorian period, now resides at the bottom. This upwardly-mobile recycling process in class has repeated (and accelerated — as we will show) with each generation, such that the gap between the late Victorians and our own contemporary average IQ is now around 10 points (Dutton & Woodley of Menie, 2018); the difference between your average high school science teacher and your average science professor (Herrnstein & Murray, 1994).

The Industrial Revolution and Its Consequences

Although this process would occur simply due to the warming environment, it would be remiss of us to ignore the impact of the Industrial Revolution, which can be regarded as a consequence of high societal intelligence, and high per capita genius levels. It can be argued that the Industrial Revolution, and its results, would simply augment this process of individualism. Through improved medicine, improved public health, and better general living standards, the Industrial Revolution has massively reduced environmental harshness.

Crucially, the Industrial Revolution interfered with, or extended, the 'Malthusian Cycle' that we referred to above. This was presented by English cleric Thomas Malthus (1766–1834). In his book *An Essay on the Principle of Population,* Malthus (1798) proffered a simple cyclical theory of how the growth and contraction of a society operates. When there is an abundance of resources and a small population, the standard of living is relatively high, because there is more than enough land and food to sustain the population. Precisely because conditions are auspicious, the population will grow and eventually it will reach the maximum possible population that the ecology can realistically sustain. However, this will also mean that living standards for most of the population will have declined — due to over-crowding and insufficient food — and, in addition, the situation will be highly unstable. It will take little more than a few bad harvests or a period of pestilence to cause a population collapse in which the genetically relatively less healthy people who have been able to amass under auspicious conditions will be wiped out. Once this happens the cycle simply begins all over again.

To give some examples, the Medieval Warm Period lasted from about 950 to about 1250, reflecting increased sun-spot activity (Mayes & Wheeler, 2002). During this time, it was so warm that grapes were successfully cultivated in various parts of England, something impossible even today (West & Scafetta, 2010, p. 129). It then started to become a lot colder. By the 1340s, there wasn't enough food to sustain the large population of Medieval Europe and many people were weakened by lack of sustenance. At this point, the Black Death occurred, as outbreaks of plague take place when it has been below a certain temperature. This is because, in these conditions, fleas are unable to pass the hardened bacillus through their system. It blocks their gut and, ravenous, and due to their rat-hosts having died of plague, they bite more aggressively and they bite humans. They transmit regurgitated bacillus in the process (Ngeleja et al., 2017). Plague, thereafter, spreads from human to human. The result was a massive population collapse, by as much as 50%, and 70% in some areas, with, in general, only the healthier people surviving (Benedictow, 2006, p. 327). This Malthusian Cycle continued, with less dramatic plague- or famine-induced collapses, right up until industrialization began. It is the process by which nature, in effect, regulates populations in a broader eco-system. Another example can be seen around a millennium earlier, at the end of the Roman Warm Period, which lasted from about 250 AD to about 400 AD (Nunn, 2007, p. 9). As it got colder, any plague would be better able to spread through the already malnourished and epidemic-ridden population (Todd, 1977, Warner, 1972, p. 18) which had ballooned in size during the warm period. Then, between 541 and 549, came the Justinian Plague, named after the Byzantine Roman Emperor at the time. Believed to be the same disease as the Black Death, the result was an absolutely catastrophic population collapse of about 60% throughout Europe (Mordechai et al., 2019).

In essence, under the Malthusian Cycle, a period of plenty made economic growth which led to over-population, poor living conditions, epidemics, and the population collapsed back to better living condition for those that remained. The Industrial Revolution can be said to have created a particularly big 'boom' via technological innovations which have meant that the pace of innovation—in terms of speeding up production, producing more food, and combatting disease through inoculation and superior medicine—has long out-paced population growth. The result has been an enormous population spike and then, as people have understood that they don't need to have lots of children in order for some to survive, or as more and more people have lost the desire to have children, the 'Demographic Transition' took place in various countries. This began in Britain, which industrialized first. The Demographic Transition is when a society moves from being one characterized by high fertility and high child mortality to being one characterized by low fertility and low child mortality. This transition, which was complete in Western countries by the beginning of the twentieth century, comes in two stages. In the first stage there is a massive decline in child mortality and this is followed, some years later, by a steep drop in fertility. In the intervening period, the population will dramatically increase because there will be *both* high fertility and low child mortality, presumably because people have not yet quite grasped that it is safe to heavily limit their fertility, and so allow their living standards to improve. By the middle of the twentieth century, most families in Western countries had only 2 children and, by the end of it, they were down to fewer than 2, to below replacement fertility. This process has occurred later in developing countries, at a point where medical technology was even more advanced, leading to an even more pronounced population spike (Kaufmann, 2019).

In addition, the Industrial Revolution reduced the need for high levels of cooperation in order to survive; increasing the extent to which individualism could flourish. It also reduced selection pressure for intelligence, with the relationship between intelligence and fertility having gone into reverse in industrialized countries. And as we'll keep reiterating, this is due to a number of factors. We were under selection for intelligence until the Industrial Revolution, with the result that intelligence remains correlated with low levels of mutation, as we were also selecting for general low mutational load. For example, intelligence is negatively correlated with gene forms related to heart disease and high blood pressure (Deary et al., 2019). Further, we would expect general mutational load to simply make the entire nervous system, and thus the brain, work less efficiently, a significant component of intelligence being processing speed and a high functioning nervous system (Nettle, 2007). As people reduce their fertility, large families tend to happen by accident. The development of reliable contraception, which is more efficiently employed by more intelligent people, thus helps to push intelligence down (Lynn, 2011, p. 67). The rise of welfare, which only a wealthy society, with huge excess, can afford, means that less intelligent people end up having large families, usually by accident. Currently, only families who are on welfare and are designated as 'troubled households' (due to a combination of antisocial behaviour, truancy, and high cost to the tax payer) (Perkins, 2016, p. 157), who tend to have relatively low IQ, have above replacement fertility in the UK (Perkins, 2016, p. 159), and such people tend to be low in personality traits such as Conscientiousness (Perkins, 2016, Ch. 2), with low Conscientiousness also predicting fertility in modern times for similar reasons (Jokela, 2012).

It has been shown that the breakdown of selection pressure has resulted in a rise in mutational load in industrialized populations, which should be obvious because easier conditions mean that the selection pressure to be genetically healthy—adapted to a harsh environment—is weakened. Accordingly, industrialization might have led to a marked increase in strongly genetic health conditions and simply in general poor genetic health (You & Henneberg, 2016, 2017, 2018). This has been termed the 'Crumbling Genome' (Kondrashov, 2017). In fact, there is evidence that, due to its relationship with low intelligence, we are specifically selecting for certain kinds of poor health. Based on a sample of 409,629 British people it has been found that we are selecting for genes associated with elevated levels of body fat and risk of heart disease, and smoking (Hugh-Jones & Abdellaoui, 2021).

Worse still, decreased selection against bodily mutational load—selecting out a poor immune system—has meant decreased selection against mutations affecting the functioning of the brain, which might predispose people toward thinking in a highly individualistic or fitness-reducing fashion. This relationship makes sense, as 84% of the genome is involved in some aspect of brain development and maintenance (Hawrylycz et al., 2012), making it a potentially large target for mutations (Miller, 2000). There is some evidence that, due to intense selection for group-orientation during our pre-industrial era, this mutation pressure might be in the direction of greater individualism. Indeed, there is some evidence that those who have individualistic, liberal traits tend to be higher in physiological and psycho-behavioural traits that might be associated with elevated mutational load, and these people might push others to act in a less group-selected way (Dutton et al., 2018). However, the implications of this have been explored elsewhere (see Dutton, 2021b) and it is not broadly necessary to the group selection model examined here.[2]

Certainly, it can be said with confidence that the Industrial Revolution, in having reduced child mortality from roughly 50% to about 1% in developed countries (Volk & Atkinson, 2008), has increased genetic diversity. The resultant population has experienced the purge of mutation, caused by child mortality, to a much lesser extent; so it is obviously going to be more genetically diverse. This genetic diversity would lead to increasing societal polarization, as more and more people were less and less genetically similar to each other, with it having been shown, as already discussed, that we tend to cooperate with people who are genetically similar—even within sibling groups—as it is a means of indirectly benefiting our genetic interests (Rushton, 2005). This would lead to greater atomization and with that the rise of individualism, leading to ever-more polarization between binders and individualists, as the latter increase in their individualism.

---

[2] This is known as the 'spiteful mutants' model. According to this model, people who are high in mutational load act in ways that reduce their own evolutionary fitness, and directly and indirectly reduce that of others, who are lower in mutational load (Woodley of Menie et al., 2017). There is at least a case for arguing that leading individualists are spiteful mutants. This has been explored elsewhere with regard to leading feminists. See Dutton (2021b).

As explained, pressure for group selection occurs under harsh conditions, in which groups are in conflict, meaning they must be high in positive ethnocentrism. This would militate in favour of a coalition of people to cooperate together in the face of a common enemy, even if such a coalition was ever-more genetically dissimilar because the enemy would be yet more genetically dissimilar (see Salter, 2007). But with the breakdown of group selection, however, these coalitions are left to decay and collapse, because there is no longer any reason to hold them together. In extreme cases, a return to the fission-fusion system, that is seen among Stone Age Amazonian tribes, where only basic needs are met, can occur. These tribes are only very weakly held together, frequently splitting into separate clans over relatively minor disagreements. In a more pre-historic sense, they are extreme individualists as reflected in their weak social organization, general lawlessness, and proneness to fighting (see Chagnon, 1968).

It has been argued that the spectre of World War II, and the Cold War, helped to hold developed world coalitions together. It halted group selection—in the sense that the threat of nuclear obliteration prevented inter-group conflict from breaking out—but it forced people to behave in a group-selected fashion nonetheless. In the absence of this threat, we would expect these coalitions to eventually Balkanize. This clearly occurred with the break-up of the Soviet Union. It might be averred that separatism campaigns within European and North American countries and even between European countries, by leaving the European Union, reflects a similar pattern (see Dattel, 2019; Ryabinin, 2017). This individualism would be further augmented by immigration, since World War II, into Western countries, by other races. American sociologist Robert Putnam (2007) has shown that immigration results in a collapse in trust for two reasons. Being genetically dissimilar, the natives and the immigrants do not trust each other. But, in addition, the process reduces trust between the natives, seemingly because they now fear that some of their own may collaborate with the immigrants against them. In other words, immigration opens up a channel via which individualists can survive, and in doing so helps to increase individualism.

The Remaining Individualizers

The key point is that, as a result of this process of weakening group selection, 'those who remain' are a growing number of individualizers. There is less pressure against them, and, thus, those who are focused overtly on 'Fairness' and 'Care', and on their own selfish interests, are able to become increasingly influential. They are also able, at least in the early stages of this process, to increasingly pass on their genes. As we will see in Chapter Ten, they will eventually cease to significantly pass on their genes, but they certainly do so at this early stage.

How do they do this? As we have already discussed, we can divide between binders and individualists. Individualists, just like the fourteenth century Lollards discussed above, will showcase individualist foundations—harm avoidance and equality—as means of getting to the top of the society; it being adaptive under harsh conditions to be at the top due to the association between high status and completed fertility. So we have people signalling their fervent belief in the importance of these traits. If these beliefs are held alongside a belief in the importance of fertility, as is often the case in Protestantism, then such people will spread as a percentage of the population, and they would also be able to spread the influence of individualizing ideas across the population, and also to question and undermine their period's binding ideas. Indeed, it could be argued that having lots of children under such a system is itself a means of playing for status. It is a way of saying that you are so nurturing that you want to have lots of children, and that you are so fit and healthy that you can successfully produce lots of surviving children; that God blesses you and orders your estate, such that you are able to have a large family —and with this comes social status and authority. Anyway, this situation creates an arms race whereby you need to signal your virtue and bravery, by your willingness to question tradition, sanctity, and authority for the good of equality and fairness, in ever-more creative and original ways, a phenomenon we briefly discussed above.

This can be accomplished through the propagation of what English scientist Bruce Charlton (2009) has termed 'clever-silly' ideas; ideas presented by intellectuals that appear superficially profound. Expanding on Charlton's idea, it has been argued that a 'clever-silly' idea is one which is persuasively and superficially logically explicated—but in reality underpinned by a perspective grounded in a certain arrangement of moral foundations and thus ultimately in dogma—and which permits you to showcase your belief in equality; your virtuous belief in harm avoidance, and also other admired traits, such as intelligence, originality, and bravery. An example would be postmodernism, which, typically mixed in with 'Critical Theory', avers that 'truth' is merely the oppressive worldview forcibly instituted by powerful groups, and should be 'deconstructed' in order to empower the disempowered and oppressed (Hicks, 2004). Postmodernist thought is almost invariably presented in highly verbose, opaque, and profound-seeming prose (see Dutton & Van der Linden, 2015). In this sense, it can be argued that most important religious innovations are, in fact, 'clever-silly' ideas. It has been averred that there will be clever-silly innovators, who will take a system of thinking and radically question it, and signal their extreme individualism in the process. This would be the case with people such as Martin Luther (1483-1546) or Karl Marx (1818-1883). In doing so, such people would take a big risk for, potentially, a big reward, in terms of future socio-economic status. And then there would be the clever-silly followers, who would hedge their bets rather more. They would question the current dispensation, in an individualistic direction, but only moderately; taking a smaller risk for a smaller reward. But they would, in their own way, help to push society in a more individualistic direction, optimally showcasing their individualistic bravery as well as, to some extent, their moderation, conformism, and reliability (Dutton & Van der Linden, 2015).

As already observed, in the early stages at least, we would actually expect this to be a fitness-promoting strategy. It would be adaptive, in an ecology in which there is little pressure to resist this process, and we would expect this adaptive desire to be correlated with other adaptive desires, such as the desire for children, and even religious belief and worship; to the extent that this is adaptive, as we will see. When there is no cost for the individual, or group, to people having such individualist ideas, then they can spread, and they can become more fervent. This runaway process could not be permitted to happen with Lutheranism or Anglicanism, as it would lead to ever-more Anabaptism, rebellion, and social chaos, threatening a group under harsh conditions of selection. Thus there were historical backlashes against the Reformation's excesses (Atherstone, 2015); and many of the extreme Protestants then fled to America (Hackett Fischer, 1989). But it could have happened if those group-selected conditions weakened.

Worse still, it can be argued that, in an increasingly easy ecology, it is actually beneficial—in terms of attaining socio-economic status—to adhere to and to contribute to such ways of thinking. In the early stages, therefore, they should be associated with fitness. And, consistent with this, there is some evidence that fitness—measured in terms of numbers of children—was less negatively associated with leftism in the early twentieth century than is the case today, and there is further evidence of this that we will explore below. Indeed, those on the left had greater fertility than those in the centre (Fieder & Huber, 2018). This may be because something like Marxism includes some fitness-inducing aspects of religiousness. It may also be because working-class people sensibly embraced Marxism as a practical means of improving their lot in life. Fertility, even by that stage, was negatively associated with socio-economic status. Since that time, however, the nature of what constitutes extreme liberalism has mutated, and it is now focused on identity politics rather than on assisting the native poor.

With no harsh group selection, this process of clever-silliness can continue until adaptive group-level institutions are questioned, not just aspects of these institutions, such as specific religious beliefs, as occurred during the Reformation. Thus, the clever-sillies will eventually start to espouse ideas that are maladaptive in terms of group and even individual level fitness. Most obviously, questioning the dogmas of the religion will lead to atheism, and then nihilism, and the belief that life is futile. This example is particularly salient because religiousness is generally fitness-promoting. There is every reason to conclude that religiousness is an adaptation, as it has all of the key dimensions of an adaptation (Vaas, 2009): it is a human universal, it is associated with physical and mental health, it is associated with fertility, it is at least 0.4 heritable (around 0.65 heritable when it comes to being 'born again', often a marker of fundamentalism), and there are specific parts of the brain that are associated with it (Dutton et al., 2018; Bradshaw & Ellison, 2008), specifically the anterior frontal cortex. When this is magnetically stimulated people become both more religious and more group-oriented (Holbrook et al., 2016). Furthermore, as we have seen, computer models have shown that, all else being equal, the group that is highest in positive ethnocentrism (in-group cooperation) and negative ethnocentrism (repelling the out-group) will eventually come to dominate other groups (Hammond & Axelrod, 2006). It has been found that religiousness is a significant predictor of ethnocentric attitudes, meaning that religiousness is crucial in optimizing group-orientation (Holbrook et al., 2016). We can understand how religiousness would have been selected for. At the individual level, the belief that one was being watched by a moral god would make one more pro-social, and less likely to be cast out by the band; to be more likely to survive social selection. The belief that God would always look after you would reduce psychological, and thus even physical, stress, making you healthier and more likely to survive (Norenzayan & Shariff, 2008). In terms of sexual selection, religiousness would be an indicator that you were pro-social, and could be trusted, meaning that a religious male would be less likely to abandon a female, and a religious female would be less likely to cuckold a male. Being pro-social, she might also be a more nurturing mother (Vaas, 2009). It would also be kin-selected, for religion mandates the monogamous mating paradigm that creates family social structures, and altruism that predominantly benefits near kin. Religious families would further gain social benefits from it being known that they were religious in a religious community. All the while the religiousness would encourage them, together, to be more pro-social in their communities, and amass honour and reputation that way. At an extreme level, religious families even engage in an honour-killing to conspicuously showcase their religious commitment (Sela et al., 2015).

But, most significantly, it would be group-selected, due to its promotion of ethnocentrism; in-group cooperation and out-group hostility. And that applies even if given a large genetically, and even ethnically, diverse polity; full of strangers whom you might never see again. A society like that would still be more cooperative, if people believed in moral gods that told them to be cooperative (Norenzayan, 2013). Consistent with this, it has also been shown that large-scale societies, that are in a state of inter-group conflict, are more likely to believe in moralizing gods, and that the development of complex societies precedes the adoption of moralizing gods (Whitehouse et al., 2019). Conversely, it has also been argued, based on analyses of many societies, that in the absence of belief in such gods there will be an absence of moral unity, and societies will become riddled by internal conflict, and will fission (Roes & Raymond, 2003). In general, under harsh conditions, anything that benefited group selection would thus become wrapped up with religion, as we will see below with regard to patriarchy.

The Critique of Religion and Its Consequences

In that religiousness was selected for under pre-industrial conditions, we would, therefore, expect atheism to be correlated with evidence of mutation, if only weakly, as it is a deviation from what was selected for. This has been shown to be the case. Atheism is predicted by autism. Atheism is predicted by left-handedness; this is a marker of developmental instability and thus mutational load, because we are evolved to be symmetrical, and symmetrical brains tend to result in right-handedness. Atheism is associated with poor physical health, poor (genetic) mental health, and even physical asymmetry; that is, not being physically symmetrical (Dutton et al., 2018). Political conservatism crosses over with religiousness; religious people tend to identify as 'conservatives' rather than 'liberals'. For example, according to America's Pew Research Center, 78% of Americans who identify as 'conservative' claim to be 'absolutely certain' that God exists, compared to 45% of liberals (Pew Research Center, 2020). Political conservatives in the US have more symmetrical faces than political liberals (Berggren et al., 2017), and relatively more attractive people, when controlling for SES, are more likely to identify as conservative (Peterson & Palmer, 2017). A significant component of beauty is symmetry because we are supposed to be symmetrical, so if we are not, then this indicates mutational load, either directly — mutations have made us less symmetrical — or indirectly — mutations have compromised our immune system, so we cannot maintain a symmetrical phenotype, because we are compelled to use proportionately more of our bio-energetic resources to fight off disease, especially in childhood. Congruous with this, as discussed earlier, it has been found that self-identified 'liberals', when controlling for age, suffer from far higher levels of mental illness, in particular depression, than do self-identified 'conservatives', something which can be regarded as further evidence of high mutational load (Kirkegaard, 2020). This relationship makes sense. Depression, for example, is fitness-reducing in terms of fertility and is significantly genetic (Fernandez-Pujals et al., 2015).[3] The clever-silly, however, will question religiosity, meaning people will be increasingly deprived of something they are evolved to experience, and which it is adaptive for them to follow.

But, moving on to something associated with religion, patriarchy can be regarded as adaptive, because if female sexuality is controlled, males are less worried about being cuckolded, so they are less likely to jealously fight each other, and more likely to cooperate, and their children enjoy confidence in who their father is, their full siblings and the rest of their extended family on their father's side. All of this elevates kin-cooperation and positive tribal ethnocentrism, thus aiding group selection. Accordingly, the acceptance, and promotion, of patriarchy becomes part of the religion (see Dutton, 2021b) with both males and females being selected to live in a patriarchal environment. Females who were submissive to the patriarchy were more likely to be invested in by males, and less likely to be cast out. Indeed, in this context, females will compete with each other to signal their patriarchal values, in order to attract the best quality men, and distrust men who do not appreciate these efforts. Men who were interested merely in their looks, and not their personality, would follow a fast LHS, meaning that they would be unlikely to remain loyal. Following on from this, males who were similarly submissive to patriarchy (to the will of their male in-laws) were more likely to obtain females who would not cuckold them (as well as just not be killed), rendering 'patriarchy' adaptive, and its rejection an evolutionary mismatch (Grant & Montrose, 2018; Apostolou, 2014). Being adaptive, it becomes promoted by the religion as the will of God.

The questioning of the religiously-sanctioned patriarchy has become feminism, and waves of ever-more extreme feminism, the mocking of

---

[3] This would be consistent with a model whereby the most extreme liberals, who push others towards extreme liberalism, are 'spiteful mutants'. However, as already observed, this element is not fundamental to the model presented here.

women who chose to be mothers, condemning masculinity as 'toxic', and even asserting that gender is a social construct. This eventually leads to an extreme evolutionary mismatch, where women take on the roles of males, despite being evolved (at least in a slow LHS, group-selected ecology) to be invested in and looked after by them (Apostolou, 2014), and in which male desires for competition and risk and suppressed by an ever-more female-dominated environment. This, among other factors, may be partly behind the collapse in male testosterone levels in Western countries since the 1970s (Andersson et al., 2007), resulting in males with less drive, a collapsing sperm count (Levine et al., 2017), and decreasing physical strength in youthful samples (Fain & Weatherford, 2016). This is not happening so clearly in non-Western countries (Levine et al., 2017).

Critiquing religiously-sanctioned ethnocentrism has become multi-culturalism, which will tell you that you should aid other genetic groups over your own, the belief that your own race should be destroyed, and the (contradictory) belief that race is not biological; it has no underlying biological basis. This contradiction may itself cause cognitive dissonance — mental discomfort caused by reality conflicting with how you expect it or desire it to be (see Festinger, 1957) — and stress. As discussed, it will also encourage immigration, and the evolutionary mismatch, especially for group-selected, slow life history people. Questioning human dominance over nature and other animals will ultimately become environmentalist anti-natalism. Indeed, the clever-sillies will subject everything that makes sense of the world (and which it is adaptive to believe) to their critique. And they will strongly morally condemn those who dare to disagree with them, as is characteristic of narcissistic individualists, especially when disagreement punctures their belief in their own superiority, a belief which permits them to cope with a fundamental sense of insecurity (Lawrence, 2008). Motivated by individual concerns, such as power, they will also gas-light society with their inconsistent and illogical, yet compulsory, worldview. If these individualizing types ascend to positions of power, they will be able to influence those with more balanced moral foundations — by persuading them, for example, that women who are dedicated wives and mothers are losers — to a very significant degree indeed, by heavily undermining the capacity of the group to engage in adaptive behaviour and to hold adaptive, fitness-optimizing beliefs.

We will turn to what this results in shortly, but, first, it should be stressed again that anti-natalism is not necessarily inherently associated with 'leftism'. This is a purely modern phenomenon. During the Reformation, it was the Protestants, who in many respects were left-wing, who were also the most fertile and who strongly advocated pro-natalism

(Clark, 2007). They were even responsible for the breakdown of anti-natalist institutions such as the celibate clergy and the celibate monasteries and nunneries (see Ridley, 1988). These would have directed the intensely religious of the heterosexual population towards celibacy, weakening the strength with which religiousness was selected for. Some manifestations of relative liberalism, therefore, are pro-natalist, and indeed it could be argued that this was also true of the Early Church, who heavily outbred the (conservative) pagans (see Stark, 2020). However, the Early Christians, despite being the 'liberals' of their time, strongly advocated an assortment of values which have been shown to be adaptive, such as fervent religious belief and practice, whereas paganism was increasingly a matter of convention, rather than genuine belief. In this sense, the Christians were reviving a moribund fifth-century Roman society, which is why they were selected for. Finding other people like themselves, they effectively attempted to create a new society that was very strong in the traits that are selected for, under harsh Darwinian conditions; the traits associated with pronounced religiosity. However, in order to do this, they had to break away from the moribund society, rendering them the radicals of their time. Even Communism — trying to build a utopia brimming with contented workers — was pro-natalist. With the postmodern left, quite the opposite has occurred. They have broken away from an adaptive society that overtly prized adaptive ideas including pro-natalism, to create one that prizes liberal values combined with fitness-damaging ideas that lead to the genetic destruction of the individual and the group.

The Death of the Individualizers

We have already set out the inexorable logic behind the postmodern left reaching this position. This happened due to runaway individualism, where people continue to do something adaptive — play for social status through signalling individualizing values — until this becomes maladaptive for society, and even for themselves. After all, they will be more convincing expositors of their ideology, if they genuinely believe it; leading to a process of 'effortful control' such that they convince themselves that they really believe it.

Overt or covert resistance to the ascendant modern leftist ideology is of immense significance from a Darwinian perspective, to the degree that it actually boosts your differential fertility over those who spread or embrace leftist ideology wholeheartedly, as we discussed in the opening. It can be argued, of course, that there is an anti-natalist dimension to modern 'Woke' ideology, though not necessarily to traditional leftism. The logical extension of white people carrying the 'Original Sin' of colonialism and slavery is that they should atone by not having children. The logical extension of casting humans, and especially Westerners, as polluters of the planet is that they should stop having children. Indeed, there are some environmental activists who have renounced having children for this reason, so called 'Birthstrikers' who will not have children 'until climate change ends' (Hunt, 12th March 2019). And not just fertility either, but in the face of an environmental disaster or an outbreak of war or lawlessness, one has to consider who is more likely to differentially survive a disastrous event like that: those with or without group-binding values? Because of this, such people could in effect be said to be *adapted* to reject such views, even at the cost of alienation and exile from their own liberal societies.

As of old, the new wave of twenty-first-century leftist hegemony induces the same sense of dysphoria in its populations to varying degrees, and by this alone we have an extreme evolutionary mismatch, because the emphasis on individualist foundations is so pronounced. But there are many more aspects to the new ascendant leftist ideology than its older predecessors in recent history. The new globalist-left ideology is different, because it has brought about, at great speed, an evolutionary mismatch that is far more extreme than twentieth-century Communism. It creates a multi-ethnic society, which is itself a situation to which humans are not evolved to desire or tolerate, as they are adapted to trust, and be with, those who are genetically similar to themselves; the more similar, the better. This may be taken for granted at the familial level, but this is true also at the societal level, as evidenced in the way that people socially and sexually select for genetically similar partners and friends, and they select them for the physical and mental traits which are more genetically heritable too (Rushton, 2005). There is also evidence from neuropsychology: the in-groupish effects of the neuropeptide oxytocin, commonly referred to as 'the love hormone', is reciprocally linked to greater ethnocentrism and lower anxiety (Bethlehem et al., 2014), and the amygdala, the brain's centre of fear, is activated when people are shown photographs of members of other races; something that happens so quickly that the conscious areas of the brain are unaware of the response (Wilson, 2012, p. 100). The existence of these deep-seated out-group-hostile psychological dispositions is what the 'unconscious bias training' industry is predicated on. And it should not be of great surprise that they exist considering how much genocidal violence and inter-group conflict occurred in our evolutionary past (Kiernan, 2008; Schulting & Fibiger, 2012; Vanhanen, 2012; Morris, 2014; Allen & Jones, 2016; Heath, 2017).

Multiculturalism, by its cosmopolitan effects, induces in people an elevated state of anxiety, as it has been found that strangers of a different race induce primal fear (Wilson, 2002, p. 100). At the same time, by its installation of new moral taboos against xenophobic emotions, it removes from people the ability to rationalize why they are more anxious in the first place. Indeed, by various strategies, multicultural doctrine inculcates natives with a guilt-complex simply for being the dominant ethnicity in their own historical nations, thus compelling them to suppress their evolved predilections to promote the interests of their ethnicity, as an extended genetic family — which is what an ethnic group fundamentally constitutes (Salter, 2007) — with 'races' being yet a further level of extension of that. It should be noted that 'races' refer to breeding populations that have been separated by a combination of geography and endogamy such that they are adapted to different environments, and such that correct predictions can be made when using 'race' as a category. The twelve races of classical anthropology map very precisely onto distinct genetic clusters, races can be identified with 80% accuracy from the skeleton alone, races differ in very important areas such as disease prevalence or likelihood of accepting donor organs from other 'races', even 'superficial' race differences (such as skin colour) are environmental adaptations with significant health consequences, when using genetic loci that differ according to environment 80% of differences are 'between races' and only 20% are 'within them', small differences can add up to significant overall differences if they are all in the same direction, and 'race' is no different from 'subspecies' in non-human animals and this is 'scientific', despite there being no clear line between different subspecies. Thus, we see no logical argument against the concept of race and those who reject it, or are even sceptical of it, appear to do so entirely for ideological reasons and are often inconsistent in so doing (see Dutton, 2020b).

Another major ideology the left uses to inflict deep-seated guilt is extremist environmentalism. Through associating apocalyptic forecasts of the geospheric environment with everyday menial necessities such as travelling, farming, utilizing water and electric utilities, building, and so on, it encourages us to feel guilty simply for being alive and to eschew or limit procreation accordingly, along with various other meagre redemptive rituals; separating plastics for disposal, and so on. These factors lead to dysphoria; to despair and to fitness-reducing behaviour — especially concerning no longer desiring to have children, with such traits obviously being negatively associated with actual fertility (Jokela, 2012). So, this is causing many people to reduce their fertility or even abandon it: only those who are highly prone to wanting children by hard-encoded genetic impulses, making them resistant to this dysphoria, end up doing so. 'Feminism' encourages females to become highly educated and to put status over children, so limiting and even obliterating their fertility. Atheism and nihilism spread a sense of existential despair, encouraging people to shun procreation in favour of materialistic abandon. Lack of religious belief also makes people less pro-social, meaning fewer friends (Norenzayen & Shariff, 2008); while religious priming allows people to better regulate negative emotions (Koole et al., 2010). Depression has been found to be contagious (Joiner, 1994) and depression makes people want to not have children, as we have seen (Schönegger, 2021).

In a sense, the ability to resist leftist-induced dysphoria is the new crucible of evolution. Where once the crucible of evolution was child mortality it is now Woke morality. Where evolution was formerly selecting for resistance to genetically based diseases, the emphasis has now switched to resistance against 'memetically' based diseases; ideological mind viruses that induce infertility in their non-immune hosts. Those who resist leftist ideology, and its direct and indirect inducements not to procreate, are those who survive. In significant part, this will be those who are, for mainly genetic reasons, religious and conservative. British philosopher Bertrand Russell (1872–1970), interestingly, predicted this, though with a specific focus on committed Catholics due to their high fertility in Britain and France at the time, when he discussed the issue.

> 'It seems unquestionable that if our economic system and our moral standards remain unchanged, there will be, in the next two or three generations, a rapid change for the worse in the character of the population in all civilized countries, and an actual diminution in the numbers of the most civilized.
>
> The diminution in numbers will, in all likelihood, rectify itself in time through the elimination of most of the characteristics which at present lead to a small birth-rate. Men and women who still believe in the Catholic faith will have a biological advantage; gradually a race will grow up which will be impervious to all assaults of reason, and will believe imperturbably that limitation of families leads to hell-fire.' (Russell, 1916, pp. 180–181, *cf.* Day, 2015, p. 257)

Eventually, those kinds of people—who will be genetically highly conservative—will reach a critical mass; a tipping point. As we will see, this has already been happening for decades.

Now to be sure, leftism promulgates its own political cults and zealous behaviour. Indeed, it has been argued that the nature of the leftism in the West is peculiarly characteristic of a Christian heresy or Gnosticism, and simply wouldn't have been able to take on the particular form that it has without that Christian cultural heritage. Specifically, many Gnostic sects argued that the world was an evil place, the province of Satan, and that, as godly people, you should renounce all worldly power and renounce even having children, procreation being a 'worldly' and selfish thing to do (Gottfried, 2004). And like just about every ideological and theological movement in history, it is rife with moral purity spiralling. This is a situation where a group of power-hungry people reason out ways in which they could appear to be more moral, and then competitively set about doing so in order to attain greater social status. With enough participation, the morally acceptable standards of behaviour in society continuously 'spiral upwards'. With ever-less accommodation made for actual human nature, these new moral standards become impossible to follow in the everyday world, thereby guaranteeing widespread hypocrisy and guilt. Then, in order to escape from this guilt and hypocrisy, a class of hypothetical evil people who are utterly antithetical to the new morality is invented as a coping mechanism and as a scapegoat. The guilty and afraid feel safer and better about themselves knowing that they are at least not like the evil people. They are at least fighting the really bad guys who, unlike them, lack the 'gnosis' — that all inter-racial socio-economic differences are reducible to 'structural racism' in which all whites unconsciously participate, for example, and that disagreeing with this is just an attempt to 'maintain our dominance within the racial hierarchy' (DiAngelo, 2018, p. 2) — or choose to reject the gnosis. However, by force of societal-obsession, these phantoms of fear, guilt, and shame begin to seem ever-more real and threatening, thus setting off a moral panic that can only be satiated with an authoritarian crackdown from above. Mercifully, the reigning moral paradigm is eventually maxed-out and exhausted — often because it creates such an evolutionary mismatch that it results in chaos and a resultant backlash, as already discussed — meaning that power-hungry virtue-signalling people have to search for a new way to seem more moral than everybody else. When they find one, the process starts all over again.

The Consequences of Extreme Individualism

An extreme societal push towards individualizing values has three key consequences. Firstly, it causes a state of dysphoria, which might help to partly explain why mental illness is currently associated with being left-wing (Kirkegaard, 2020). People who are left-wing believe things, for reasons of status attainment, which make them deeply unhappy; though it may also be that such people are inherently deeply unhappy, and are thus attracted to a pessimistic worldview, which at least seems to give the world structure for them, and which renders their unhappiness almost like a kind of superior gnosis. Neuroticism is associated with Borderline Personality Disorder and the 'splitting' associated with it, whereby people with Borderline Personality Disorder assuage a fundamental sense of uncertainty by adopting a highly black-and-white worldview. Convincing themselves that they are morally superior to others, absolutely correct, and are part of a crusade to purge the world of 'evil' could help to assuage their profound feelings of inadequacy, self-doubt, and their fear of abandonment; these being key components to Borderline Personality. Indeed, it has been found that virtue-signalling and being morally judgemental act to strongly elevate mood; so they can be highly addictive for these mentally unstable people, like a drug (see Miller, 2019). We can both think of examples where we have been happily chatting to Neurotic leftists and one stray remark about science triggers them, very suddenly, into an all-out moral attack during which they feel insecure, 'split', and regain a sense of their own worth by attacking us. Often, if you spend further time with such people, the evening culminates in them crying about how dreadful their lives are. Moreover, high Neuroticism tends to develop in a context of weak group-selection that is easy yet unstable. This 'fast Life History Strategy' causes you to 'live fast and die young', meaning you are acting in a manner that evolutionarily presupposes a violent, antisocial, and short-lived ecology, where it makes little sense to be anything more than an individualist.

Secondly, and related to the first point, being depressed and genuinely believing that life is futile and that nothing makes any sense, they are less likely to have children, through a feeling of dysphoria (but not full-blown mental illness), which is self-medicated through the ordinary hedonistic frivolity, that modern consumerist capitalism is very efficient at placating; rather than devotion to any kind of ersatz-religious political ideology.

Thirdly, and further similar to this, the situation creates dysphoria even for those who are not fervent supporters, but who have been inculcated with these ideas or even exposed to people who have been. This is consistent with evidence that there is a contagious element to depression. Those in contact with those who are depressed are more likely to become depressed (Joiner, 1994). Due to the highly sociable nature of humanity, we are evolved to be around other genetically healthy people, who believe and espouse ideas that are fitness-elevating. Furthermore, humans are highly environmentally plastic. Less complex organisms are born ready to get on with life; following their instincts. More complex organisms, often evolved to a harsher but more predictable ecology, benefit from having a 'childhood', in which they are able to learn about their harsher, more difficult-to-survive-in environment, and, so, be more likely to thrive. Accordingly, they are born helpless, and relatively low in 'instinct'. They learn adaptive behaviours from their parents and from their broader group. They are socialized into the most adaptive possible ways to behave; directed to follow a road map of life that will make them the most likely to survive, to develop optimally, and to pass on their genes. In addition, this 'road map' directs them to optimally thrive in the very specific and narrow environment to which their species, or subspecies, has long been adapted, and any instincts they have will be optimally useful in that environment. Thus, if the environment rapidly changes, members of such a species may experience an 'evolutionary mismatch', resulting in their behaving in fitness-damaging ways. And if the nature of the group changes—such that it ceases to be composed overwhelmingly of genetically healthy people or overwhelmingly of group-oriented people—then it will cease to socialize its offspring properly, resulting in more and more offspring adopting fitness-reducing behaviour or even developing abnormal sexuality.

This could, potentially, be even worse for females. Greek psychologist Menelaos Apostolou (2014) has argued that, being adapted to patriarchy, females are adapted, to a greater extent than males, to a situation in which choices are made for them, usually by their parents, and particularly by their fathers. Left to their own devices, they are, accordingly, more likely to make maladaptive choices. These choices would be rendered even more maladaptive by a runaway individualistic society positively encouraging them to make maladaptive choices. This would be in line with evidence that being wealthy is far more damaging to the fertility of females than to the fertility of males. Equivalently wealthy women in Britain are far less likely than men to have children. Indeed, wealth—though not IQ—weakly positively predicts fertility among British men (Nettle & Pollett, 2008). Moreover, it has been found that more intelligent people express a preference to remain childless when they are young, but only more intelligent women actually do so. This is the case even controlling for factors that might limit female fertility such as education and earnings (and the consequent trading of fertility for a career) (Kanazawa, 2014). This implies that females are more maladapted than males in a non-patriarchal environment. In addition, females pursue a slower Life History Strategy than males (Daly & Wilson, 1988, p. 140), obvious in the way in which they invest proportionately less energy in sex and more in nurture than do males. Slow Life History strategists are more environmentally plastic than fast Life History strategists, meaning that they are more sensitive to their environment. This environmental sensitivity allows the organism to be optimally adapted to its environment at any given time, giving it a competitive edge in the highly competitive ecology which produces a slow Life History Strategy (Kuzawa & Bragg, 2012).

As such, the adaptive development of females is far more reliant on a precisely optimum environment than is the adaptive development of males. If this environment deviates from the one in which female development is evolved to take place, we would thus expect females to become far more psychologically maladapted than males, as evidenced in the fertility patterns outlined above. In effect, runaway individualism, of the kind that is possible under weakened conditions of group selection, creates an extreme evolutionary mismatch in which we live in places of low trust, high genetic and ethnic diversity, and constant change and questioning of tradition. This results in a sense of chaos, a pronounced sense of disgust (towards the fitness-compromising behaviours that are unleashed and promoted in the name of equality — a sense of disgust which must be repressed), and a power structure which tells you that life has no meaning, and that everything that adaptive people believe is 'good' is in fact 'evil'. This will all create extreme dysphoria and unhappiness, resulting in people increasingly not having children.

Intelligence and Not Wanting Children

It appears that this is more likely to happen to people who are more intelligent; something that was also noticed during the declines of Greece and Rome, where wealthier people (this being a robust marker of intelligence) limited their fertility even in the absence of contraception and in face of a tax on childless people (Glubb, 1976). This could be seen in Greece, then part of the Roman Empire, during the time of Polybius, that is, the second century BC. Polybius wrote that:

> 'In our own time, the whole of Greece has been subject to a low birth rate and a general decrease of population, owing to which cities have become deserted and land has ceased to yield fruit although there have neither been continuous wars nor epidemics... For men have fallen into such a state of pretentiousness, avarice, and indolence that they did not wish to marry, or if they married to rear the children born to them or at most, as a rule, have one or two of them.' (Quoted in Zimmerman, 2014)

Now, obviously, this is highly impressionistic — Polybius doesn't present us with hard data — and he is merely a source with his own motivations and should be treated as such. The above quote is likely to be mainly referring to the kinds of Greeks with which Polybius was intimately acquainted, members of the elite, rather than Greeks in general, or the population collapse would have been incredibly rapid. Later, however, the same phenomenon was remarked upon in Rome. The poet Ovid (43 BC-17 AD) recorded this change at the time in his poem *Nux*:

> 'But since more plenteous honour has come to planes that yield a sterile shade, than to any tree, we fruit-bearers also (if as a nut tree I am counted among them) have begun to luxuriate in spreading foliage. Now apples grow not every year, and injured grapes and injured berries are brought

home: now she that would seem beautiful harms her womb, and rare in these days is she who would be a parent.' (Ovid, 2016)

Intelligence develops in an environment of extreme competition in which a long childhood is necessary such that you can learn how to negotiate a highly complex and difficult ecology. Thus, intelligent people are more environmentally sensitive and they are less instinctive as being attracted to non-instinctive possibilities allows you to solve cognitive problems better. Hence, intelligence correlates weakly with Openness-Intellect (Dutton & Van der Linden, 2017). Congruous with an intelligence-sensitivity nexus, some studies have found that people with high IQ are more environmentally plastic. For example, in a sample from 11,000 twin pairs: 'individuals with high IQ show high environmental influence on IQ into adolescence (resembling younger children), whereas individuals with low IQ show high heritability of IQ in adolescence (resembling adults), a pattern consistent with an extended sensitive period for intellectual development in more-intelligent individuals' (Brant et al., 2013). Intelligent people are more sensitive to their environment and are more likely, therefore, to become maladaptive in an evolutionary mismatch.

As such, intelligent people are more reliant on being placed on the optimum road map by the group. If the group genetically changes, due to weaker selection pressures, they will be less likely to be pushed along the precisely correct path, causing them to limit their fertility to a greater extent than less intelligent people, who will simply have an instinct to breed. Intelligent people are more likely to be inculcated with the dominant ideology and act accordingly, including if it is an individualistic, fitness-reducing ideology (Dutton & Van der Linden, 2015). In line with this, it has been found that intelligent children in the West appear to become more 'liberal' with age, as they absorb the dominant worldview (Woodley of Menie & Dunkel, 2015). And, further, being more environmentally sensitive, intelligent people will more easily experience dysphoria in an evolutionary mismatch, leading to a sense of depression and futility which militates against wanting children (Schönegger, 2021). Indeed, it has been found that, when you control for Neuroticism levels, intelligence predicts suffering from depression (Navrady et al., 2017). Those with *very* high intelligence are simply more prone to depression, possibly due to their intense sensitivity to the world, a sensitivity which means they absorb more information and are, thus, better able to solve problems (Karpinski et al., 2018). As such, we can see why an evolutionary mismatch — in which the group's traditional society is falling apart — would result in the more intelligent people disproportionately wishing to limit their fertility and, being less impulsive and more efficient users of contraception, successfully doing so. Only those who are able to resist all this, to not be inculcated with it or impacted by it, are likely to pass on their genes, in the face of what is, in effect, a self-created simulation of the survival of the fittest. As already stated: Wokeness is the new child mortality; the new crucible of evolution.

The result of this is that individualizing liberals will have fewer and fewer children, something we are now seeing. In that liberals have higher IQ on average than conservatives, liberalism and IQ will be culturally and genetically correlated due to social selection. As a result, their proportion of the entire population will continue to decrease, including among the 'smart fraction'—the highly intelligent people who tend to influence the rest of society with their ideas (Rindermann, 2018, p. 199), such as the 'clever-sillies' in academia (Charlton, 2009). Eventually those with high *Binding* values—especially for genetic reasons—meaning that they can resist the onslaught of Woke-induced dysphoria, and low *Individualizing* values, which would especially cover Nationalists/Identitarians over your typical Neoconservatives, will start to become genotypically dominant. Such resistant people will ultimately start 'engineering' the environment, in ways that redound positively to their fitness also. Once a tipping point is reached, possibly about 20% among the elite population, the culture will shift very quickly back to an adaptive norm. However, this will ultimately be also accompanied by a major societal decline and conflict, due to the fact that IQ is in decline, as we will discuss again later, and due to a variety of related factors such as declining trust wrought by multiculturalism and collapsing monogamy. This will mean that conditions become harsher, but this is where the cycle will be complete: the weak men will have created the hard times, and the hard times will go on to create the strong men, as the saying, or meme, goes.

Why Bad Ideas Come from the Middle Classes

This raises another question worth exploring which is, 'Why do these bad ideas always seem to come from the middle class?' Class differences in environmental harshness, combined with the high heritability of social class, help, in part, to explain why fitness-reducing ideas tend to emanate from the elite while 'traditional' (that is, 'group-selected') ideas—such as nationalism—are stubbornly held on to by the working class. 'Traditional' ideas would tend to be those which went relatively unquestioned prior to the Industrial Revolution: belief in God, the maintenance of custom as a good in itself, the acceptance of societal hierarchy, reverence for the ancestors and their achievements, and loyalty to family, region, and nation (Scruton, 2002). Holding group-selected ideas in the working class would be further elevated by our cognitive bias towards such ideas under stress, with those of low socio-economic status tending to live more stressful lives. It has been shown that when people become stressed they become more prone to many different cognitive biases, including religiousness. Religiosity is also specifically elevated by mortality salience, as well as by feelings of social exclusion or persecution (Norenzayan & Shariff, 2008). One of the anti-group-selected elite ideas is to reject traditional, hierarchical religion; this has negative effects on those who are pushed away from the group-selected norm of religiosity, as it creates psycho-social distress and dysphoria. As if this wasn't problematic enough, the more complex the society is, the more sensitive it would be to the breakdown of group selection. This is because, to use an organism metaphor, the more interactive and reliant upon each other each organ system is for its optimum functioning, the more drastic the effects of the breakdown of one of these systems of the whole organism would be.

In addition, intelligence tends to be associated with generalized altruism, with holding liberal social views, and, in particular, with holding to the dominant worldview (Jensen, 1998). As already discussed, there is evidence that if the dominant worldview is liberalism, then intelligent people will be more likely to force themselves, through effortful control, to adopt that view. This is because intelligence predicts the ability to notice what the dominant worldview is, to understand the socio-economic rewards inherent in being, in effect, conformist to that view, and, so, adopting that view as one's own. Less intelligent people would be less able to successfully execute this strategy, as already noted. In a sense, people who are less intelligent are less able to use reason and intellectual self-control to suppress their spontaneous or implicit beliefs, and this includes suppressing spontaneous beliefs with regard to ethnocentrism. Thus, moderately low intelligence acts as a protective factor against the adoption of ideologies that challenge group-selected values, which, in the presence of relaxed group selection, more intelligent people will adopt, due to their intellectual conformism, and their general high Openness to counter-intuitive ways of thinking. After all, solving complex problems — the essence of intelligence — involves critiquing and overcoming implicit or 'commonsensical' solutions, and thinking in often very counter-intuitive ways (Dutton & Van der Linden, 2017).

So, for all of these reasons, we would expect those high on IQ, social effectiveness, and *Individualizing* (that is, non-group-selected) moral foundations — who push society in a direction that is damaging to group-level fitness — to emanate from the higher social classes. And this might be particularly pronounced among the professional middle class because, lacking the wealth and hereditary status of the upper class, it has been noted that they have long tended to play for status by stressing their education, religiousness, and morality, in contrast to immoral classes below and above them (McEnery, 2004, p. 11). Sixteenth-century English Protestantism, for example, was very much spearheaded by intellectuals, merchants, and craftsmen (Ridley, 1988, p. 114).

The Consequences of Collapsing Group Selection

Having explored the central role played by climate and social conflict in creating conditions of cultural group selection, we can begin to see how it would be possible for societies to become increasingly culturally 'liberal' while fertility was, at the same time, associated with being 'conservative'. Large and complex cultural groups only form under conditions of intense climatic stress (such as during times of severe cold), and only persist under conditions of intense inter-group competition. Historically, the populations comprising of such groups would have been composed of people, as we have already noted, who would manifest the traits which were selected for under pre-industrial conditions: traditional religiousness (specifically the collective worship of a moral god, and a belief in life's eternal significance); a worldview that was, by modern definitions at least, 'conservative' (it stressed the moral foundations of Purity/Sanctity, Authority, and Loyalty); robust mental and physical health; a strong desire to have children; and a strong abhorrence for any way of thinking that would undermine one's, or one's group's, genetic fitness. Accordingly, these people would pass on their genes and culture, and they would be highly resistant to a culture that might implicitly, or explicitly, tell them not to do so, or somehow point them towards heavily delaying reproduction or severely limiting their fertility.

Many of those in such populations, especially those with low social status, would not have been able to participate fully in the reproduction of the next generation. Thus there would have been significant downward social mobility from the upper and middle classes, which would have raised the levels of 'group-selected' traits in these populations, gradually over time. In the first half of the twentieth century the sorts of values that we have identified as being costly to group-level fitness (but not necessarily to one's personal fitness) were, to a great extent, increasingly marginalized. Most people in England, for example, identified as religious, and as adherents to the Church of England, and the Church of England itself espoused a highly 'traditionalist' form of Christianity. Religion, in general, has taken fitness-elevating ideas — such as pro-natalism, altruism to kin, and even group selection (with assertions that 'God is on our side' in times of war) — and turned these into the will of God, making them more likely to be adhered to. This can be regarded as a key evolutionary function of traditional religion (see Sela et al., 2015), with fitness-damaging religions, often more accurately termed as cults, that failed to do this not having survived, along with the populations which adopted them. An obvious example is the eighteenth-nineteenth-century American sect known as the Shakers. It advocated not procreating and eventually died out (Stein, 1992). An example of the one-time conservatism of the Church of England can be seen in its reaction to Princess Margaret's (1930-2002) plan, beginning in 1953, to marry the divorced courtier Group Captain Peter Townsend (1914-1995). The Queen's consent was required for her sister Margaret to marry, but the Queen was also head of the Church of England, and the leading bishops were clear that marrying a divorced man, whose wife still lived, was unconscionable (Holmes, 2016).

However, as a higher and higher percentage of the population came to actively, or passively, support liberal views—as spearheaded and continuously pushed leftwards by socially successful elite *Individualizers*— things would have gradually changed. This led to a reversal of what was normal, because, as we discussed earlier, experiments have shown that once roughly 20% of a population question a system of thinking then a tipping point is reached, people start to lose faith in the system, and they begin to defect to the new way of thinking (Centola et al., 2018). This is, seemingly, what happened, meaning that by around 1970, when Larkin was writing the poems for *High Windows*, we had a society that was very much 'liberal' and continuously moving in a more 'liberal' direction. Even though liberalism became negatively associated with fertility after the 1960s, sufficient 'liberals' had children and the influence of high-IQ 'liberals' over culture was strong enough that society could, nevertheless, continue moving ever-more towards individualist, leftist values.

This change helped to facilitate a liberal 'march through the institutions', meaning that liberals increasingly controlled the purveyors of culture: the universities, the schools, the Church, the legal system, and any organ that had significant power (Gabb, 2007). This increasing 'switch' meant that younger people were more 'liberal' and, as older people, who were more conservative, retired, they would then be replaced by people who held liberal views. In line with this, the BBC was once mocked as little more than an arm of the Conservative Party. Now it is regarded as a bastion of left-wing politics (see Mills, 2016). Not only that, but as the 'culture' became 'liberal' then liberalism became associated with intelligence, and intelligent people began to outcompete each other to espouse ideas that were ever-more focused on individualizing foundations. These liberals could work together to completely take over university departments, for example, and eventually the entire university system. In America, only in the 1960s did self-identified 'liberals' start to become increasingly common among academics. By 1969, only 27% of

American college professors self-identified as 'conservative'. It was 12% by 1999, and just 7% by 2010 (Shields, Fall 2018). The same phenomenon has been found in Britain. In 1964, 35% of academics claimed to vote Conservative. In 1976, it was 29%, in 1989 it was 18%, and by 2015 it was a mere 11% (Carl, 2017, p. 5). This shift can partly be explained by the retirement of academics born before World War II, who were not youthfully inculcated with liberal values, and their replacement with younger academics who were certainly inculcated with liberal values.

So, as the Industrial Revolution took off in around 1800, the frequency of group-selected traits would have then been quite high within various Western populations. As the climate started to simultaneously warm and stabilize, as between-group peace increased, and as medical advances wrought by the Industrial Revolution took hold, creating further environmental stability, child mortality collapsed—beginning among the wealthy, who could provide better conditions for their offspring. At the same time, levels of mortality salience, and thus stress, were falling, meaning that, for an environmental reason, people were becoming less religious, and thus, more receptive to atheism, and other such group-level fitness-reducing ideas. Weaker selection pressures also meant that individualism could spiral out of control. There was a sense in which this was happening 'beneath the surface', because at the time prominent, non-group-selected 'liberals'—who strongly and openly questioned the traditional society—were either fringe figures, or they were just not taken especially seriously by the majority of the population, dismissed as decadent, or callow. However, their numbers and soft influence on society continued to grow, in a society in which traditional religiousness still held sway, as the strength of group selection gradually reduced over time. In this sense, by the 1950s, religious society, significantly weakened, but still living, was a dam holding back a tsunami of individualizing values.

Eventually, pressure of numbers meant that a tipping point was reached, the Church was subverted, and people began to defect en masse to the new—'liberal' individualizing—way of thinking. Larkin identifies the year 1963 as the turning point and, in a British context at least, he may be right. That this change happened quickly is consistent not only with research on tipping points (Centola et al., 2018), but also with Peter Turchin's (2016) research, explored above, on the way in which cycles of relative peace and relative conflict appear to operate across the history of the West. The society becomes increasingly polarized, leading to particular decades being marked by crisis and disorder, and it is in these decades that dramatic changes—such as serious wars—take place. These are followed by periods of relative stability until once more societies become polarized, leading to a dramatic decade or so of instability. Turchin's modelling, it should be noted, predicted that the 2020s would be just such a decade of strife, akin to the 1960s; the latter being polarized between liberals and conservatives, though one in which conservatives began with the upper hand. Indeed, in a monograph entitled *Multilevel Selection: Theoretical Foundations, Historical Examples, and Empirical Evidence* (Hertler et al., 2020), the cycles predicted in Turchin's model were explicitly linked to shifts in the degree of group- vs. individual-level selection operating across history.

The key point is that, on this basis, we can begin to understand why the second half of the twentieth century, in Western countries, saw such an extreme move towards liberalism while, concomitantly, it is the religious and the extremely conservative who produce the largest share of offspring — starting in the 1960s. Those with individualizing moral foundations would have flourished, with the weakening of group selection, becoming a growing proportion of the population since around 1800. Eventually, their penetration into the elite was sufficient to trigger a 'tipping point', wherein the society switched, relatively quickly, to their point of view; the traditional defences against group-level fitness-depressing worldviews having been gradually subverted, for the various reasons outlined, such as declining religiousness (due to falling mortality salience), increased individualistic questioning of tradition, increased dysphoria, and so on.

Once this occurred, then there was a system of runaway liberalism, because the way in which you competed for status in the new dispensation was, within certain limitations, through being ever-more liberal, and pushing the society in an ever-more liberal direction. After all, if everyone overtly accepts that traditional marriage rights should not be restricted to heterosexual couples, then you can no longer signal your virtue, your originality and thoughtfulness, by asserting that you believe this. In order to successfully compete in and climb the liberal social hierarchy, you have to move on to a new target, or in some way be slightly more extreme. You must be even more 'clever-silly'. The only limitation was that you could not do so, with such speed or radicalism, that your innovation was 'too much' for the population, and so provoked a populist backlash. The speed with which this has happened, and the extent to which conservatives will tend to cede ground to liberals anyway, has meant that conservatives can outbreed liberals, even though the society continues to become ever-more liberal. This is the power of what American thinker Noam Chomsky has called *manufacturing consent*, as the domination of media and elite institutions by those with individualizing moral foundations has more than compensated for the relative lack of reproductive success such individuals have had since the 1960s (Herman & Chomsky, 1988).

But, clearly, this cannot go on forever, due to what it creates. It brings about a society that promotes as the 'norm' ways of thinking that are negatively associated with fitness, such as female careerism and even altering your gender. The runaway liberal society has told people that life has no meaning and that life has no eternal significance, implicitly discouraging reproduction in favour of simply enjoying life, and even feeling guilty about reproduction due to being 'white' or simply 'human'. As the environment directed by morally individualizing liberals successfully encourages more and more people—who are subject to group-influence, and manipulation, in a way that negatively impacts their group-level fitness, and increasingly also their individual-level fitness—not to breed, it will eventually reach those who cannot be manipulated in this way. It will reach the remnant population from pre-industrial times who, for genetic reasons, will be resistant to liberal ideas, and will be strongly so. And these—along with those who are low in intelligence and low in impulse control—will be the only people who will pass on their genes to any significant extent. As such, eventually, the percentage of the population who are 'conservative', and who are strongly resistant to liberals, will be so high that a new tipping point will be reached, and the society will once again swing in a more 'conservative' direction.

In the next chapter, we will look at why this switch is happening, and we will examine ways in which it might unfold. But it may be noted here that, in this sense, the ideology of multiculturalism might, ironically, be regarded as adaptive in evolutionary terms. If intelligence is strongly selected for, then the society creates conditions which reverse historical Darwinian selection pressures. This permits decreasingly intelligent people to survive. Due to the relationship between religiousness and mortality salience, the more intelligent of these people start to question religiosity, adopt nihilistic views, and start to limit their fertility. Multiculturalism will also live in an evolutionary mismatch, creating dysphoria, something seems to impact the more intelligent worse, causing them to limit their fertility. If society became ever-more developed, eventually almost everybody would adopt these views, and the population would die out. However, less intelligent people, in this context, have children by accident and are more inclined to have children anyway, so the human population continues.

Chapter Five

The Future Belongs to Those Who Turn Up

'A serious house on serious earth it is
In whose blent air all our compulsions meet
Are recognised and robed as destinies.
And that much never can be obsolete.'[1]

And That Much Never Can Be Obsolete

Sometime around 1955 — by which time church-going in England had long been in decline (Bruce, 2002, p. 67) — Philip Larkin wandered into an old church, leading him to muse on the decline of Christianity, and on what the future of this particular building might be. Would it fall completely out of use? Might it be employed to house sheep? Could churches be avoided completely in the future; regarded as somehow unlucky? Who would be the last person ever to come to this church to use it for its original, sacred purpose? But, as he continued to contemplate his surroundings, he realized that he liked being there, and that there was something about places like this which, surely, meant that they could never simply become obsolete. As Larkin puts it:

'Since someone will forever be surprising
A hunger in himself to be more serious
And gravitating with it to this ground
Which he once heard was proper to grow wise in
If only that so many dead lie round.'

Data indicate that Larkin's pensive prognostication is correct. The 'death' of traditional religion has been predicted for a long time. Sociologists such as Aberdeen University's Steve Bruce (2002) are very fond of death metaphors for Christianity in the West (see Dutton, 2008a). They give us

---

[1] 'Church Going', Larkin (1955).

journal articles with titles such as 'Christianity in Britain: RIP' (Bruce, 2001) and books with titles such as *The Death of Christian Britain* (Brown, 2001). And they are correct, to the extent that they describe a trend whereby British people, especially over the last 150 years, have decreasingly attended church, and decreasingly believed in the existence of God. In 1948, 2% of Americans had 'no religious affiliation'. By 2010, this had grown to 14%. In 1900, 27% of British people regularly attended church or tithed to a church. By 2010, this had fallen to a mere 11%. In 1957, 78% of British people believed in either 'God' or a 'Spirit or Life Force'. By 1993, this had fallen to 70%, which would seem to imply that, though religious belief is breaking away from traditional institutions with speed, it is actually declining quite slowly (Dutton, 2014, pp. 248–251).

However, the proponents of the Secularization Thesis assume that this process will go on forever, until, as Larkin whimsically predicted, churches are used to house sheep and nobody worships at them anymore. Similarly, there are those who have forecast the death of conservatism in Western countries, arguing that an increasingly liberal and urbanized society means that 'conservatism' is essentially finished; with right-wing populism being the last gasp of an ideology engulfed in total panic. The 'conservative' way of seeing the world is going to die out. The future will be one of 'Care' and 'Equality', of 'Individualizing' (e.g. Beckett, 28th May 2019).

The Heritability of Conservatism and Religiousness

The problem with these kinds of arguments is that they are not informed by genetics. If we look at the situation from a genetically-informed perspective, then the future will be very different from that predicted by sociologists such as Steve Bruce. It is not religion and conservatism that are going to 'die out'—if we employ this hyperbolic metaphor for substantial decline and loss of societal influence—it is liberalism and atheism.

Firstly, we have to be aware of the heritability of one's political perspective; the extent to which it is influenced by genetic factors. A number of twin studies have explored the heritability of political perspective. There are slight differences between the results of these studies, and there are also heritability differences between specific measures of conservatism and liberalism, such as attitudes to gay rights, or views of women's rights. But, overall, these studies seem to concur that the genetic influence on whether you are 'liberal' or 'conservative' is in the region of 0.6 (Schwabe et al., 2016). Studies using other methods, such as Genome Wide Association Studies (GWAS), have found a lower heritability, leading to the conclusion that the figure is between 0.3 and 0.64 (Fieder & Huber, 2018). There are margins of error to such studies, and heritability may be a little less than this, but 0.5 is, therefore, the approximate heritability figure around which these studies appear to converge. But this is, obviously, a conservative estimate, with the heritability level possibly being somewhat higher.

This level of heritability appears to be slightly higher than the heritability of religiosity; of how religious you are. This is measured through twin studies that ask subjects to rate, for example, how strongly they believe in God, how certain they are that there is an afterlife, how often they pray, how important religion is in their life, and the extent to which they have had religious experiences in which God has seemed to somehow present Himself to them. Again, there is variation in the heritability of these different components of religiousness. The genetic component of being 'born again', for example, is around 0.65, as noted earlier. But, overall, the genetic component of religiousness is approximately 0.4 (Bradshaw & Ellison, 2008). It should be emphasized that these are approximate numbers, but they illustrate that a very significant component of religiousness and of conservatism relates to genetics and, as such, if we want to try to predict the future with regard to these traits, we have to take into account the extent to which they are being selected for.

Who is Reproducing?

A number of studies have examined, as precisely as they can, the fertility differentials between atheists and the religious, and between conservatives and liberals. For those who espouse the Secularization Thesis, these should certainly make for thought-provoking reading.

Austrian psychologists Martin Fieder and Susanne Huber have conducted a number of analyses on the relationship between political viewpoint, religiosity, and fertility. In this regard, they have drawn upon a number of large-scale surveys that encompass many countries, such as the World Values Survey; the Survey of Health, Ageing and Retirement in Europe (SHARE); and the General Social Survey (GSS) in the US. The results for the World Values Survey were consistent across cohorts, and between countries, possibly because the survey draws upon both developing and developed nations. However, in all six waves of the World Values Survey, the most fertile group was the 'far right', with political viewpoint assessed via a survey of opinions, rather than by self-identification. In some cohorts, however, those who were 'far left' were more fertile than those who were 'left', 'centre', or 'right', but they were always less fertile than the 'far right'. We have already looked at reasons why this might have been the case. In all cohorts, overall, being right-wing predicted fertility. As we will explore in more detail below, some survey questions are better indicators of being 'right-wing' — in the sense that we have already defined it—than others. On these indicators, across the entire survey, being right-wing is clearly associated with fertility. As the authors summarize: 'For the survey questions on "homosexuality always justifiable vs. never justifiable," and "abortion always justifiable vs. never justifiable," a clear linear relationship is seen, with rejection of homosexuality and abortion, respectively, being increasingly associated with higher number of children.'

In SHARE, which only surveys Europeans, there was a clear and direct linear relationship between how right-wing you were, and how many children you had. The same was true for the GSS, which only surveys Americans. As the authors note:

> '…in the recent European sample (including also Israel) (SHARE), we find no reproductive benefit at all for extreme left positions. On the contrary, the average number of children increases with increasingly conservative political attitude. The same association holds true for the US-sample (GSS), albeit only if analysing the overall data set.'

Interestingly, and as we would predict, the relationship between fertility and being right-wing has become more pronounced across the five waves of the GSS between 1972 and 2014. In 1972, the relationship did not exist. It only emerges clearly around 1990 and then begins to strengthen. By 2010, the mean number of children born to the 'far left' in the US was about 1.8, while the mean number born to the 'far right' was 2.8. Separate from politics, Fieder and Huber's analysis of these studies also finds that religiousness is associated with fertility. This is consistent with data from America, analysed by Sarah Hayford and Philip Morgan (2008), which found that reproductively complete females, who regard religion as 'very important', had 0.4 more children than women for whom religion was 'somewhat important' and 0.8 more children than women for whom religion was 'not important'. According to the GSS, conservatives have a fertility advantage of 41% over liberals (Haddock, 17th September 2006). This means that for every child born to a liberal, 1.4 is born to a conservative. For every child born to an atheist or agnostic, 1.8 is born to a religious fundamentalist, and these numbers were similar in the cohort born in the year 2000 and in the cohort born in 1990. These findings are broadly consistent with what we noted earlier. There have always been individualizers and binders, and the influence of individualizers has been kept in check via group selection. With its collapse, individualizers were able to breed substantially, until runaway individualism led to highly maladaptive ideas, which led to a more recent fertility advantage for binders, which is likely to continue to increase.

In addition, Danish researcher Emil Kirkegaard (2020) has analysed the GSS and shown that, consistent with the World Values Survey, there is increasing evidence of political polarization. The percentage of the American population that self-identifies with the left- or right-wing extreme has doubled, from around 5% in 1975 to roughly 10% in 2018. Approximately half of these, for much of the period, were far left, and half were far right. Kirkegaard notes that this increase in identification with the political extremes could help to explain 'The Great Awokening' in which increasingly extreme left-wing policies—to the point of wishing to create a new Year Zero—have been pushed for by 'Woke' activists, while right-wing populism has concomitantly increased (see Kaufmann, 2019; Kaufmann, 22nd June 2020).[2] This could be put down to declining intelligence, in the sense that IQ is negatively correlated with adopting extreme positions, when asked questions with multiple options. However, this would not be consistent with evidence that low IQ is very specifically associated with right-wing extremism, and aspects of this such as negative ethnocentrism (Jensen, 1998). Overall, Kirkegaard finds that, between 1975 and 2018, the trend has been for Americans to become slightly more 'far right' than they have 'far left'. This would potentially be congruous with cultural processes pushing more people to the extreme left, while underlying partly-genetic processes have pushed more people to the extreme right, or towards extreme traditionalist religiosity. Evidence of the latter is quite clear from American data. Between 1960 and the year 2000, liberal Protestant churches saw their component of the American religious market halve, from 16% to 8%. However, conservative Protestant groups increased their market share from 7% to 16% (Kaufmann, 2010).

---

[2] We can only speculate on what might have caused this rapid cultural change. One possibility is a combination of the underlying processes already outlined combined with the rise of social media. This has permitted individualizers to easily find each other, create strongly motivated coalitions, and exert influence on conservatives, and feed runaway individualism, in an extreme fashion. It has also been found that social media seems to directly contribute to societal polarization. Posts that condemn an out-group are most likely to be shared, resulting in a kind of runaway polarization (Rathje et al., 2021). It has further been argued that, together with these processes, 'Wokeness' has been deliberately promoted by corporate entities in order to draw leftists away from campaigns for economic equality that interfered with corporate financial interests, such as 'Occupy Wall Street'. In this sense, it is akin to the 'Bootlegger-Baptist Coalition' which favoured Prohibition in the United States: a moral-economic coalition (Carl, 22nd July 2021).

From One Extreme to Another?

However, returning to the GSS data, there is a case for arguing that the increasing percentage of the population who are politically extreme may actually be partly genetically mediated. Using samples aged over 40 at the time of the survey, intolerance is associated with fertility to at least the same extent as religiosity. Tolerance of homosexuality is weakly negatively associated with fertility as is tolerance of militarism, or racism. In all cases, these are weak correlations, in the region of 0.1. However, this would imply that, at the genetic level, people would be becoming increasingly intolerant of those who hold different viewpoints from theirs. This would be expected to manifest at the extremes, where there would be a small but slowly growing proportion of people who were highly intolerant of those at the other extreme and who would regard those at the other end of the political spectrum as, essentially, evil. So, this would actually be in line with research by Fieder and Huber (2019) discussed above. At the genetic level, society would be becoming increasingly fundamentalist and right-wing overall, but it would also be polarizing, due to the fertility advantage associated with intolerance, and due to it becoming increasingly left-wing at the environmental level. Thus, we have what we might call a 'Co-occurrence Model'. Overtly, Western societies have increasingly become left-wing for many decades, pushed in this direction by the breakdown of group selection, and its sequelae, as already outlined. However, at the genetic level, society is becoming more right-wing. Due to the fact that political perspective is substantially heritable, we would eventually expect the genetically right-wing percentage of society to reach a critical mass (Centola et al., 2018) after which the society would tip back towards being right-wing in some way. At an earlier stage of this process—seemingly the stage through which we are now living—we would expect the society to be intensely polarized, as people who had previously repressed their 'right-wing' feelings, would become aware that right-wing sentiment was a growing force, and would, therefore, move towards it. Following the Cultural Mediation Hypothesis (Woodley of Menie & Dunkel, 2015), this would increasingly be more likely among the most intelligent of those previously repressed right-wing people, and these people might also reach a point where they find the extreme liberal evolutionary mismatch too obnoxious to any more tolerate.

Quite why this is happening is unclear; it could be that fundamentalism predicts fertility. Some children of fundamentalists retain aspects of fundamentalism even after they defect from their fundamentalist beliefs; meaning that they can go on to have highly intolerant left-wing views. These leftist views slightly reduce their fertility, but they would also, to some extent, inherit the desire for fertility associated with fundamentalism, and low mutational load. Thus, they are a variation on the theme of traditional religiousness, as they seem to maintain some of the beneficial traits that are associated with it. The idea that there exist variant 'morphs' of traditional religiousness can be seen in the religious dimensions to multiculturalism, including fervent belief in dogmas, a sense of fate, belief in 'forces' (akin to magic) that nebulously influence events (such as reified 'History' or 'Racism'), and a strong sense that the out-group is (implicitly) demonic. It is a 'morph' in the sense that it promotes individualizing values rather than binding values, and because there is no belief in a metaphysical reality let alone a moral god; though there are collective rituals that might be compared to collective worship, such as white BLM activists publicly prostrating themselves to atone for 'white racism'. Also, there is some indirect evidence for the hypothesis that the offspring of fundamentalists are the ones who are becoming, in some cases, the polar opposite; multiculturalists or Marxists (Zuckerman, 2011), as we will see below.

Indeed, as already noted, it has been argued that multiculturalism constitutes a Gnostic Christian heresy, with Gnostics having combined strong individualizing values with anti-natalist beliefs, preaching that the world is Satan's province, and that nobody should have children at all, because doing so is bringing people into a diabolical world created by the Devil. In this sense, it could be argued that, to some extent, some forms of historical Gnosticism reflected runaway individualism, in which the desire to gain moral status through espousing individualistic values pushed over into a fitness-damaging worldview (see Gottfried, 2004).[3]

Consistent with the relationship between fundamentalism and multiculturalism, firstly, it has long been noted that a common means via which you become religious involves a dramatic move, from being extremely and fervently irreligious, to being profoundly religious and zealously anti-secular, as part of a conversion experience. In a sense, a portion of those who embrace fundamentalist religion appear to move from one form of dogmatism to another (Bloch, 1992); congruous with evidence that religious-seeking is associated with periods of pronounced mental instability and anxiety, and a consequent need to make absolute sense of the world (Hills et al., 2004). As discussed above, this would be in

---

[3] Interestingly, these runaway individualist, Gnostic ideas spread during a relative warm period in which group selection was weak; the Roman and Medieval Warm Periods. They were purged as the climate became colder, and group selection intensified. This possible relationship would be a fascinating topic for future research.

line with the dynamics of Borderline Personality Disorder, whereby a weak sense of self, extreme anxiety, and a tendency to flit between different pronounced models of identity (in order to assuage a sense of meaninglessness) are all interrelated. There is relatively little large-scale research on apostates from fundamentalist Christianity. However, one recent study indicates that apostates score higher in Neuroticism than religious people; being around as high in mental instability as the general non-religious population (Saroglou et al., 2020), while another finds that emotional instability is the only personality trait which predicts exiting a religion (Hui et al., 2018). This is consistent with a number of studies that have found that apostates are less happy than either religious converts or those who stick with their childhood religion (Wood et al., 2009, pp. 134–135). Accordingly, it seems that we have a 'conversion in reverse', with 'de-converts' tending to embrace a kind of secular religiosity, rather than merely being ordinary, secular people. In line with this, a study of 87 American apostates found a relationship between apostasy from conservative religiosity, and the adoption of 'left-leaning, progressive or radical political views' (Zuckerman, 2011, p. 11).

Indeed, as already noted, psychologist Hans Eysenck (1954) presented evidence that some people are simply attracted to political authoritarianism and extremism—they are 'tough-minded' rather than 'tender-minded'—and, depending on the circumstances, can be equally content as Nazi activists or as Soviet agents in the German Democratic Republic. They may also simply be attracted to extreme identities. There have been documented cases of individuals who have converted from socialism to Fascism, such as Benito Mussolini (1883–1945) (Settembrini, 1976) or British Fascist leader Sir Oswald Mosley (1896–1980) (Dorril, 2006). Suffragette and convicted arsonist Mary Richardson (1882–1962) went on to be a Labour parliamentary candidate and then Chief Organizer of the Women's Section of the British Union of Fascists which was led by Sir Oswald Mosley (Webb, 2020). Adela Pankhurst (1885–1961), women's suffrage campaigner Emmeline Pankhurst's (1858–1928) daughter, went into Communist activism and then the extreme nationalistic Australia First Movement (Coleman, 1996). This would be congruous with very high Neuroticism, which predicts periods of fervour as a means of dealing with feelings of chronic anxiety (Hills et al., 2004), and even with Borderline Personality Disorder. Underpinned by a pronounced fear of abandonment, this condition predicts an intense desire for order and for pronounced black-and-white thinking, frequent changes in identity (and thus political perspective) due to neurotic self-doubt, and violent outbursts (Fox, 2020).

There are also many cases today of 'far right' activists who have become 'far left', so-called 'Anti-Fascist' activists, such as British 'National Front' member turned anti-racism campaigner Matthew Collins (Boycott, 10th March 2002), and Finnish Nazi leader turned Anti-Nazi campaigner and Green Party activist Esa Henrik Holappa (Waris, 19th September 2016; Soisalon-Soininen, 27th February 2017). Though religiousness appears to be an adaptation, it is also a bundle of other adaptations that have become selected for together. Certain multiculturalists may manifest a number of these adaptations; possibly even including a desire for children, even while concomitantly advocating anti-natalism. Being high in individualistic traits such as Machiavellianism, they would find ways of justifying these contradictions to themselves. Of course, an alternative explanation for fertility among the 'far left' may simply be that it mainly reflects higher fertility among the working class, with it being adaptive for the working class to support the 'Old Left' (as opposed to Woke Left) because the working-class Old Left effectively promotes the interests of the working class by redistributing wealth.

Understanding Heritability

All of these data, especially when dealing specifically with Western countries, show that the right has higher fertility than the left, and the far right has the highest fertility of all. This raises the question of the heritability of these traits. As we have previously discussed, political perspective is approximately 0.5 heritable, while religiosity is roughly 0.4 heritable.

By 'heritability' here, we mean the percentage of variation explained by differences in genetics versus environmental influences — so a heritability of 1.0 means the entire story is genetics, whereas a heritability of 0.0 indicates a trait that's completely plastic to its environment. Note, however, that these numbers are population averages. If we say, for argument's sake, that the heritability of diabetes in the overall population is 0.5, we know that the reality on the ground is that some people are essentially born diabetic because of genes that they inherited from their parents (1.0), whilst with other people, diabetes was induced by an unhealthy diet (0.0). It's only by lumping those two together that you get an averaged figure of 0.5. You might then erroneously conclude from the figure of '0.5' that the forces of genetics and environment are equally balanced in the population and that, therefore, unhealthy genetics can always be 'cancelled out' with a perfectly healthy lifestyle. One might even go so far as to claim that the condition is therefore not 'heritable' at all, because diabetes can always be 'cured' by healthy lifestyle choices. But that's not how it works in practice: some people are indeed able to cure themselves of the diabetic condition by improving their diet and exercising more, but other more unfortunate diabetics cannot, and can only at best make their condition less severe by doing so, because for them environmental influences most certainly do not overpower genetic influences, in defiance of what's usually the case on average.

Moreover, just because something is more environmental than it is heritable, this doesn't erase the heritable component of it. You can never erase the genetic risks you are born with that predispose you to certain conditions like diabetes, and among those who have escaped from their diabetic condition by making positive lifestyle choices, they will forever be less able to indulge once again in unhealthy foods than your average person without lapsing back into the condition. Their genetics are still compelling their lifestyle choices to avoid a disease they are otherwise momentarily cured of. This should be obvious, but it's a common tendency to over-essentialize and cast something as either heritable or environmental, despite the fact that virtually nothing is as simple as this in practice. Though there are virtually no psychological traits that are completely heritable or environmental, there are, however, many such traits that are *mostly* environmental or *mostly* heritable. The prime example of the latter is, of course, IQ, where for most populations it has a heritability of around 0.8 in adult samples (Lynn, 2011, p. 101). It is less heritable in child samples because the child's IQ reflects the environment created for it by its parents, and thus the parents' IQ, rather than the child's innate IQ. However, even in adulthood, there is an environmental component. Some people will have a maximum possible IQ of 100, achieved only through living in the most intellectually stimulating environment. For others, with different genes, 100 will be their minimum possible IQ, achieved by living an intellectually non-stimulating life. Both people, however, may end up with the same IQ (see Flynn, 2016).

The Advantage of the Right

Resuming our discussion of political traits, we have observed that those who have remained 'traditionally religious' and 'extremely conservative' in the face of a culture which has increasingly pushed them in a left-wing and irreligious direction are likely to be extremely resistant to these kinds of fitness-reducing influences on their behaviour, and on their thought processes. Indeed, if and when a more conservative culture takes hold, we would expect many of these people to adopt this as their worldview, perhaps with equal fervour. As we have earlier noted, left-wing extremism is associated with mental instability. However, mental instability is also associated with extrinsic religiousness, and with dramatic changes of worldview, or 'conversions' (Hills et al., 2004). The first relationship is likely because those who are high in anxiety fear the consequences of not socially conforming, and so over-compensate for this by ostentatiously socially conforming, leading to an arms race of being more openly 'religious' (in a religious context) than the next adherent. The 'conversions' reflect the fact that such people go through phases of mental instability, and in their unstable phases they find themselves questioning everything, and feeling that nothing makes sense, causing them to be attracted to new and different systems of making sense of the world; especially those that significantly differ from the system which they find themselves questioning.

But returning to the heritability of these traits, there is evidence that they are much higher among extremely counter-cultural religious groups. As we already noted, genetic factors explain 0.4 of the variation in how religious people are. However, this rises to 0.65 when it comes to being 'born again' (Bradshaw & Ellison, 2008). In theory, being 'born again' refers to a dramatic religious experience in which God somehow reveals Himself to you and you realize the truth of Christianity. In practice, this is simply an indicator of being a fundamentalist Christian, as all such Christians appear to find some evidence of having been 'born again', such as looking up at the stars as a young child and feeling God's love, and later interpreting this as having been 'born again' (see Dutton, 2008b). The extent to which extreme or counter-cultural religious beliefs are transmitted from parents to children is even stronger, because the genetic factors will potentially foster an environment which optimizes the likelihood of the ideas being passed on. Eric Kaufmann (2010), whom we met earlier, has noted that the retention rate among the Amish, for example, is 85%. This is despite the fact that almost all young Amish leave their communities for a rite of passage known as *Rumspringa*, in which they enter the secular world for a period, in order to decide whether or not they wish to remain Amish. The Amish are an Anabaptist sect that eschews child baptism; Amish adolescents are baptized if and when they decide to return to the community (Shachtman, 2007). Kaufmann actually notes that the retention rate has moderately increased over time. He also observes that the retention rate of fundamentalist Protestants in America is almost 70%. This would actually be consistent with being 'born again' — a marker of being a fundamentalist Protestant — being 0.65 genetic and the shared environmental influence on this trait being 0.06, as noted in American psychologists Matt Bradshaw's and Christopher Ellison's (2008, p. 38) study of the heritability of religiosity. Thus, we can estimate the heritability of fundamentalist religiosity to be about 0.71.

It is reasonable, especially considering the significant crossover between conservatism and religiosity, to posit the heritability of being 'far right' as likely to sit at the upper boundary of the estimates for political viewpoint. In this regard, a meta-analysis by Peter Hatemi and colleagues (Hatemi et al., 2014) found that political perspective was 0.4 genetic and about 0.2 a matter of shared environmental influence. However, digging deeper into these studies, something fascinating is revealed: critics of the 'far right' usually label it as 'racist'. Of course, this highly loaded term can be criticized as unscholarly. The word 'racist' has become an insult; a means of morally condemning those with whom one disagrees on a topic. As such, its use in everyday life is likely to be extended far beyond its original meaning to, in essence, mean 'a person who is even slightly unorthodox in their thinking with regard to issue X'. There are many terms of this kind. As Australian historian Alexandra Walsham (1999, p. 108) summarizes, in her analysis of Early Modern religious non-conformity in England, the accusation of 'atheist' was 'available for the expression and repression of disquiet about "aberrant" mental and behavioural tendencies—for the reinforcement and restatement of theoretical norms'. Both 'atheist' and 'papist' were 'categories of deviance to which individuals who were even marginally departed from the pre-scribed ideals might be assimilated and thereby reproved'. But, this prob-lem aside, it has been found, based on twin studies, that 'racist attitudes' —a term which definitely refers to negative ethnocentrism, and may also refer to positive ethnocentrism—are roughly 0.45 a matter of genetics and 0.25 a matter of shared environment (Hatemi & McDermott, 2012). This means that, as with fundamentalism, it can be cautiously said that being far right—or even being politically extreme more generally—is about 0.7 heritable. There is a retention rate, therefore, at fundamentalist Protestant levels.

Why is this Happening?

So, with many large-scale surveys, all of which prove that being religious and being right-wing are associated with fertility, this raises the question of the causes. Are religion and ideology causal in terms of fertility differences? The answer appears to be 'Yes'.

German biochemist Gerhard Meisenberg (2019) has also explored the factors behind fertility differences in the GSS. We have examined the evidence that there exists, in Western societies, a negative relationship between intelligence and fertility. Until the Industrial Revolution, there is evidence that there was a positive relationship between these two variables. As noted above, wealth is a robust correlate of average IQ; pre-Industrial Britain, for example, was marked by the 'Survival of the Richest' (Clark, 2007). The completed fertility of the richer 50% of the population, in early seventeenth-century England, was approximately double that of the poorer 50%, based on parish registers (Pound, 1972). The result was that in every generation, those who were poorest—and on average the least intelligent—died out. There was a society of social descent, wherein most men, often younger sons, would occupy a social rank lower than their father did. They were forced to move downwards to fill the positions vacated by those who had died out in a society in which, in general, population size, though it fluctuated, was never more than about six million; this being the maximum the land could sustain. Living standards changed little between 1100 and 1800. However, as we have already seen, consistent with the hypothesis that we were selecting for intelligence, average head size (a robust correlate of IQ) increased, literacy and numeracy increased, and interest rates went down; less intelligent people tending to save less, because of their short time horizons—being focused on what they want now rather than in the future. Intelligence is associated with empathy, and murder rates decreased across the period. And, most importantly, levels of per capita genius and per capita major innovation increased, with a peak in the latter around 1870 (Huebner, 2005a), as we already saw in Figure 4.1.

As noted above, a number of factors conspired such that by around 1900 this relationship had gone into reverse. Climatic warming reduced inter-group competition, removing a major selective pressure favouring high IQ, and other group-selected traits. Furthermore, the Industrial Revolution produced improved living standards and medical care, further weakening the relationship between being poor and dying young, before one could have children. Reliable contraception meant that people could now control the size of their families and, as they became decreasingly religious, people increasingly elected to have smaller families. Large families happened by accident, because people were too impulsive (a correlate of low IQ) to use contraception, or they were not intelligent enough to use it effectively. As the use of contraception spread downwards from the upper classes, a negative correlation between fertility and intelligence emerged. This negative correlation is higher among women. This is partly because—under the influence of 'liberal' gender ideologies—more intelligent women will tend to dedicate their 20s to their education and their career (i.e. to the pursuit of personal, rather than societal, 'goods'), in a way that less intelligent women will not. As a result, less intelligent women will have more children, and even more generations, sometimes becoming grandmothers in their late 30s, when their more intelligent contemporaries are first becoming mothers (Dutton & Woodley of Menie, 2018). Indeed, there is evidence that, the more intelligent people are, the more not only do they not have children, but the more they simply do not want to have children, as noted earlier (see Kanazawa,

2012, Ch. 12). Perhaps such women are more likely to adhere to a leftist and anti-natalist ideology by virtue of their higher intelligence.

It might be argued that the intelligence decline that we have noted is not consistent with everyday life, in which society becomes ever-more technological, and living standards seem to improve across generations. It can be countered that the innovations of the Industrial Revolution were so enormous and boosted living standards so substantially that the Industrial Revolution was akin to a huge amount of capital (Dutton & Charlton, 2015). With the Industrial Revolution, we managed to make an enormous amount of money. We became quite spectacularly rich, because of the brilliant inventions we came up with. This permitted us an extremely high standard of living: the stereotypical American Dream of the mansion, the country retreat, the jet-setter lifestyle, and so on. But, thereafter, our rate of inventiveness slowly decreased. At first this didn't matter, because of the huge interest that our capital was generating; the capital was making more capital, with very little input on our part. Our input was just minor tinkering, little inventions here and there. But, eventually, our rate of inventiveness completely dried up, and once this happened, we were no longer making any new money. So, we had to start living off the capital and, in order to sustain this, standards of living would necessarily decline.

We can think of a pyramid of invention. The inventor of the car is cleverer that the developer of the car. He is smarter than the person who can manufacture and fix the car, while he is more intelligent than the person who can maintain the car, and he in turn is brighter than the man who can merely operate the car. Each generation, the top level is boiling off, meaning we are living in an increasingly over-promoted society. Eventually, we will decline to a level where we cannot any longer manufacture cars. Then we will run out of cars, and, on that measure, civilization will go into reverse. However, as we will discuss, there are likely to be refuges of civilization during this decline, because of the inevitability of intelligent people migrating away to richer places, where other intelligent people exist. Intelligence has consistently been shown to predict migration. This is because intelligent people are more open-minded to new possibilities (which allows them to better solve problems), they are more future-oriented and better prepared to make sacrifices now for a better future, and they are wealthier and more organized, meaning that they are more able to migrate (Jensen, 1998).

We have not reached this situation yet, but it can, perhaps, be seen, in a decreasing ability to solve novel and difficult problems, of the kind that would have been relatively easy for the geniuses of 1850, when our cognitive elite were at their IQ peak. In this regard, it has been shown that the number of scientists required to double the speed of technology has itself doubled since 1979 (Bloom et al., 2020). This is clearly consistent with the hypothesis that we are becoming less intelligent; we are becoming less good at solving problems. This decline is likely to increasingly reveal itself as we are confronted with unforeseen difficulties, such as the Covid-19 pandemic. Those with outlier high IQ, one hundred years ago, would almost certainly have come up with a solution to this problem, such as a vaccine, much more quickly than we can now. As we become less intelligent, there will be more and more people, making increasingly short-term and bad decisions, leading to more and more accidents and crises, such as Covid-19, dragging on longer and longer, before they can be dealt with. The result is that, even if we continue to slowly technologically advance for the next century, or at least not regress, life will still become more stressful, as everything becomes ever-less reliable. This in turn will elevate religiousness, and also ethnocentric attitudes, with our cognitive biases becoming more pronounced during periods of stress.

Moreover, on many other measures, it might be argued that declining intelligence is obvious in everyday life. Surely we must agree that freedom of speech has declined under Woke-pressure; something that is central to democracy. Believing in democracy is associated with intelligence and trust (Lynn & Vanhanen, 2012). That said, however, historical religiousness suppressed freedom due to its strong focus on the holy and binding values; and this is elevated at times of stress, as already stated. Thus, what has probably occurred over the course of time is this: mortality, and thus mortality-salience, collapsed quite rapidly, causing us to become less religious, whilst still being sufficiently intelligent and trusting to question religiosity and other taboos, in civilized discourse. Thereby, we enjoyed a period of freedom and Enlightenment, thanks to the moderately low religious influence, coupled with the immense amount of cognitive and social capital our society still possessed, which religious influence had built up and bequeathed to us. There was an optimum balance between 'binding' and 'individualistic' values, for a thriving intellectual culture. However, this period could only be fleeting. The decline in religiousness started off a lot of processes that would erode our cognitive and social capital over time. A long decline in ethnocentrism began, resulting in immigration and, with that, declining trust; something that immigration causes, because, as we have stated several times before, people are less inclined to trust those genetically dissimilar to themselves, and because they fear that individualist co-ethnics may collaborate with foreigners against them (Vanhanen, 2012; Putnam, 2007).

The collapse in child mortality, and relaxation of selection pressures generally speaking, permitted even greater genetic diversity to arise, something that further exacerbated declining trust. Declining religiousness also led to the rise in the influence of females, and thus a greater emphasis on 'equality' and 'harm avoidance' over systematizing and truth, a coddling moral psychology that goes far in justifying restrictions on free speech in the name of protection from hurt feelings and grim realities. The entire situation led to an increasing evolutionary mismatch, higher levels of mental illness, greater paranoia, and, thus, further overall declining trust, feeding into desires to restrict free speech in order to promote 'safe spaces'. Declining intelligence itself meant decreasing belief in democracy, declining trust, and increasing dogmatism. Genetic diversity also permitted more and more depressed and individualistic people, who would be low on trust, and black-and-white in their thinking; pushing society away from beliefs in freedom of speech and democracy. With no group-selection pressure to keep society united, and with traditional religiousness being weak, these people could hijack the culture —due to the way in which group-oriented people sympathize with individualists—pushing it in an ever-more extreme individualistic direction, and so challenging democracy and freedom of speech, because individualistic values would need to be placed ahead even of truth.

Further to this context, the collapse in sexual restraint and monogamy would also be congruous with declining IQ, as low IQ is associated with low impulse control and thus with illegitimacy, and increasing Life History speed. This increase is because there would be more individualists in the population and these people would have a faster Life History Strategy; effectively adapted to a less harsh and group-selected environment than that which existed when Darwinian selection pressures began to weaken due to the Industrial Revolution and global warming. It is also because a broadly religious culture would push fast Life History strategists in a group-oriented, and thus 'slow', direction. With the collapse of this culture, such peoples' natural Life History Strategy—one that is antisocial, sexually promiscuous, and neurotic—would be actualized. And then, as society flipped over to individualism, many naturally group-oriented people would be pushed, by the culture, to operate a faster Life History Strategy—based around sexual liberty and not suppressing their emotions—than they otherwise would. Think of the libertine attitudes that are prevalent on many university campuses—the culture of sexual experimentation, alcohol, and drugs (see Dutton, 2008b). Some people—on British campuses there are fundamentalist groups such as the Christian Union—are completely resistant to this, possibly for genetic reasons. Others are induced into it, at least to a degree, due to being influenced by the culture in which they are living. Once they have left university, they might actually revert to a more conservative and slow Life History Strategy.

Why is Religiousness Associated with Fertility?

Gerhard Meisenberg (2019), whom we met earlier, has attempted to isolate the factors that cause this relationship, through examining the different cohorts of the GSS, born between 1885 and 1973. In almost all of these cohorts, religiousness is significantly positively associated with the IQ-fertility nexus. In other words, if two people are of similar intelligence, then the more religious of the two is likely to have more children. Being 'Liberal' or being a registered 'Democrat' both have significant effects on the relationship, especially in younger cohorts. If two people are of equal intelligence then, on average, the liberal will have fewer children than the conservative and the Democrat will have fewer children than the Republican.

This implies that liberalism reflects something which makes you directly not want to have children, or impacts you in such a way that circumstances mean you do not want to have children—but probably a combination of both. One possible explanation is that if you believe that life has eternal significance, then you will desire to have children. Such a worldview will incentivize you to have children, but it will also be correlated, as religiousness is adaptive, with other adaptive desires, such as the intrinsic desire to have children, with mental health (which provides you with a positive view of life), and with a desire to perpetuate the group of which you are a part.

If you are a liberal, you will be less likely to believe that life has eternal significance, meaning less of a desire to have children. You will also be more likely to be mentally ill, and nihilistic, you will be less group-oriented, less *K*-selected (meaning less inclined to nurture), and your liberalism may correlate with other non-group-selected traits, such as a desire to extinguish your genetic line, and even that of your group. Indeed, in that we were selected to be religious and group-selected, we would expect individualism to be associated with forms of self-interest, and with traits that are inimical to the well-being of the group and placing energy into nurture.

The overall negative association between intelligence and desiring children may exist in part because intelligent people tend to be less religious on average (see Dutton, 2014), and because, as we relentlessly keep on reiterating, intelligence is associated with thinking in non-instinctive ways, with intelligent people being more likely to imbibe the dominant value-set which, in this instance, is nihilistic, materialistic, liberal values (Woodley of Menie & Dunkel, 2015). An important part of intelligence, and the ability to solve cognitive problems, involves a form of intellectual self-control, where you suppress the instinctive reaction to a situation, and calmly and rationally analyse it. It follows that instincts, or cognitive biases, are weaker in intelligent people, meaning they would be more able to rationalize away their desire to have children, in a way that less intelligent people simply cannot. To the extent that religiousness is a cognitive bias, this might also explain why intelligent people are less religious (see Dutton & Van der Linden, 2017).

Modelling and Reservations about Modelling

So, now we have examined what the available data tell us about who is breeding and the possible reasons why, we come to the tricky task of modelling the future. To do this, we will use the American General Social Survey data mentioned before, with ultimate depth — we will simulate the reproduction of every person in the GSS survey population (1994-2018).

The figures examined earlier could allow us to make cautious estimates about the growth of fundamentalists and extreme conservatives within Western societies, simply among the native populations. As Kaufmann (2010) has noted, in 30 AD, there were about 40 Christians. A combination of conversion (female converts in particular who would influence children's views to a greater extent, through greater nurture) and very high fertility meant that by the year 312 there were 6 million Christians, and the sect was so influential that, in that year, the Emperor, Constantine the Great (c.272-337) adopted it as the official religion of the Roman Empire. Similarly, there were 400 Hutterites in America in 1880, and there are now 50,000. There were 5,000 Amish in America in 1900. There will be more than half a million Amish in just a couple of decades, with this being virtually entirely due to high fertility, because the Amish have always been a highly insular sect without any tradition of accepting converts.[4] American conservative Protestants have double the fertility of the rest of the population, according to the GSS (Perry & Schleifer, 2019). As we have discussed, they have almost double the number of children than do those for whom religion is 'not important'.

It might be tempting, based on these data, to attempt to make predictions about precisely when traditional religious, or conservative, influence might reach a point where it is so significant that we begin to

---

[4] However, some Mennonite groups — these being more liberal groups that are related to the Old Order Amish — do accept converts (Camden & Gaetz Duarte, 2006, p. 5).

move back towards a more conservative society. Such a model would involve many assumptions. Most obviously, we would have to assume that the heritability of political ideology remained constant across time. But this is improbable. As earlier explored, as the society increasingly pushes people in directions whereby they are discouraged from having children, only those who were 'conservative' for strongly genetic reasons would likely end up having children. Consequently, we would expect the heritability of conservative political ideology to increase. Related to this, as the perspectives associated with liberalism become increasingly fitness-damaging — espousing anti-natalism both directly and indirectly — then the fertility advantage enjoyed by conservatives, and in particular extreme conservatives, is itself likely to increase across time. Furthermore, we might expect those liberals who do have children to increasingly have them later, meaning that conservatives will end up propagating more generations sooner than liberals, something that will compound the conservative fertility advantage over the long run. A lot of educated guesswork would be required simply to factor in these issues.

Then there are problems with measuring 'conservatism' and 'liberalism'. Even if we remove the economic dimension to these categories, and focus purely on the cultural, that which is regarded as 'liberal' or 'conservative' will itself change across time. For example, it was once considered 'liberal' to proclaim that you should be 'colour-blind' in your treatment of people from different races, judging them 'not by the colour of their skin but by the content of their character', in the words of American black civil rights activist Martin Luther King (1929-1968). This now appears to have become a 'conservative' viewpoint, with 'liberals' demanding that you actively positively discriminate in favour of black people in order to right past wrongs of racial discrimination. As such, it becomes difficult to trace the fertility of self-identified conservatives — or even people who are classified as conservative through filling out a questionnaire — across time, because what constitutes 'conservative' will itself change across time, and the questions in the datasets from which political perspective can be inferred will have to be the same questions, such as one's opinion on 'abortion' or the morality of 'homosexuality'. Opinions on these matters are also likely to change over time due to political fashion, which would mean that it would be preferable to discern a person's political perspective from longitudinal studies, which track them across time, and then average out the results.

'Conservatism' is a cluster of different traits and views, so accounting for the fact that the specifics may change across time, it is more useful to look at the precise aspects of conservatism that are likely associated with fertility — such as religiousness or ethnocentrism — rather than simply conservatism itself. For this reason, it is just as useful to look at religiousness, and other proxies, as it is to look at conservatism itself directly, if we want to understand how, and by what point, a society might become more 'conservative' in the future. This is because the current conservative-nature of religiousness involves traits that are clearly adaptive, such as ethnocentrism and pro-natalism.

Also, such a model would have to take into account demographic changes which could themselves have an impact on the point at which we might return to a more conservative society. For example, as we have already stated several times, it has been found that multiculturalism — specifically a local neighbourhood becoming ethnically diverse — reduces social trust, because the natives are disinclined to trust foreign immigrants, but also because this process reduces social trust between the natives. This happens because more ethnocentric natives will naturally blame their less ethnocentric counterparts for allowing the multicultural situation to have occurred (with the latter in turn increasingly feeling threatened by their right-wing accusers), but also, building on this, because the loyal ethnics now fear that disloyal co-ethnics might collaborate against them with the immigrants, ironically lowering their own ethnic loyalty (Putnam, 2007). In this sense, the increasingly multicultural societies in which Westerners find themselves would predict further reductions in binding values, if that were possible; at least in the short term. On the other hand, it has been found at the national level that ethnic diversity is strongly associated, at 0.66, with ethnic conflict. The more ethnically diverse a nation, the more riven by ethnic conflict it tends to be (Vanhanen, 2012). This actually elevates binding values, and creates stress and mortality salience, due to an increasingly felt threat of war, which will in turn elevate religiousness and thus ethnocentrism, as we explored earlier. So, for this reason, we might expect a long-term increase in binding values in Western countries, especially in ethnically homogenous rural areas that neighbour the more ethnically diverse urban centres. We should expect increasing rural–urban political polarization, especially once this territorial distinction becomes politically self-aware. We may yet see a time when 'city folk' are treated with suspicion and hostility, as if they were from a foreign country.

Furthermore, the fertility of non-Western immigrants, and especially those from Islamic countries, is very considerably higher than that of Western people, though it does seem to decline moderately, the longer they live and integrate into Western societies. The fertility of Muslim immigrants is extremely high, so there will be a growing, highly religious minority in Western countries, and these people will increasingly come into contact with Westerners. For example, in Denmark, the average fertility of Danes is less than two children whereas for Somalis in Denmark it is five children (Kirkegaard, 2013). This persistent contact could potentially spread binding ideas to native Westerners, just as much as native Westerners would spread individualizing ideas to Muslim immigrants.

It also appears that Eastern Europe is following a very different political trajectory from that of the West. It is much higher in binding values, as expressed in relatively strong ethnocentric attitudes (Aschauer & Mayerl, 2019), religiosity (in some Eastern European countries, at least), and intolerance of homosexuality (Doebler, 2015). There could be a number of reasons for this, including later industrialization, and the relative poverty of Communism, making the populations more inclined to trust their implicit beliefs, and a lack of ethnic diversity, due to Communism not allowing immigration from the developing world. One also has to consider how specifically *south* Eastern European Balkanization effectively recreates the increasingly sinister multiculturalist conditions that the West is itself heading to, by a plethora of young and small ethnically distinct nation states that deeply distrust each other. But the most straightforward reasons would obviously be that Eastern Europeans have very strong resistance to leftist ideas culturally, born out of having recently suffered under Communism for almost a century, and simply because they are just, intrinsically—that is, genetically—more ethnocentric than north Western Europeans (see MacDonald, 2019). For example, the average Eastern European has half the number of ancestors compared to the average Western European (Ralph & Coop, 2013). This would mean that Eastern Europeans would be more genetically distinct from outsiders and, thus, it would be in their genetic interests to be more hostile towards them (Salter, 2007). In addition, it might, itself, be a reflection of small communities that have been selected to be hostile to outsiders. If such countries continue with these attitudes, we can predict that, eventually, at least in the more northern states, they will be manifestly safer, and more stable, than Western European countries, because they will be lower in ethnic conflict and thus higher in cooperation. Their success may then motivate Westerners to act to imitate them.

Then there is the issue of declining intelligence in Western countries, which we have already touched upon a few times. Intelligence is associated with liberal values, and with racial tolerance; at least when liberalism is the dominant way of thinking. Intelligence is also associated with generalized altruism, and with an ability to overcome cognitive or instinctive biases; rendering one interested in possibilities which might not necessarily elevate genetic fitness (Dutton & Van der Linden, 2017; Kanazawa, 2012). For these reasons, as intelligence declines—holding everything else constant — we would predict that people would become higher in negative ethnocentrism. Intelligence is also negatively associated with religiousness, meaning that, as intelligence declines, we might expect people to become more religious, and, potentially, more ethnocentric as a result. Furthermore, as intelligence continues to decline, we would predict that, ultimately, living standards will get worse, and, therefore, mortality salience and general stress will increase. This can be predicted to elevate both religiousness and ethnocentrism as we have already argued.

One caveat in this regard, however, as we have also already discussed, is that religiousness is adaptive, and has been selected for. It is composed of a bundle of inclinations, including agency over-detection (such that you tend to believe in God), pattern over-detection (such that you find evidence of God's activity in the world), obedience to authority (such that religious institutions can develop), group-orientation, collective worship, belief that life has eternal meaning, and many other components (see Boyer, 2001). Those who were relatively high in mutational load, or relatively easily environmentally influenced, might, therefore, under conditions of stress, be prone to fitness-reducing forms of religiosity; religiosity that involved only certain components of traditional religiosity and which, theologically, encouraged fitness-damaging behaviour. Congruous with this, it has been found that being extremely religious, though not engaging in collective worship, and accepting conspiracy theories, and the paranormal without religious belief, are associated with poor mental health, and especially with depression and schizophrenia (see Dutton et al., 2018).

In much the same way, as already noted, it has been argued that multiculturalism is rather like a replacement Church in which there are dogmas, fervent belief, the casting of dissenters in Devil-like terms (such as 'racist'), a belief in Fate (that equality *will* be achieved), obedience to the group, a sense of salvation (achieved by admitting your 'White Privilege' and by aiding non-whites), and over-detection of (evil) agency; taking the form of ever-present 'racists' that are perceived to rule the world. People inculcated with this religious cult would potentially become more fervent during periods of mortality salience. It has been argued that this contributes to understanding the 'Black Lives Matter' movement among young people in the wake of the Covid-19 pandemic of 2020 (Dutton, 2020b).

As far as we can see, the Black Lives Matter movement — and the religious fervour, violence, iconoclasm, and polarization that it represents — is a significant landmark on the road to the future down which we are now walking. And it is modelling this future to which we will now turn.

Chapter Six
Modelling the Future

'In this decayed hole among the mountains
In the faint moonlight, the grass is singing
Over the tumbled graves, about the chapel
There is the empty chapel, only the wind's home.
It has no windows, and the door swings,
Dry bones can harm no one.
Only a cock stood on the rooftree
Co co rico co co rico
In a flash of lightning. Then a damp gust
Bringing rain.'
—Extract from part V. *The Waste Land*, T.S. Eliot

A Waste Land?

Most will generally admit that T.S. Eliot (1888–1965) was the greatest poet in English history, but few dare to admit that he was one of the last great poets in English history. These are the rich and evocative words of *The Waste Land*. In all its vivid imagery and audibly-luscious detail, it exudes and shares a bleak and despairing post-war depression: bespoke for the time, yet lastingly applicable.

In his life, Eliot described himself as a 'classicist in literature, royalist in politics, and Anglo-Catholic in religion'. He said that he 'combined a Catholic cast of mind, a Calvinist heritage, and a Puritanical temperament' (Eliot, 1957, p. 209). His work reflects a man of that ilk quietly suffering through the painful birth of our post-Christian modern world. As per the theme of his greatest work, Eliot's world has indeed passed away into a wasteland of sorts, and what is now 'poetry' is but a game of pretentious rants, packaged in a modern, or more accurately postmodern, style of drivel, such as the poetry of Carol Ann Duffy (see Gabb, 2009). All the while popular culture carries on disinterested; endlessly binging itself on TV, Netflix, social media, and video games.

But this is the inevitable result of a world that is haemorrhaging intellect in a slow and strange process of breeding that cannot be stopped and cannot be undone. We will not return to making great poetry like this again in this age, nor great literature, nor great art, nor great architecture, nor great music, nor great drama—nor great much of anything anymore. Instead we can only attempt to copy our past achievements; as can be seen in the constant repeats and, worse still, remakes; updated remakes and revivals of long-ended comedy and drama series that besmirch our screens. We either lack the originality to make anything new or, if we do make something new, it's just not very good. We are collectively spoiled, privately-educated, and dim-witted children living off our inheritance, bequeathed to us by our intelligent, assiduous parents who struggled out of grinding poverty into breath-taking achievement. In contrast to their lives, we are squandering ours away in the most appalling show of decadence that history has ever known. Through a process of tacking on increasingly minor innovations to our technological landscape, we join with our ancestors to take credit for the whole of the modern world, as if we could have started the Industrial Revolution ourselves.

We congratulate ourselves for our permissive morality, not imagining that our tolerance is just a reflection of our full bellies, central heating, and comfortable beds. We overlook the fact that we've never known what it is to suffer serious natural stressors, such as war, plague, famine, or the death of our children. Our supposedly moral society has really yet to be tested—but it will be. Most of us have not been raised to be obedient members of the group, as was once the case with parents explicit about thus raising their children (Dutton & Madison, 2020a). We have instead been brought up to be ultra-contented individuals, with nothing upsetting permitted to occur to us; not even losing a race at school, lest it hurt our precious feelings. As a result, so many young people—raised in this way —require 'safe spaces' to protect them from those who might make them feel 'literally unsafe' simply by questioning their worldview.

And all of this poignant picture would appear to be increasingly the case the more intelligent or 'middle class' the subsection of the population we look at. This is precisely what drives the decline in IQ in the first place —the relatively more intelligent among us are the worst offenders in this modern barren and sterile cacophony of self-pursuit and idle consumption. But because of this, it counts for more, much more, when somebody among the middle class bucks the trend, and chooses a traditional lifestyle instead. For as we shall see, it is this conservatism that is the shell, the protective outer coating, by which the essence of civilization—intelligence —is safeguarded, and shielded from modern cultural diseases; the symptoms of which most critically include infertility.

The Decline of American Intelligence

Our results predict, as expected, that American IQ will continue to fall. Our modelling, which we will introduce in a moment, found that the average IQ of the US, now set at 100, was at a peak of 105 circa 1970, congruous with evidence of a 'Negative Flynn Effect' occurring at about this speed of decline (Dutton et al., 2016). However, it will be about 85 by the end of this century. Only slightly higher numbers have been predicted using a variety of other methods and datasets (Rindermann, 2018, p. 433). Data from Denmark implies that the native Danish IQ would be around 92 by 2085 and as low as 86 by 2100 (Nyborg, 2012), giving us confidence in our findings.

All the while intelligence is declining—being powered by the rising underclass and receding middle class—we also expect a turning point to occur in population growth, where the growing underclass actually manages to fully compensate for demographic recession everywhere else —that is, the deficit of births among those who are not on 'benefits'. Thereafter, the population growth rate will dramatically accelerate, renewing old fears of an over-population crisis. Until this point, the climax of the Malthusian Cycle will have been held at bay, with production, and thus the ability to attain the necessary resources to live, always outpacing population growth. But, eventually, it will cease to outpace population growth. This is because the population will be so high and the average IQ will have fallen so low that we will not be able to sustain the current innovations that we have, in a context in which the masses are reliant on welfare to varying degrees. Welfare systems in place to support the underclass throughout the developed world will, therefore, collapse. Increasingly wealthy and prestigious countries with maxed-out budgets on public spending will see their welfare provisioning entities fail to meet demand. The provision of healthcare and centrally heated housing will be among the first to go. Homelessness and crime will ensue. A population that has been artificially propped up for centuries by generous welfare payments and free or heavily subsidized healthcare will, in fits and jolts, be gradually reintroduced to normal Darwinian conditions.

As we will explain, our GSS simulation projects the average number of children per family to soar well above replacement fertility, and for the average age at birth-of-first-child to collapse from about 29 to 19. This is based on the actual fertility rate. Although in the last century this has proven to be largely a matter of social and economic conditioning, our model has shown that, on the whole, as the fertility rate has diminished, the consequential differences in fertility between the various political demographies has only intensified. Indeed, it has intensified to the extent that the long-term outcomes stay roughly the same and this includes with regard to rising fertility. To put it into an analogy, as the volume gets turned down on fertility, the lyrics of the music being played are all the more fervently instructing the operator of the hi-fi to turn the volume back up.

The Rise of the Underclass

Perhaps that's a strange analogy and doesn't help, but again, all we are saying is that within the overall developed world population, which is now receding because of sub-replacement level fertility, there is nevertheless a rapidly multiplying sub-demographic, with far-above replacement level fertility, which we label the underclass. They're very roughly about one fifth of the population in most Western countries at the moment, and their many descendants will begin to consume every population in the West as we move into the latter half of this century. British readers will be familiar with the case of Mick Philpott (b. 1956) of Allenton in Derby in the English Midlands. In 2012, as part of an insurance fraud, Philpott set fire to his own house, with six of his young children—whom he'd intended to rescue from the flames—dying as a result. Philpott, a long-term benefits recipient, is the father of seventeen children (Paprota, 2020, p. 76), children who will inherit the psychological traits that render their parents part of the underclass (Perkins, 2016) and, indeed, their parents' propensity for having children, as this is significantly heritable. Analyses of this issue have, thus, concluded that, precisely because we are selecting for fertility, the world population is going to continue to rise (e.g. Collins & Page, 2019).

The GSS simulation found this process of underclass takeover to be much slower, indeed practically non-existent, if it were to go by desired fertility, instead of by actual fertility. So this implies, correctly, that the middle class want more children than they're actually having, and the underclass are having more children than they actually want, and earlier than they want. This would also be consistent with declining average IQ and accelerating Life History speed; we would expect accidental births to be negatively associated with IQ and Conscientiousness.

If we projected the actual fertility of Generation X, we would predict that the population of the US would increase ten-fold over the next 50 years; that would be 75 years if it were based on the 'ideal' simulation, i.e. desired fertility. This is clearly impossible, especially so if amplified to a global scale, and radically out of line with the consensus among many demographers who base their projections on the assumption that the whole world is predestined to adopt middle-class standards of below replacement reproduction; they tend these days to worry about population implosion, not over-population. But our research is based upon a less conventional evolutionary demographic approach (e.g. Sear et al., 2016; Collins & Page, 2019) and we disagree with 'mainstream' demographers here, on the grounds that their models ignore variation in personality traits in the population, and they tacitly assume an environmentally deterministic perspective. They do not consider the hereditarian effects that our fertility models are based upon, and we're not the first to raise this objection (see Burger & DeLone, 2016, and Kolk et al., 2014). Nevertheless, we do not go all the way with hereditarianism ourselves either: we cannot possibly see how the developed world could ever support such a ludicrous pace of growth as the model would have it.

Given that, against increasing hereditarian upwards pressure on birth rates, the real-world environment of finite space and resources counter-demands that birth rates *must* continue to fall (and especially teen pregnancies), it's fascinating to consider how much of the modern world's anti-natalist influences are simply economic in origin, not cultural. Consider the difficulties for today's generation of young people to afford housing compared with their grandparents in the 1960s, a large component of which is the price of scarce land in urban areas speculatively bought up for rental yields and capital gains by investors with financing from banks (Ryan-Collins et al., 2017). Consider how, compared with the price of real estate, real wages have stagnated since the 1980s for the average worker (Desilver, 7th August 2018). Consider the changing nature of the jobs market, and how it's becoming increasingly difficult to find unskilled work that pays a living wage in the developed world at all (Fitzgerald, 22nd March 2019). For decades, young people have been increasingly compelled to invest more of their fertile years in higher education, especially in STEM subjects, and then be further subject to years of industry training and junior positions after that, before they finally earn a salary that makes owning or renting a family-sized home anywhere near a densely populated area possible. It was recently reported in the United States, citing a report from the Low Income Housing Coalition, that 'there is no state, county or city in the country where a full-time, minimum-wage worker working 40 hours a week can afford a two-bedroom rental' (CNN, 15th July 2021).

It's a mistake to think, however, that all of these factors necessarily work against fertility in all young adults—they don't have to; they can put up with poverty and begin having families at a young age, just as the rest of the undeveloped world does. It's the social and psychological forces that determine how each individual actually responds to these tightening economic forces. Those of the middle class will have higher expectations of their standard of living, set by their family and peers, and by simply being more intelligent and *K*-strategic. They will indeed respond by delaying procreation, until they're satisfied with their economic situation much later in life. It's instinctual for this personality type: if they have offspring, they want to be able to invest in them and ensure that they can compete successfully in a tough world, so they will delay having offspring until they're satisfied that they have sufficient resources to make that investment. But culture conspires to exacerbate this trend: the liberal political culture that presides over the Western middle class thoroughly encourages hyper-educated young adults in their endeavour to procrastinate and limit procreation, as we have discussed throughout this book.

For those of the underclass, however, there is a very different reaction. It is the norm among their family and peers to drop out of education early on, and to live off a mixture of welfare, menial jobs, and even crime; thus conceiving their children in relative poverty. They go against the ruling liberal political culture by doing this, of course, but, unlike the middle class, they lack both the intelligence and the Conscientiousness necessary to absorb and follow the liberal party line. They are also of a personality type that is adapted to a much easier ecology, in which one need care little for investing in one's offspring; basic resources like food are plenteous — the children will raise themselves.

So it is that, under further increasing economic pressure to delay and diminish having children, we should expect these class differences in fertility to intensify, not diminish. There is evidence that social class differences in fertility have been moving in this direction for a long time, possibly centuries, across the world (Skirbekk, 2008), and, as already stated, our model does indeed show further intensification of these fertility differences at present; intensifying with each succeeding generation. The downward trajectory projected continues to steepen the later the samples we use. We regard it as extremely probable that, by the end of this century, the world's population will have peaked, at a point far too high to be sustained, and the consequence will be intense individual and inter-group conflict over land and basic resources. This means elevated death rates will rise to meet the elevated birth rates. And that, unfortunately, among other things, means the return of war, poverty, and widespread crime; as was commonplace in our pre-industrial history. These grim conditions will be especially intense at first as the world population declines back down to a level that is in line with its population average IQ.

Incidentally, such a harsh turn in our environmental conditions would elevate religiousness and conservatism, due to the increased mortality salience that our renewed Medieval conditions would bring us. For it's an elemental dynamic of all violent conflicts that they inevitably fall along familial, tribal, ethnic, or even racial lines (Vanhanen, 2012), thus mandating group-binding values in order to survive. Such a huge population, built up by what will then be the failing technological supply chains and infrastructure, which until this point had mass produced and distributed food, hygiene products, warm housing, and so on, would, under the pressure of a long-term conflict-ridden civilizational collapse, break down. As we march ever-more solemnly towards the end of this century, the collapse of everything around us will culminate in the most appalling outbreaks of disease, famine, and mass homicide; the apocalyptic scale of which has not been seen since the Bronze Age Collapse, three thousand years ago — a collapse which we will explore.

Such a mass death would drag on until the population fell down to sustainable levels; presumably the natural carrying capacity of the environment, *pre-industrialization*. That nightmare being the end result of the ongoing processes occurring today, we will until then admire the amusing and scenic political journey, to this grim end. Let us now turn to the evidence that strongly points towards this scenario.

The Death of Liberalism

The first graphs from our simulation, that we are going to present in a moment, on the whole convey one singular message: liberalism is now dying — everywhere. It is dying among the more intelligent; it is dying among the less intelligent. It is dying among blacks; it is dying among whites. It is dying among men; it is dying among women. Only, it hasn't been dying up till now of course; liberalism has been thriving. It is liberal *genes* that have been dying.

One of the more interesting ways our GSS simulation projects this is by examining what is happening with white women in America at the political extremes, based on extrapolated fertility, and by this we mean projecting on the assumption that white liberal women are having children that are exactly the same as them on all political opinions and go on to have exactly the same number of children, starting at the same age. Extremely liberal white females implode from 5% of the white female population in the year 2000 to below 2% during the 2040s. Conversely, extreme conservative representation among white women almost doubles in that same time period to about 7%. Whereas at the moment there is a little less than two far-left white women for every far-right white woman in the American working-age population, in just a couple of decades time, by heritable fertility, the USA would be an extraordinarily different place: there would be approximately four far-right white females for every one far-left white female.

What is occurring with women is of particular importance in genetic promulgation because, in this era, women are having children at significantly younger ages than men. That means that women have a disproportionately larger effect on the gene pool than men, who usually start to breed at older ages. Tracing your family tree is a relatively easy and inexpensive hobby now, in the age of the internet, and has thus become quite popular: if you traced yours, you would notice this effect by counting the number of generations backwards in your paternal line to before 1600 and comparing that with the number of generations in your maternal line to the same century. Chances are you will count an extra generation on your maternal line. This difference in speed of breeding effect is likely a factor in why the birth sex ratio varies the way it does across the world, with some studies finding the likelihood of having a daughter increases in proportion to the age of the father, but not the mother (Ruder, 1985; Jacobsen et al., 1999). It can also be said that a female's contribution to the gene pool is a 'safer bet' or more egalitarian: it has been shown that, especially under polygamous conditions, females select for the highest status males and thereby create greater inequality among males in terms of who passes on their genes, with many being excluded from procreation completely (Lippold et al., 2014).

Over time, women actually power two thirds of the story in our heritability simulations, because of the compounding nature of their 'age-at-birth-of-first-child' advantage over men. This is problematic to the assumption of heritability, because sons are naturally going to express more masculinized political opinions than their mothers, but our model cannot account for that. The GSS data shows that females tend to be less extreme in their politics and drift in their opinions at a slower and steadier pace than men at the societal level. Thus, when looking at our graphs, remember they are 'feminized' quite a bit and thus likely to *understate* the true size and speed of the swings in politics that we should expect, as well as the amount of polarization.

Another curious nuance to our model is that the overall average trend in identification as broadly 'conservative' increases substantially the younger the generation we start our model at, despite having less time to evolve. This is consistent with the anti-natal economic and social effects we discussed a moment ago: that the increasing downwards pressure on fertility is disproportionately penalizing the fertility of the more liberal middle class.

All the graphs and commentary made will be based on simulations starting with the youngest generation for which we have completed fertility; Generation X. Completed fertility being defined as reaching the age of 41 for women and 44 for men. In all likelihood, the class differences in reproduction have become even more pronounced with the Millennials, who will complete their fertility over the next twenty years. Thus, in the fullness of time, our simulation will probably turn out to underestimate the pace of change, due to intensifying economic stress placed on the dwindling middle class, with each subsequent generation.

There is also a marked difference between the 'ideal number of children' and the 'actual number of children' fertility trends, when looking at conservatism. But this is least the case when looking at 'regular church attendance', which we can employ as a reasonable proxy for religiousness. Religious people desire a certain number of children—rather more children than do non-religious people—and that is close to the number they actually have. Using the simulation of actual fertility, we would predict that the level of 'genetic religiousness' will increase a little, about 5%, over the next twenty years, as the working population transitions from Boomers to Zoomers, but then recedes again thereafter. This signifies that the underclass set to take over the American population is, though more socially conservative along a number of dimensions, not all that religious. Ultimately the fertility of the irreligious underclass will overpower every other demographic.[1] This growth in the religious population is slower when extrapolating by desired fertility, but never actually reverses, because under conditions of desired fertility, where everyone had the number of children they wanted, the underclass wouldn't take over the population; the religious would.

So in contrast to the religious population, which doesn't intersect all that much with the underclass, conservatives, who do, find themselves having far more children than they actually desire. This would also be consistent with research showing social conservatives have lower IQ (Jensen, 1998). We'll argue that, especially to begin with, the driving force behind the rise in conservatism in America will be yet further decreasing IQ, and the rise of the political underclass; who are too unintelligent and impulsive either to use contraception effectively or to conform to politically correct dogmas.

However, it will not be exclusively for this reason; religiousness does predict fertility, even when you control for IQ (Meisenberg, 2019). Over the medium term (the next couple of decades) the religious personality will be making gains at every level of IQ in society; most especially

---

[1] We appreciate these are imprecise labels, without clear borders, but this is true of any system of categories. In science, categorization is useful to the extent that it permits correct predictions to be made, and there are, in these data, clear differences between the behaviour and attitudes of these different generational cohorts.

among the elite, as we'll see. However, as we move into the second half of this century, the underclass will be dominated by its irreligious subfaction (though not necessarily atheistic or sceptical), because they multiply their numbers even faster than the religious. They have children at even younger ages (by accident), as adolescent teenagers; where the religious generally begin their families as young adults, on purpose. And they are content, as r-strategists, to keep on having children by accident, leaning on the government to provide for their welfare; the religious population, being more *K*-strategic, will have their children on purpose, and plan carefully to provide for their well-being.

What these trends mean for tangible social issues in America, like homosexual marriage, is rather complicated, and will require a lot of explanation. As we'll see in many examples, for a lot of these issues, fertility and cultural trends are diverging quite dramatically. That is to say: the adults who report having more sceptical attitudes regarding homosexual marriage are having more children at faster rates, but, in flat contradiction to that pattern, each generation is expressing more liberal points of view on these same topics—although that isn't controlling for age; people do generally express more conservative points of view as they get older (Glenn, 1974). Parents also tend to be more conservative than non-parents (Kerry & Murray, 2018). That said, many Millennials simply won't become parents, having been inculcated not to.

Political conservatism bottoms among Millennials, but then markedly rebounds with the Zoomers. By actual fertility, those who identify as 'extreme liberal' are projected to vanish into extinction from 5% at the beginning of this century to below 1% by the end. You might have thought that this meant there would be no increasing polarization, as there's a clear movement towards conservatism. With the acceptance of homosexuality and homosexual marriage, for instance, you would predict at the very least a moderate decline in the coming decades, based on these heritability trends. These trends do indeed predict moderate declines of this nature; another instance would be a slight 5% decline in the average belief that it is 'Not Better for Women to Be Housemakers' over the next couple of decades, and a slightly smaller decline in the acceptability of premarital sex. Whereas political conservatism changes direction quite dramatically between Millennials and Zoomers, viewpoints on these tangible social issues changes relatively more modestly, according to our model, likely indicating that this rising young underclass American 'conservatism' has a discernable libertarian flavour to it. To examine this further, let's look at this 'Generation Z' effect and use our knowledge of Zoomers to try to posit some more realistic hypotheses of the course of politics in America.

Generation Z's Rebellion

As we've said, left-wing identification, or viewpoint, peaks among the Millennial generation and then there is a sudden 'Generation Z' reversal. This would be indicative of the notion of the West having reached 'Peak Woke' and Generation Z or 'Zoomers' reacting strongly against it. And indeed, many indicators illustrate this. Support for the Republican Party takes a sharp dip among Millennials and then sharply rises among Generation Z in the white male sample. A similar phenomenon can be seen, though it is less pronounced, in the white female sample. Those identifying as 'extreme liberal' peaks among Millennials and then collapses, based on the actual GSS data as they are — not our fertility extrapolations. The same is true of almost every other measure, but a note of caution must be adhered to in estimating the exact size of it, because at this stage the Generation Z sample in the GSS is relatively small. It remains the case for the moment that Generation Z is still dominated by a left-wing political point of view — just significantly less so than their older Millennial counterparts. Nevertheless, these political trends, that we will discuss, are consistent with other studies of Generation Z (Twenge, 2017). They really do appear to be reacting against the extreme leftist culture which has been the 'norm' during the era in which they were raised.

Whether this is for environmental reasons, or genetic reasons, we'll explore in the next chapter in greater detail, and make further predictions with regard to what the future might look like based on this. Suffice it to say, it's surely a combination of both. Our fertility extrapolations show that, at the genetic level, the population has been becoming more temperamentally conservative for quite a number of decades now. That the political culture has been pushing the population in the opposite direction over that same period would naturally create an increasingly severe sort of 'collective psychological disequilibrium'. It seems reasonable to assume that this disequilibrium would ultimately be punctured by a major shift in the cultural environment; be that the invention of the internet and gaming consoles, providing a social platform or 'gamer culture', in which young people can outpour their disinhibited unconscious, or a transition in the foremost dogmas and rules by which teenagers express their rebelliousness, from older imperatives such as 'tuck your shirt in', 'no smoking or drinking', and 'speak politely', to newer, more viscerally offensive commandments given by the new regnant Woke morality: 'Don't use micro-aggressive language', 'stop perpetuating stereotypical gender roles and norms', 'don't culturally appropriate your shirt'.

Examining Our Data

But now, rather than continually just offering the results of our simulation in text with our interpretation, we'd like to show you a few of the graphs that were generated by our Python codebase and GSS dataset directly. To read them, however, you need to understand the three different simulations we are using for analysis, which define the graph legends.

The solid black lines show 'Actual Fertility', extrapolated. That is, the completed fertility among those over the age of 40 or so. We use information from the GSS about the number of children each applicable survey subject had, and what age they first started having them, and we extrapolate from that. We assume that their children have exactly the same number of children as their parents, starting at exactly the same age. Obviously, in real life there is more randomness than this, but underneath the noise, fertility does substantially correlate within families (see Kolk et al., 2014).

The dashed lines show 'Ideal Fertility', extrapolated. By ideal fertility we mean the number of children the GSS subject reported as being ideal for a family to have. Unfortunately, 'ideal age to start having children' is not included in the GSS, so we have to use the actual age data instead. If it were, perhaps the dashed lines would conform more to the solid lines in the graphs, as conservatives are more likely to idealize having children at an earlier age (Stone, 2020).

The dotted lines show 'Sterile Fertility', extrapolated. This is the plotline of the movie *Children of Men*, where everyone is infertile; nobody can have children. The population eventually goes extinct, as everyone in the GSS is just left to grow old and die, childless—except that people are removed from our graphs when they reach the US retirement age of 67; not at death.

All of our several million graphs are made available online. For more information on the simulation and how it works, see Rayner-Hilles (2020).

There's a lot to notice about extreme liberalism in graphs 1, 2, and 5. One thing that may have stood out is that extreme white liberals of both cognitive strata do actually idealize having an above replacement level number of children, albeit if at much later ages; it's just that they don't end up following through on their ideals. It's the case that the proportion of extreme liberals in marriage is far below the population average, which perhaps speaks volumes—a lot of them are likely failing to pair off.

Ideal fertility is given merely for academic insight, however. What's crucial to look at is how the solid and dotted lines interrelate. The dotted lines show what's actually happening in the real world at the time of the GSS surveys, taken forward. However, sterile fertility starts with just the eldest among GenX and culminates in the youngest adult Zoomers.

Graphs 1 to 6 make it perfectly plain that, genetically, we are becoming more conservative on average, and that devout liberals are going the way of the dodo. However, the dotted lines are indicative of what we all know to be true by anecdote; a culture that is continually moving ever-more leftwards.

Such diverging trends between genetics and culture obviously cannot continue indefinitely; the population has to psychologically capitulate to their genetic predisposition over their cultural conditioning sooner or later. And as you can see, in varying degrees, with graphs 1 to 6, that appears to be exactly what is happening among the youngest adults of Generation Z. It's represented by the dotted spikes and dips towards the late 2050s, because the only people still of working age by this period are Millennials and Zoomers.

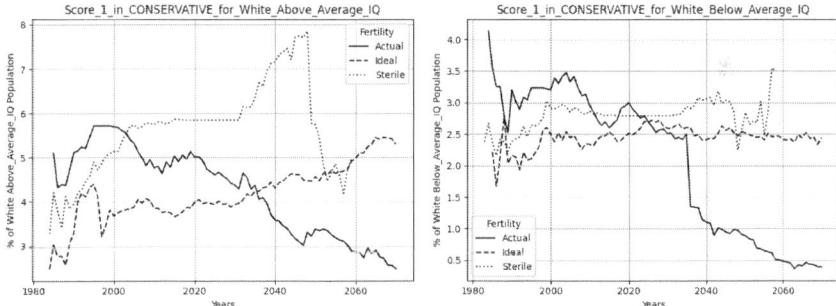

Graph 1 and 2. Extreme Liberals Among the White Population; Above & Below Average IQ.

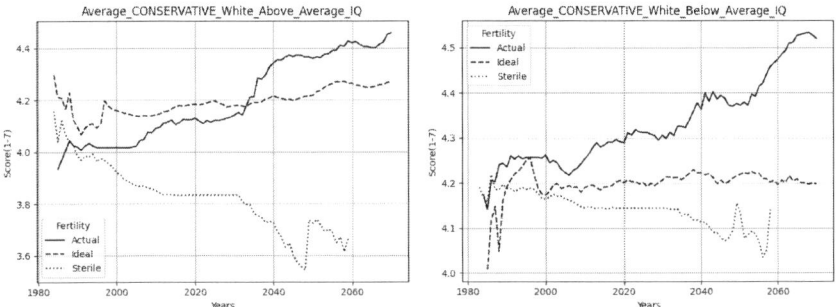

Graph 3 and 4. Average Conservatism Among the White Population; Above & Below Average IQ.

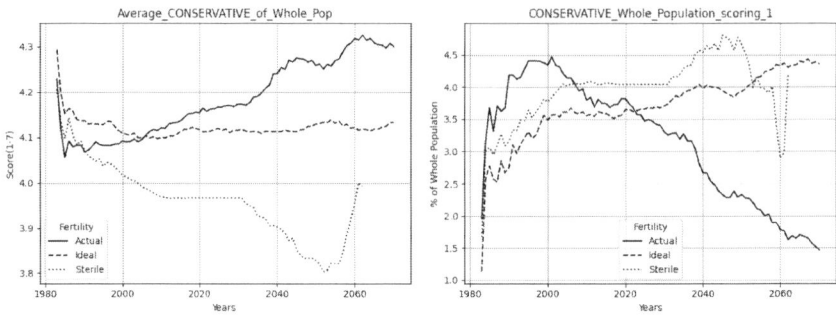

Graph 5 and 6. Extreme Liberals and Average Conservatism Among the Whole Population.

For the next set of graphs about extreme conservatism (7 to 12), you'll notice a very curious discrepancy between the patterns for the whole population compared to just the white population. For the whole population, extreme conservatives make substantial gains in both the above and below IQ section of the population, but you'll notice the gains are larger and more stable in the upper half. For the white population, however, the difference is more dramatic: conservatives make extremely quick gains in the upper half after the more intelligent Generation X begin retiring out of the working population during the 2030s; whilst in the lower half extreme conservatives actually make losses in representation. What's the explanation for this?

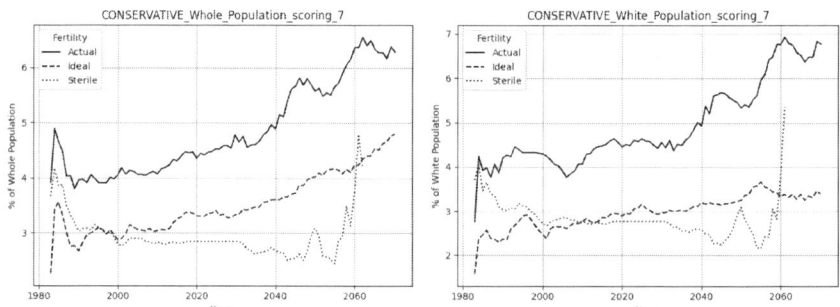

Graph 7 and 8. Extreme Conservatives Among the Whole Population and the White Population.

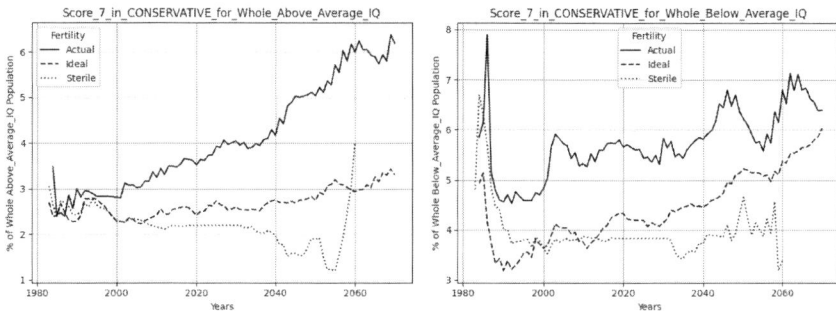

Graph 9 and 10. Extreme Conservatives Among the Whole Population; Above and Below Average IQ.

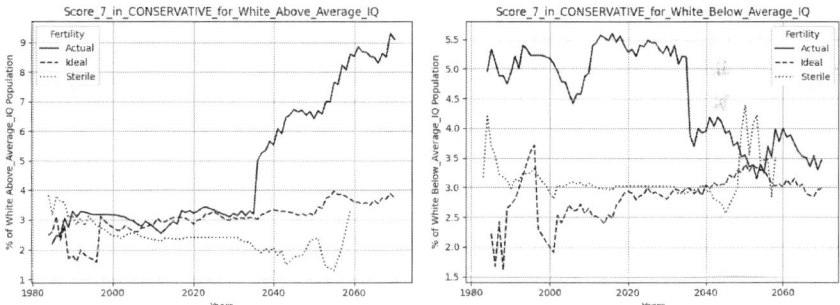

Graph 11 and 12. Extreme Conservatives Among the White Population; Above and Below Average IQ.

The Conservatism Promotion Effect

This isn't simply a matter of differential fertility any more: the average IQ, via which the population is categorized by the model, as being either above or below, is trending downwards over time. This means someone who had below average IQ in 2025 can suddenly be reassessed as being above average IQ in 2035, despite their IQ not actually changing; the bar has simply been lowered for them. So what we have here is a 'promotion effect' — extreme conservatives are disproportionately jumping above the mean IQ as it trends downwards. The implication is that there's something about being an 'extreme conservative' that makes your IQ 'more likely to survive' the selection pressures of contraception and political anti-natalism.

You might be wondering why the promotion effect wasn't visible in graphs 3 and 4 of conservative averages, where roughly 10% increases in the averages were shown for both above and below average IQ populations. You would expect part of this to be because more moderate levels of conservatism will give you diminishing levels of resistance to anti-natalism broadly defined. But the main reason is that, at least within the white population, the rising underclass powering the downward trend in IQ is discernibly conservative. It is just not extremely so; presumably because lower IQ is associated with political disengagement (Jensen, 1998) and because extreme conservatism is associated with impulse control and an intense disgust reflex that the fast LHS underclass can't possess. Certainly, it has been found that outlier high IQ predicts extreme environmental sensitivity, because you can better solve problems by taking in more information. The consequence of this, at the extreme, is very high IQ people that are overwhelmed by stimuli and are extremely sensitive to even very minor negative stimuli (Karpinski et al., 2018). But, as stated, the underclass are decidedly conservative, to the extent that conservatism represents a cluster of taboo instinctual human values that one is born with, such as ethnocentrism, patriarchy and homophobia, and so on. In this context, intelligent liberalism conversely represents the learned moral inhibition of these prejudices that we receive from the regnant social order. With IQ comes greater social and cultural inhibition; greater conformity with presiding mores and taboos (Woodley of Menie & Dunkel, 2015). The underclass, lacking in IQ most of all, are thus the furthest removed from the liberal 'cultural override' on human moral sentiment.

That IQ determines people's susceptibility to having one's inner moral life regulated, by social or political influences, has further implications at the other end of society. IQ being largely associated with socio-economic status, we have a curiously circular cause–effect loop here, where the ruling class, that determines the socially approved paradigm of morality within a society, is at the same time the most likely to be inculcated by that same ideology. Standard political science theory will tell you that the reason why politicians generally gravitate towards the centre of politics is as a conscious strategic effort to win support from undecided moderate 'swing' voters. Yet here we have a psychological explanation, not incompatible with the Machiavellian one from political science, which is that politicians are relatively higher in IQ and its associated personality traits, Openness and Agreeableness. This means they are more predisposed to absorbing the 'average' political orthodoxy currently established by their polity, than the more polarized and disagreeable rabble who walk the streets. Cyclical reinforcement aside: if conservatives, especially extreme conservatives, continue to infiltrate the smarter section of society by sheer demographic force of numbers, this will push what's now widely considered to be the politically unsafe opinions into the smarter fraction of society.

The Low IQ Rebellion, Led by
High IQ Autistics and Psychopaths

Nevertheless, inasmuch as the left has cultural and institutional hegemony for now, we expect those with lower IQ (especially the underclass) to be the ones disproportionately more willing to rebel against the ruling culture, and advocate for their instinctual genetically determined preferences. With the white GSS population, each generation is lower in IQ than the previous one, going back to the 1970s. So inasmuch as we should expect a conservative revolution in politics, we should expect it to emanate from two very different groups. On the one hand, there will be those who have extremely high intelligence, causing their autistic obsession with truth to override their 'cultural mediation'. This will be all the more pronounced if they have moderately psychopathic traits, causing them to be attracted to danger, or if they are simply strongly instinctively group-oriented to the extent that 'cultural mediation' is overridden. They will ally with those of relatively low intelligence; including young people, with raw intelligence increasing up to middle age. These will be people who you wouldn't expect to occupy positions of political power in society, or even be all that engaged in politics, but nevertheless, through casting their votes in elections as much as they do, they are able to decisively influence the outcome of an election, in favour of socially conservative political actors, to the dismay of the ruling liberal elite—who will be held in high regard by their peers, but decreasingly voted for by the people.

Once such a revolution approaches completion, the left will have had its hegemony taken away, which has compounding effects, because, to reiterate, the left is reliant on cultural-political hegemony to gather support from the smarter fraction of its voter base. Once gone, you have a 'liberated' higher cognitive strata and they would become *more* zealous in their conservatism, than the lower strata that liberated them, because said conservatism would likely be established as the new political orthodoxy for the intelligent and socially-adept people to conform themselves too; regardless of their own inborn dispositions.

But again, as to our previous point on demographic survival of conservatism in the higher cognitive strata of society—a process that has likely been ongoing since at least the 1970s—those intelligent, genetically conservative people would have thus far been repressing the extremes of their conservatism to fit in with the previous established orthodoxy. However, they would now have their innate moral preferences fully liberated, and endorsed, by the new conservative moral paradigm that was voted in from below, by the rebellious underclass. Thus, in the timespan of a single political generation, intelligence would change from being associated with liberalism to being associated with conservatism, and a 'Woke arms race' would ensue in the opposite direction, as a new psychological equilibrium would be sought. More intelligent people will attempt to virtue-signal their group-binding values, and thus try to outdo each other in their apparent conservatism. The underclass that commenced the whole process of installing the new moral paradigm into power will, ironically, come to be seen as the most liberal in the population, and will likely be looked down upon for that reason. The future may closely resemble certain conservative religious groups, where people, often not so subtly, show off their Biblical knowledge or allusions to their purity (see Dutton, 2008b). And, it's fascinating to consider: the high IQ autistics and psychopaths who will also have been involved in the process of destroying the Woke world will now find themselves appalled by the 'Noble Lies', group-promoting taboos, and other repressions enacted by the new conservative dispensation, and they will be attracted to, or stimulated by, the dangers of opposing it.

American Politics as a Racial Game

The next set of graphs (13-24) that track GSS Democrat–Republican affiliation show even clearer promotion effects. There, the difference in fertility trends, between the above and below average in IQ, for these explicitly political tribes, is as stark as it gets. Examining these trends, devout Democrats of *above* average IQ will nearly halve their number over the next two decades, as will devout Republicans in the *below* average IQ sector of the white population. Conversely, it would seem that devout Democrats are set to make future gains in the below average IQ white population, where devout Republicans will be making gains in the above average IQ white population. (You might have wondered if this could be a 'demotion effect' – the opposite of a promotion effect. However, a true demotion effect would only occur when the average IQ in the population was trending upwards and a particular political demographic was being 'left behind' in this regard, and thus falling below the rising average.) These trends are not confined to the fringes of politics; you can see that the graphs of averages of Republicanism have concomitant drops and rises in average IQ – especially pronounced around the 2030s when the Generation X population retirement process kicks in.

Chapter Six

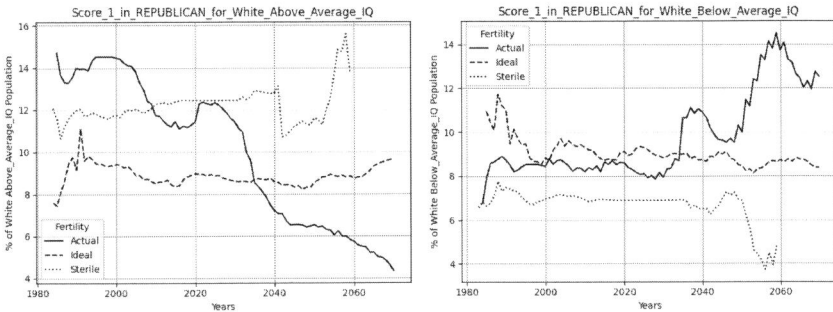

Graph 13 and 14. Devout Democrats in the White Population; Above & Below Average IQ.

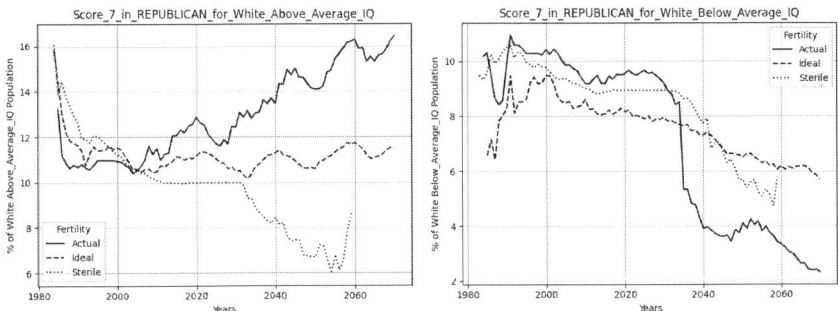

Graph 15 and 16. Devout Republicans in the White Population; Above & Below Average IQ.

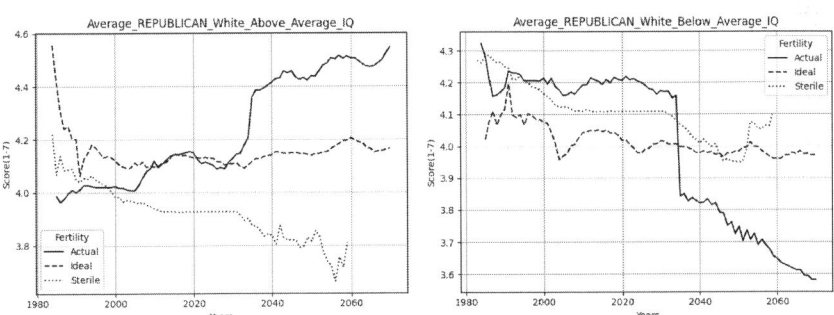

Graph 17 and 18. Average Republicanism in the White Population; Above & Below Average IQ.

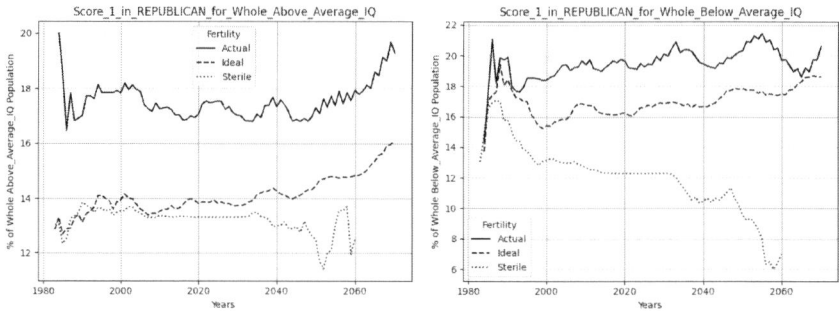

Graph 19 and 20. Devout Democrats in the Whole Population; Above & Below Average IQ.

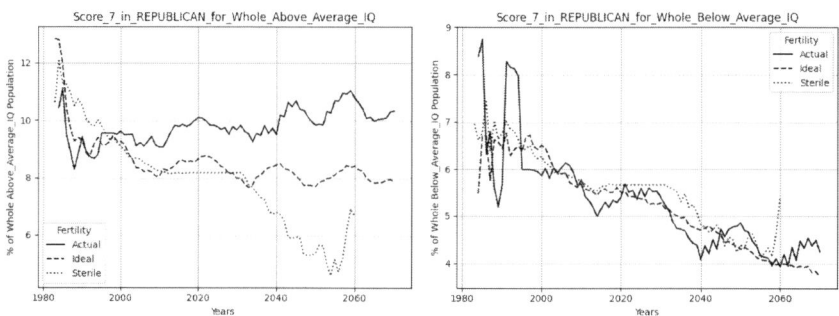

Graph 21 and 22. Devout Republicans in the Whole Population; Above & Below Average IQ.

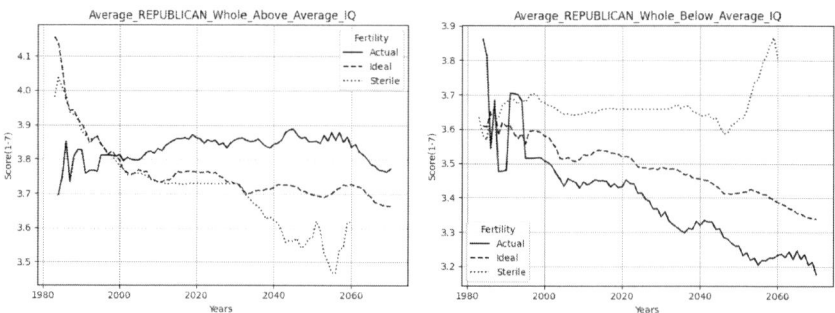

Graph 23 and 24. Average Republicanism in the Whole Population; Above & Below Average IQ.

These much stronger, and universal, effects in political IQ shifts would appear to contradict what we were saying earlier: about the rising underclass being decidedly conservative, though not extremely so. However, this was in reference to social conservatism; especially of the taboo and contentious nature, which conflicts with the new 'Woke' morality. It's important to realize that, until recent times, coarse social conservatism, and the politically conservative party in America, the Republican Party, were not ever so strongly aligned; not least because of competing economic issues. 'Republicanism' in these graphs is defined by all of the GSS survey years we sampled from 1994 to 2018. The election of Donald Trump, and his nationalist populism, in America saw swathes of working-class voters defect from the Democratic Party (Shaw & Petrocik, 2020, p. 10). Conversely, a substantial amount of middle-class Republican voters were put off by the character and politics of Donald Trump, as these were tied to (taboo) social conservatism (Jacobson, 2019, p. 201). The more intelligent and agreeable middle-class personality is a creature of 'super-ego' and thus takes care to conform to cultural pressures exerted by the enthroned left, as we have discussed. The less intelligent and conscientious working-class personality is conversely 'libidinous' in character, and thus is always aching to openly rebel against what can be broadly regarded as a psychologically frustrating morality and elite (see Dutton, 2013b). Remember, despite conservative *genes* being upwardly mobile during the long decline in heritable IQ, we expect the conservative *cultural* revolution to come from the lowest in society, as they are the most able and willing to rebel against left-wing cultural hegemony.

That being said, it makes sense, more perennially, for working-class, and especially underclass, voters to prefer the party of the left, even if they are socially conservative, because the Democratic Party always better represents their immediate economic interests in terms of welfare and other socialist provisions, regardless of which party they might think would run a better economy. Over the short to medium term, the underclass shall continue to vote for the nationalist populist party of choice over taboo social issues; over the long run the underclass will surely vote for the socialist welfare it relies on to live.

American Political Affiliation

But we haven't yet discussed the ethnic-racial dimensions of political affiliation, the growing underclass and IQ trends, and here the plot thickens. You'll probably have glanced at the latter six graphs (19–24), the Republican–Democrat affiliation trends for the *whole* population split by IQ, and noticed they're quite different from the trends in the white subsection shown in graphs 13 to 18. And this is in stark contrast to the trends for conservatism we showed earlier, for which white and whole populations were pretty much identical. The IQ-transference effects are almost completely wiped out when generalizing from whites to the whole US population, for Republican–Democrat affiliation. The only thing that stays consistent between the white and the whole population is that, on Republicanism, in terms of devout followers and average support, Republicans still make significant losses in the lower IQ sector. But there are no corresponding increases in the higher IQ sector, and, in fact, devout Democrats actually make modest gains in the higher IQ sector on fertility later on in the century.

Taken altogether, what this in effect means is that, even for those ethnic minorities of a conservative temperament and above average IQ — which would otherwise align them with the Republican Party both socially and economically — they are nevertheless still more inclined to vote Democrat over Republican; purely because they perceive the Democratic Party (unconsciously or otherwise) as better representing their extended ethnic interests. If it beggars belief for you that an individual could go that far politically in sacrificing their own personal views and interests to favour what they perceive as better for their ethnic in-group, it must be emphasized that every other ethnicity in America — and for that matter the entire world — is significantly higher in ethnocentrism than white populations (see Dutton, 2019a). It's the general rule in human nature to put your own ethnic in-group's political interests before your own; ethnic Western Europeans are the exception to this.

This potentially has game-changing implications for the future of American politics that we have thus far been outlining, because whites are being bred out of the US population, as the trends in the next set of graphs show (25-30). Being more intelligent is an especially strong negative predictor of fertility if you are a white liberal, and the underclass is majority-composed of ethnic minorities, as we'll see when we discuss the ethnically segmented data on illegitimate births.

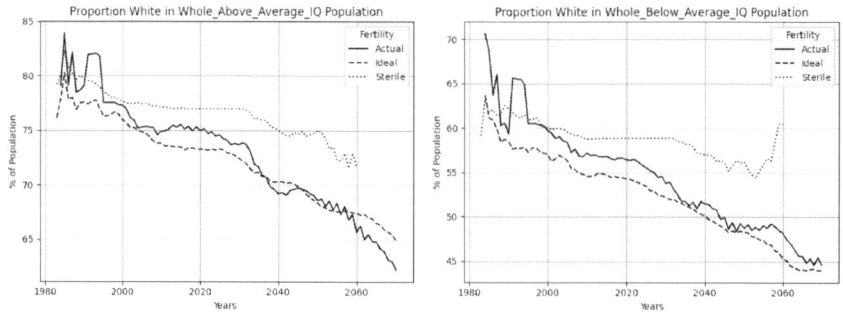

Graph 25 and 26. Percentage of the Whole Population White; Above & Below Average IQ.

Chapter Six

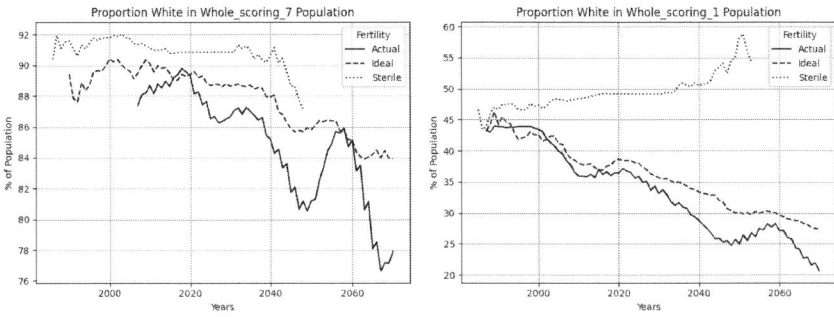

Graph 27 and 28. Percentage of Devout Republicans & Devout Democrats White.

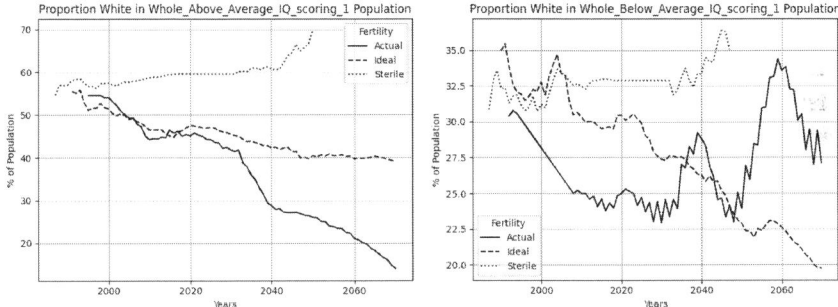

Graph 29 and 30. Percentage of Devout Democrats White; Above & Below Average IQ.

By the middle of this century, whites will be only two thirds of the above average IQ population, and only half of the below average IQ population. Extrapolating fertility, we would expect devout Republicans to be only about three quarters white by this time. And for devout Democrats, white representation is falling twice as fast, and will shrink from about half white as it is today, to about a quarter white mid-century. This means, overall, ethnic disparities in political party identification in America are only going to increase, despite white representation falling fast overall in both parties, and the whole population. Moving into the second half of this century, we would expect the committed Republican population will be about three quarters white, whereas the committed Democratic population to be only one quarter white. Breaking this racial demography further down by IQ, we see it is the smarter half of white Democrats that are imploding; by fertility, committed Democrats of the above average IQ white population will not make up one third of that demographic a couple decades hence, and not one fifth another couple of decades after that.

These fertility trends might seem unlikely, considering that smarter white Millennials in America are unprecedented in their liberalism and Democrat affiliation, nevertheless it must be remembered that this group has extremely low fertility, and is set to be voted out by religious/libertarian Zoomers and the rising politically incorrect underclass. For the Democrats to survive, they must forsake all other 'Woke liberal' social policies not related to race, and remove their image as a party composed of rich and powerful white neo-liberals. Instead, it must market itself as a party *by* the racial-minority-dominated underclass *for* the racial-minority-dominated underclass. Its policies must focus on ever-more extended welfare benefits to the underclass, including universal basic income, and race reparations. It must in all things be seen as anti-elite and anti-white, and in that sense be quite indistinguishable from the Black Lives Matter organization. The leadership of the Democrats will ultimately come to be dominated by African and Hispanic Americans, aggressively selling crude and simple racial grievance politics to an impulsive and low IQ underclass. In that sense, it would seem that 'Wokeness' will live on; however, these racial minority leaders in the Democratic Party will be almost entirely composed of homophobic and patriarchal religious men; as the religious section of the racial minority population in America will be the only sub-demographic sufficiently intelligent, conscientious, and pro-social to make it in politics, whilst holding social views and behaviours that the underclass could relate to, or sympathize with. Feminist and sexual minority activists, as well as other liberal-left preoccupations such as environmentalism, will all come to be seen as a 'rich white thing' that 'rich white people' use to virtue-signal and gain status (which, let's face it, is exactly what they are) and thus have no place in the Democratic Party of tomorrow. It seems likely the Republican Party will poach the votes of feminists and sexual minorities, when the Democratic Party abandons and turns on them, under a protective life-raft of pro-tolerance libertarian rhetoric. Beyond the tolerance of their existence, however, these groups will very likely lose their privileged positions in the ruling political culture, and issues such as abortion, trans-sexuality, non-binary children, gay marriage, and sex education will be regarded as an 'excess' of the decadent past, when we worshipped the Golden Calf and Baal, something for which God has now well and truly punished us.

'It Don't Matter If You're Black or White'

This grim picture of the politics of tomorrow, being entirely based upon racial–class divisions, might seem overly black and white. And that's precisely what it will be: or rather, it will likely be a fuzzy black and white. As the left continues to evolve, it will push a vague and amorphous political conflict, between two 'super-ethnicities' called: 'white-aligned' and 'non-white-aligned'. And there is evidence that this is already happening. If you are non-white but you pursue a culture of education and success, and even speak like educated people do, then you are 'white-aligned' (Mozafari et al., 2020). The reason for this is that there simply won't be enough European white people in the latter half of this century to sustain a simpler narrative. The 'white-aligned group' will be less than 50% European white; the rest will be made up of English-speaking Hispanics, Asians, and 'black traitors', as they shall be likely labelled. Conversely, the 'non-white-aligned' group shall be broadly made up of an ethnic mix of blacks, Spanish-speaking Hispanics, and underclass whites and Asians. And ironically, though being labelled as a racial conflict, the actual substance, and division lines, of this demographic, political feud will be in terms of culture and wealth, or ultimately speaking: IQ.

The next set of graphs, 31 to 40, are a lot to take in, but, in essence, they are showing that there is an IQ promotion effect in believing that race differences are inborn versus believing that race differences are discriminatory. Interestingly, our model found that when you split the higher IQ half of the population into quartiles, and look at the sterile population, you can see it's the lower quartile in the above average IQ Gen Z population that's showing signs of rebelling against the accepted orthodoxy; upper quartile in IQ remains flat. This is further evidence that taboo breaking, here the taboo on inborn race differences, will necessarily promulgate up the IQ ladder from the bottom up, regardless of the intellectual merits of the position, simply because intelligence is so strongly associated with social inhibition and conformity to dogma. The punch line is that the effects are substantially stronger for ethnic minorities than they are for whites. That is to say, blacks, Hispanics, and Native Americans would be increasingly coming apart by IQ on the question of what's responsible for race differences, if this were a heritable viewpoint.

It might seem surprising to you that this divide should come about in the future, if you consider that it is in flat contradiction to the Woke ideology, that intelligent minorities are supposed to absorb through public educational institutions, but perhaps it's precisely America's educational systems that are responsible for this effect, knowing that education is the ultimate negative predictor of fertility. The more educated you are, the less children you have. Thus views on the causes of racial disparities among intelligent minorities should work as a good proxy for how much 'education' (or indoctrination by the Neo-Gnostic Church) they have put themselves through, and delayed having children in the process; this versus how soon they went into the real world of work, to discover how things actually are for themselves, and have many children in the process. Also, minorities with higher IQ are more likely to examine the relative poverty of their co-ethnics from a removed, higher socio-economic position; whereas those of lower IQ will more likely be suffering ghetto poverty themselves. Lacking the cognitive capital to make it in an increasingly cognitively demanding labour market (see Rindermann, 2018), the optimal Darwinian strategy for low IQ ethnic minorities is to use their victimhood status as a minority to extract welfare payments from a pathologically altruistic welfare society.

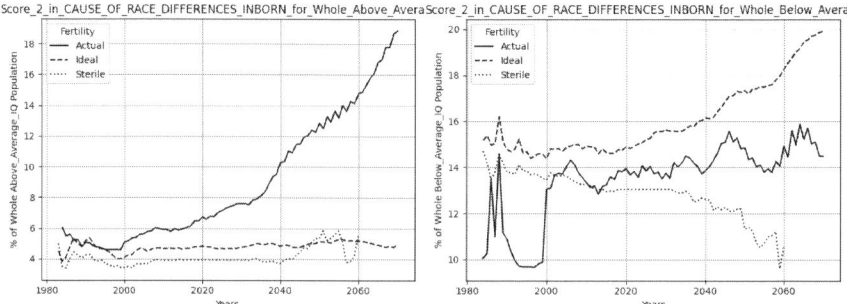

Graph 31 and 32. Percentage of Whole Population, Race Differences Inborn; Above & Below Average IQ.

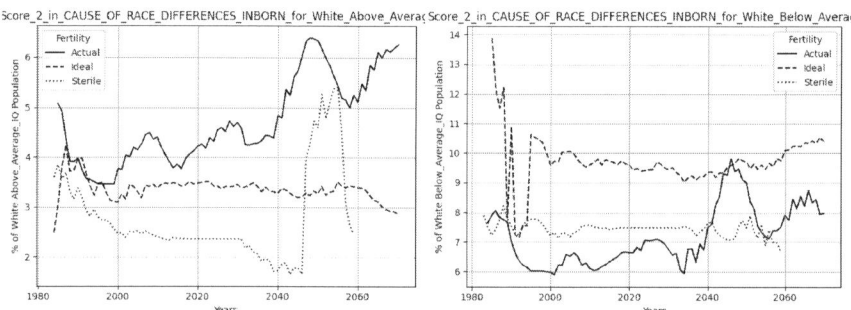

Graph 33 and 34. Percentage of White Population, Race Differences Inborn; Above & Below Average IQ.

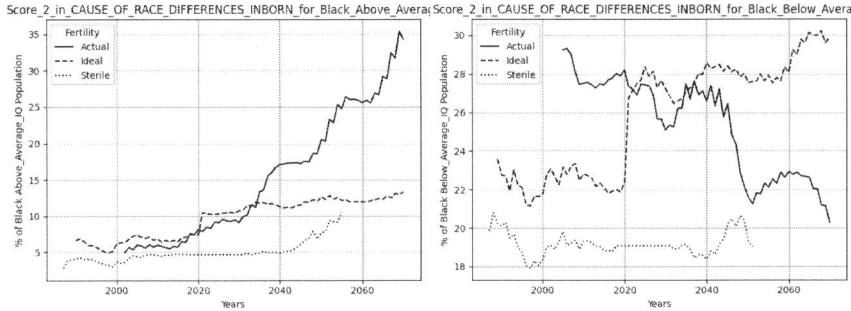

Graph 35 and 36. Percentage of Black Population, Race Differences Inborn; Above & Below Average IQ.

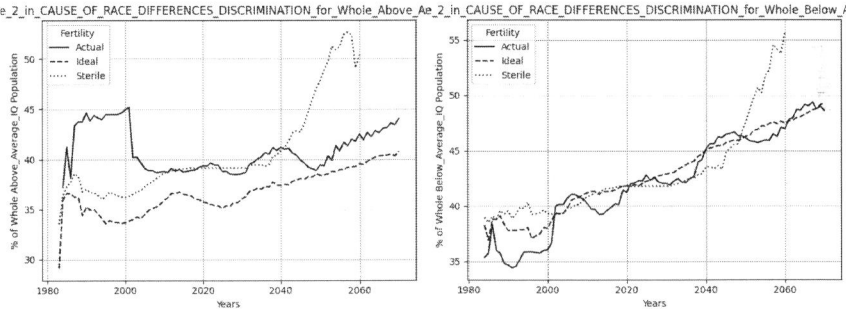

Graph 37 and 38. Percentage of Whole Population, Race Differences Discrimination; Above & Below Average IQ.

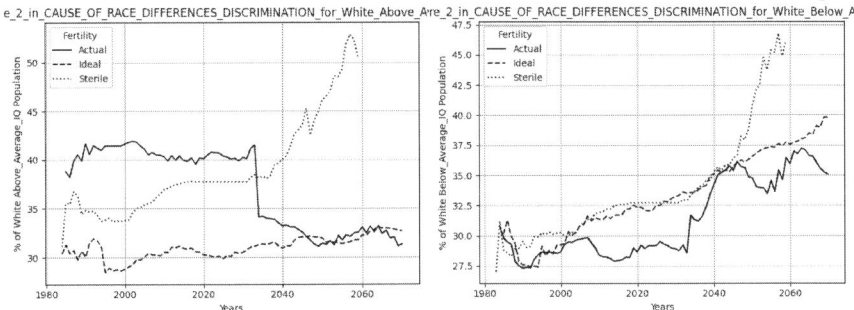

Graph 39 and 40. Percentage of White Population, Race Differences Discrimination; Above & Below Average IQ.

It also makes sense even for low IQ non-ethnic minorities to do this, purely on the basis of class; however, membership of the victimized underclass will require more than mere poverty — it will be increasingly associated with the culture of the 'non-white-aligned' super-ethnicity; admission to which is currently restricted, for those of a pure European white ethnic makeup, because of taboos on 'cultural appropriation'. That being said, we would expect there to be an ever-vanishingly smaller number among the underclass who are purely composed of any one ethnicity; let alone white European, inasmuch as the underclass is defined by its fast Life History Strategy, as this is a key predictor of low socio-economic status (Perkins, 2016). This is because, despite fast LHS predicting negative ethnocentrism, it ironically also predicts sexual preferences for racial outbreeding; in the context of short-term and promiscuous relationships, that is, where women beget children from different and varied men. There are a number of lines of evidence indicating an association between outbreeding and a fast Life History Strategy. Mixed race high school students in Alaska have been found to be more likely to suffer from depression (Garcia et al., 2019). Another study, drawing upon America's 2002–2003 National Latino and Asian American Study, reported that, controlling for age and other important variables, 17% of mono-racial people in the sample had suffered from mental illness, compared to 34% of bi-racial people (American Association for the Advancement of Science, 17th August 2008). A similar conclusion was reached when analysing the National Longitudinal Study of Adolescent Health (Udry et al., 2003). According to the US 2002 National Survey of Family Growth, interracial marriages, overall, have a higher divorce rate, which would be consistent with the argument that elevated mental illness in their offspring is simply a reflection of fast Life History strategists being more likely to contract mixed-race unions. The divorce rate is higher the more genetically distant the races are. Thus, white-Asian marriages end in divorce as often as white-white marriages, though more often than Asian-Asian marriages. White-black marriages are the most prone to end in divorce (Bratter & King, 2008). This relationship exists because, if you are evolved to an unstable environment, then you may as well marry those who are strongly genetically different from you, because they might carry some useful adaptation. You'll be attracted to risk and, in that the female will expect no investment in the offspring, you will select for traits which, if inherited, will permit the offspring to survive instability. Thus, she will trade genetic similarity for evidence of strength, for example, from any race. By contrast, *K*-strategists are strongly adapted to their own specific niche, rendering it adaptive—for the offspring—that they marry genetically similar people. They'll also be averse to risk and, nurture-inclined, people tend to bond more strongly with those who are genetically similar to themselves.

It should be said that even in long-time multi-racial societies, such as the United States, mixed race marriages are extremely rare, as predicted by 'Genetic Similarity Theory' whereby we tend to maximize our genetic fitness by breeding with people who are optimally similar to ourselves. Couples have been found to be more genetically similar than two random co-ethnics, and more similar on more heritable physical and mental traits. People find opposite sex photos more attractive if their own faces are morphed into them. Best friends are more genetically similar than two random co-ethnics. And even within families there is evidence that people bond more strongly with those who are the most genetically similar to themselves (Rushton, 2005). There is evidence, from Iceland, that the 'sweet spot' for a successful and fertile marriage is your third cousin or the genetic equivalent thereof (Helgason et al., 2008). This is all congruous with the evidence outlined above that we are adapted to maximize our genetic interests — pass on as many of our genes as possible — by breeding with those who are genetically similar to ourselves. But people will, of course, balance this with other evolved desires. Having nothing to lose from the sexual encounter, males are evolved to primarily select for youth and beauty, as young women are more likely to become pregnant, and beauty is a sign of low mutational load and thus of healthy genes. Females, though they are interested in genetic health, are more evolved to be attracted to high status males because, under harsh conditions, high status males can invest more in the offspring and in herself, making it more likely that both survive. In addition, the offspring will carry whatever genes have permitted the male to attain status, with status being associated with fertility under pre-industrial conditions (see Buss, 1989). Thus, trade-offs between these different factors can be made.

But, even so, marrying people who are very genetically different — such as of a different race — is rare and it becomes even rarer the larger the genetic distance between the races. In 2001, Americans were 75% less likely to know a person of another race 'with whom they discuss important matters' than would happen by chance (McPherson et al., 2001). Among 2015 newlyweds in the US, white people chose a spouse of another race just over 11% of the time. Of the mixed race marriages in America in 2015, 42% were white/Hispanic, with Hispanics being, on average, about 50% white. Further, 15% were white/Asian and 11% were white/black (Livingston & Brown, 18th May 2017). Based on analyses of the genetic distances between races, this is exactly what we would predict (Salter, 2007). It is also worth noting that Asian-Americans were more likely to marry non-Asians in 1980 than in 2015 (Livingston & Brown, 18th May 2017), presumably because the percentage of fellow Asians in America was lower back then. This implies that those who believe that different races are all going to inter-blend at every level of society into 'a uniform coffee colour with a pleasing tinge of yellow' (Walker, 1977, p. 9) are simply incorrect. Congruous with this evidence of the rarity of race-mixing, it has been found that people will invest more of their resources in strangers of their own race (Rushton, 2005), they will assort along racial lines on university campuses in terms of living arrangements (Clark & Tuffin, 2015), they trust people of different races less (Putnam, 2007), and they feel an instinctive fear towards strangers of different races which they do not towards strangers of their own race (Wilson, 2012, p. 100).

A faster LHS is optimized to a more antisocial environment; where genetic similarity of the children to the population counts for less. Faster Life History speed is associated with being higher on the Dark Triad traits (Machiavellianism, Psychopathy, and Narcissism), which are themselves associated with the behaviour and desire to inflict guilt and exploit sympathy, through extracting charitable transfers of wealth from their altruistic opposites, as well as to gain socio-economic status by signalling virtue and victimhood (Ok et al., 2020). The future politically left underclass will potentially be likened to a political guild of mixed race sociopaths; the admission requirements to which will permit as much white admixture as you have just so long as you do not appear completely white in ethnicity. To the extent that you satisfy those requirements, you will be permitted, and even required, to wear a certain uniform associated with 'gangster-ghetto' culture, which includes a style of clothing, music, speech, and general way of living, antithetical to the white middle-class culture. The benefits of belonging to this guild will be access to the welfare and benefit payments of government and charities, which one requires in order to live without legal paid employment; as well as other privileges, such as exemption from being policed by white officers, and access to certain well-paid white-collar jobs in large corporations, not requiring any former experience or training, or even basic education.

Why Non-Whites Might White-Align

The significance of a fast LHS predisposition to promiscuous racial out-breeding cannot be understated because, ultimately, it is what is going to cause the underclass to decidedly swing back to the left, under the future paradigm we've been describing; ironically just after it has triggered a conservative revolution in the upper echelons of society, by voting in deplorable taboo-breakers to positions of power. Today's underclass in America is composed of just as many whites as racial minorities, who are content to vote in Donald Trump's ethno-nationalist populism, but all the while they're doing that, they're frequently having their illegitimate children with other ethnicities; and in any case, to the extent that they're not, they're being outbred by racial minorities of equivalent economic status. Thus they're becoming ever-more acculturated to the aforementioned 'ghetto-gangster' culture they're being subsumed into, thus guaranteeing that most of their many dozens of grandchildren alive in twenty years' time will be mixed race, even if some of their illegitimate children being born now aren't.

But let's get back to the future mindset of higher IQ minorities. Contrary to what you might have expected, though by no means wooing over the majority, Donald Trump's nationalist-populist political campaigns in 2016 and 2020 made record-breaking gains for the Republican Party among ethnic minorities (Nagesh, 22nd November 2020). How could this have happened if it can be taken as a given that Trump's platform was predicated on a soft-core version of white nationalism? Part of the answer here is genuinely due to white-alignment of Hispanics, Asians, and all mixed race Americans who are dominantly white in admixture. A study by the Pew Research Center (2016) examined the Latino vote in the 2016 election, and made certain telling findings about the nature of Hispanics who were voting for Trump. They were more likely to be born in the US, they were more educated, more likely to be men, more likely to speak English over Spanish, and more likely to vote at all. Republican Hispanics really can be said to be more 'white-aligned'. Just as 'non-white-alignment' can happen by assimilation into urban ghetto-gangster culture, white-alignment occurs by assimilation into white-collar middle-class American culture. By virtue of being higher in IQ, you belong to a more 'white-aligned' population cluster in America. IQ and socio-economic status predicts an awful lot about an individual's personality, and lifestyle choices, right down to their choice in beer and music, as Charles Murray (2012) shows extensively in his book on the growing US class divide, *Coming Apart*.

From a more biological, Darwinian perspective, true white-alignment, though, would only be determined by the choices one makes in ethnicity of partner to mate with, and what one encourages in their children's mating preferences also (consciously or otherwise). In America's contemporary mating market, white people command a premium. Data from online dating websites shows that white females in particular are significantly choosier about the ethnic makeup of their long-term partners; regardless of whether or not they are willing to consciously admit to having a racial preference. Yet the data shows that this preference can be compensated for, by ethnic-minority men, by being higher in socio-economic status (Hitsch et al., 2010).

It needs to be kept in mind that, in America, though ethnic minorities fall into certain identifiable camps (e.g. Africans, Hispanics, Native

Americans, Filipinos), a long running legacy of interracial mixing means that some members of these ethnic groups are much closer to a white European ethnic makeup than others. Notwithstanding this, in a slow Life History Strategy mating paradigm, involving long-term marital bonding, with nuclear and extended families, unless there's a critical mass of their own mixed-ethnicity around to mate with, in-group preferences in ethnic mating, and sheer regression to the mean, causes the descendants of mixed ethnic individuals to inevitably merge back into just one cluster of their ancestral ethnic groups. Which ethnic group they and their descendants choose would ultimately determine which ethnicity they were truly aligned with.

In America there certainly is a critical mass of intelligent, *K*-strategic people who blur the line between Hispanic and white European; making white-alignment for middle-class Hispanics relatively easy. There's also a mainstream trend of middle-class white males marrying East Asian females and producing mixed children. However, when it comes to white and black marriages, these partnerships appear to be too rare, and produce too few offspring, to provide a significant emulsifying class of European-African Americans (Dutton, 2020). It's never impossible for an intelligent, middle-class, slow Life History minority to find and marry a partner of another race, and in that sense 'align' with that race; these marriages occur all the time. We're just saying that there are varying degrees of difficulty in this, depending on what race you happen to belong to, and that this has far-reaching political implications. A large part of what attracted ethnic minorities to Trump's Republican nationalist-populist campaign, over and above white-alignment, was simply the fact that the Democratic Party had become too liberal on social issues for some minorities to stand. It must be emphasized that social conservatism, especially of the taboo kind, isn't an intrinsically white-aligned phenomenon; on a lot of social metrics in the GSS, white populations score more liberal than other ethnic minorities.

A Darker Left Throws the Woke to the Wolves

As we discussed, the Democratic Party will ultimately abandon all of its 'liberal Woke' policies, as a 'rich white' aberration, and double down on racial–class grievances. It will be a traditional Marxist left-wing party, with a leadership composed entirely of patriarchal, homophobic, religious minorities. This means that all of the ethnic minorities who are voting for the Republican Party today, on social issues and economic issues, will be drawn back to voting for the Democratic Party again, down the line, if they are not 'white-aligned'. That means that intelligent Hispanics and Filipinos will on the whole 'white-align' because they can, and they have an economic incentive to do so; inasmuch as they are probably paying more to the government in taxes than they are getting out in terms of social welfare. Intelligent blacks however, despite having an economic incentive to white-align, will find that, unconsciously, socially much more difficult, and thus shall likely nobly stick by their own political faction of ethnic interest. Some, however, will, of course 'white-align'.

The implication here is that the American underclass of tomorrow, though largely ethnically mixed of all of the ethnicities, will have a discernibly African identity and leadership to it, because that's where the intelligent and pro-social part of this, admittedly very unintelligent and non-sociable, group will be concentrated. Moreover, in terms of the practical application of Marxist-racial grievance politics, the history of American colonial enslavement uniquely qualifies the most African-looking members of the underclass to espouse victimhood narratives.

Rising Liberalism Among Some Non-Whites

Unfortunately, the future is even more complicated than this elaborate description would have you believe, because in terms of the direction of trends, ethnic minorities aren't going to hold a reputation for traditional views on religion, sex, and gender roles forever, as the next graphs 41 to 52 show. Though they are more socially conservative in absolute terms today, the black population is trending more liberal in terms of fertility on just about every metric, where whites are trending in the opposite direction. The ultimate explanation for this is that the underclass is dominated by its most fast LHS breeders. It was stated earlier in the chapter that religiousness would initially be rising in the underclass somewhat, before being taken over by its irreligious subcomponent. These are the fast Life History strategists, who fall pregnant at very early ages, with a great variety of men, in brief liaisons and romances. Fast LHS is associated with being low on all five moral foundations (Gladden & Cleator, 2018), and, along with stupidity, is associated with disengagement with politics and a lack of cooperation with the ethnic in-group (Figueredo et al., 2011).

It wasn't the case for the previous Boomer generation that blacks were trending downwards in conservatism; the black population was trending more conservative just as the whites are now. The reason for the change is the sexual revolution. It had a vastly disproportionate effect on racial minorities. An explosion of teenage pregnancies and births, out of wedlock, came out of the 1960s for ethnic minorities (Raley et al., 2015). According to CDC data on births today, about three quarters of blacks, two thirds of American Indians, and half of all Hispanics are born out of wedlock — whereas the proportions are only a third for whites and a fifth for Asians (Martin et al., 2019). These out of wedlock births occur at significantly younger ages on average, meaning a much faster rate of reproduction. Though some of these ethnicities retain a highly religious-conservative subculture, fast Life History strategists now dominate their reproductive trends overall, and thus they shall become a demographic force for increasingly permissive (anti-)social values. That said, we might discount the political consequences of this; though looser sexual mores are associated with political liberalism (Wolfinger, 2018) this is in the context of a more intelligent population. When it comes to the low IQ population of fast Life History strategists, even the GSS data we have on political engagement itself show this explosive underclass is half as interested in politics as the current average.

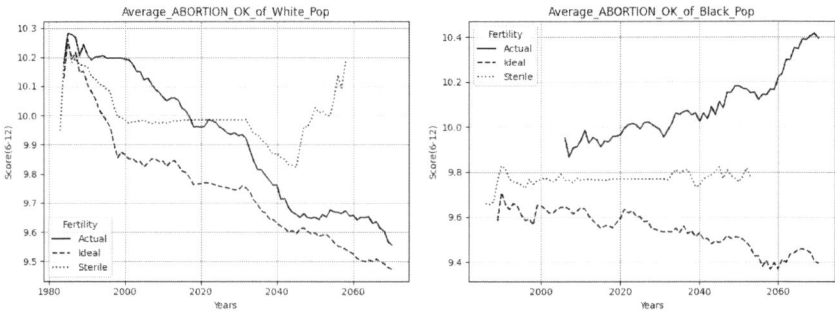

Graph 41 and 42. Average Views on Abortion OK; White & Black Populations.

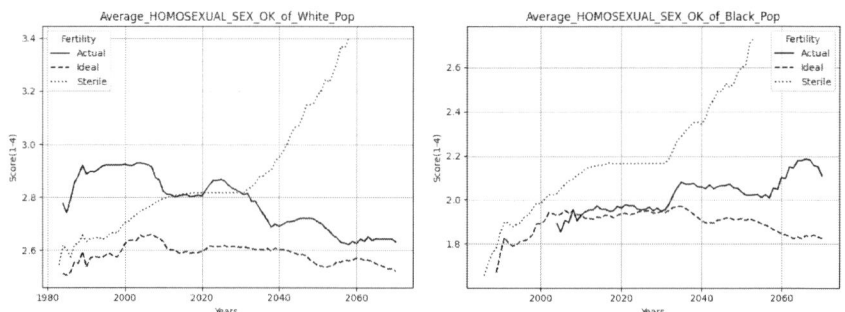

Graph 43 and 44. Average Views on Homosexual Sex OK; White & Black Populations.

Chapter Six 153

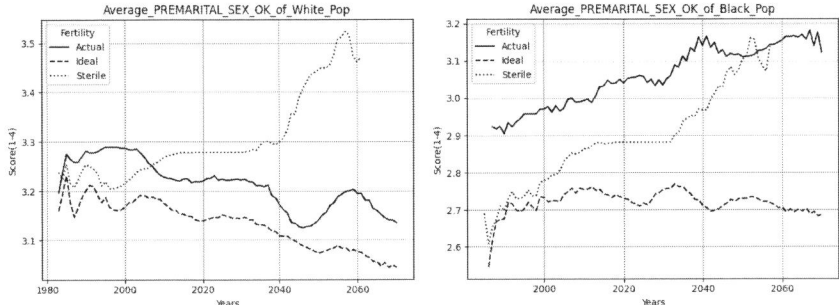

Graph 45 and 46. Average Views on Premarital Sex OK; White & Black Populations.

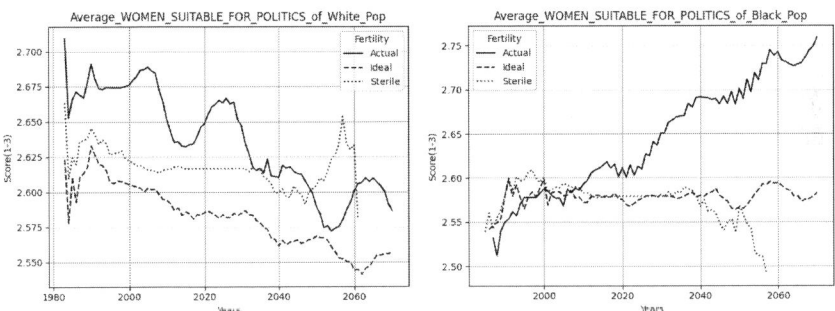

Graph 47 and 48. Average Views on Women in Politics; White & Black Populations.

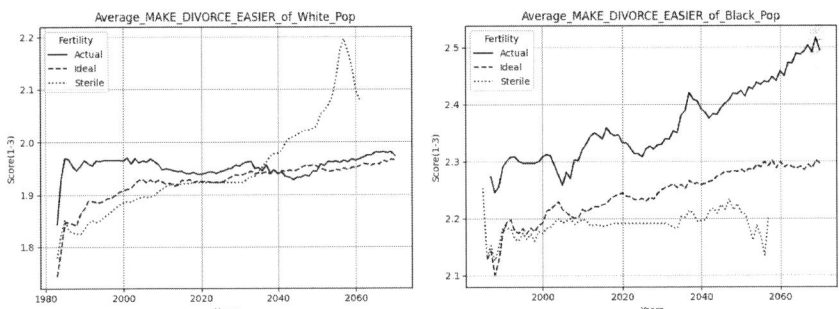

Graph 49 and 50. Average Views on Making Divorce Easier; White & Black Populations.

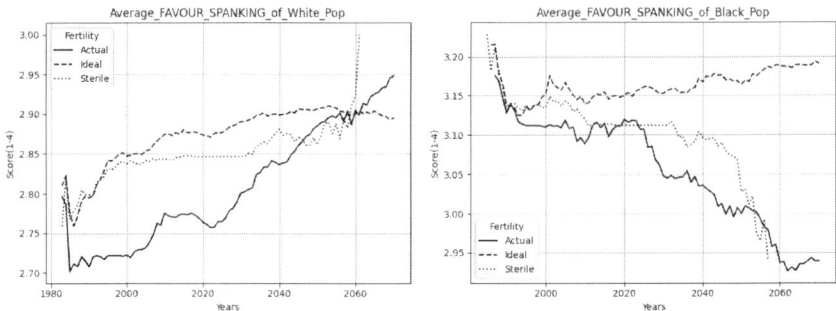

Graph 51 and 52. Average Views on Spanking Naughty Children; White & Black Populations.

When the United States of America finally comes to split apart into separate independent states, along Republican–Democrat battle lines, this pattern of breeding does not bode well for those intelligent and religious blacks living and ruling in what will then be Marxist states: for they will find themselves with the rather tricky task of taxing and governing a population of ever-multiplying people of low intelligence and low Conscientiousness.

The Nearer Term

Coming back to the matter of what's going to happen over the next couple of decades, the thrust of this analysis has been to show that America is coming apart racially along political lines, and that the more intelligent, higher SES minorities will white-align culturally, and even genetically, and the less intelligent, lower SES whites will non-white-align culturally and genetically. The political implications of this process should be put in the context of a 'second stage' in the culture wars, where not just members of the underclass or the Zoomers fight against Woke-taboos for a conservative culture, but, whilst the Democratic Party remains so dogmatically socially liberal in all things, an increasing number of intelligent, socially conservative minorities will white-align with the Republican political faction in America, and make intelligent and persuasive arguments in favour of socially conservative policies; all while enjoying the relative immunity that comes from belonging to a protected group. We can, perhaps, already see this process in America, with figures such as Candace Owens, who has married a white man. Whatever happens in America, we would expect to reach Britain, perhaps in a less pronounced form, eventually. White-alignment is probably even more obvious in Britain; there being a number of highly influential Hindus in senior positions within the Conservative Party. Most obviously, there is Priti

Patel, an ethnic Indian whose parents were Ugandan Asians and who is also married to a white man, who was seemingly pressured into playing down her previously expressed support for reintroducing capital punishment when she became Home Secretary (Doyle, 2nd August 2019).

Conversely, the subtlety, restraint, and intellectual calibre of the political voices on the left will continue to gradually degenerate over the coming years, due to collapsing IQ and white representation; until it is nothing more than a naked shriek for the interests of racial minorities, and the wider economic underclass. Could 'calibre' already be becoming an issue among younger leftists? Could this explain why the Democrat choice for the 2020 Presidential Election came down to two elderly white men? Could this even explain why there was no obvious, inspiring candidate to lead the Labour Party in the UK after its 2015 defeat, resulting in the election of extreme-left radical Jeremy Corbyn? Could this help us to understand why Labour's deputy leader, at the time of writing, who was born in 1980, is not a sometime academic or barrister, but a woman who dropped out of school at 16 after becoming pregnant, and later became a social worker (Torr, 11th November 2014)?

The significance of the political force of intelligent white-aligned conservative minorities for breaking the liberal social and cultural conditioning among the ruling elite and unleashing a sizeable portion of the middle class's deeply repressed conservative instincts, must not be underestimated. Nationalist populist voices among the American working class are easily dismissed because of their origins, but the second wave voices of the intelligent white-aligned ethnic minorities will penetrate right into the heart of elite institutions and circles. The great irony is that affirmative action will likely accelerate this penetration process in a lot of cases. We are not proposing here that a movement of intelligent white-aligned ethnic minorities will emerge into the political foreground to outright advocate white nationalism. Merely that they will identify with, and advocate, civic and religious nationalist symbols, that they mostly ascribe to the white European population, and some of them appear to be doing so already.

The most infamous white European institutions of all time are, arguably, the Christian churches, and the next six graphs (53–58) demarcate the effects this strange and special form of traditionalist conservatism has on IQ and fertility. These graphs examine the GSS measure of religious attendance but the results are almost identical if you examined 'religious commitment' and 'religious belief'. The curious difference between religiousness and other conservative measures is that its effects on IQ-fertility are much more felt at the ends of the population bell curve, here presented as the top and bottom quartiles (25%) in intelligence; whereas the other conservative metrics we have been looking at generally push and pull people just over the population average in IQ. This is because religiousness is a much more potent trait to affect these breeding forces; it is the *sine qua non*, the *par excellence*, in IQ conservation. Religiousness is capable of sustaining fertility at much higher levels of absolute intelligence than ordinary conservative political views can. As a consequence, we can expect the cognitive elite of tomorrow to be distinctly religious in nature; whereas the wider smarter fraction of the population might be merely just conservative and white-aligned.

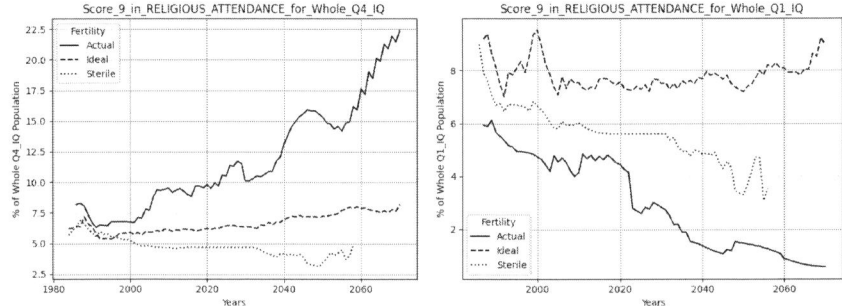

Graph 53 and 54. Very Frequent Religious Attendance; Top & Bottom IQ Quartiles.

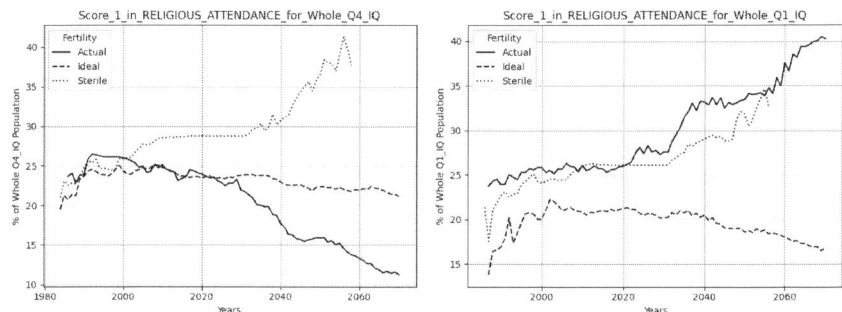

Graph 55 and 56. No Religious Attendance; Top & Bottom IQ Quartiles.

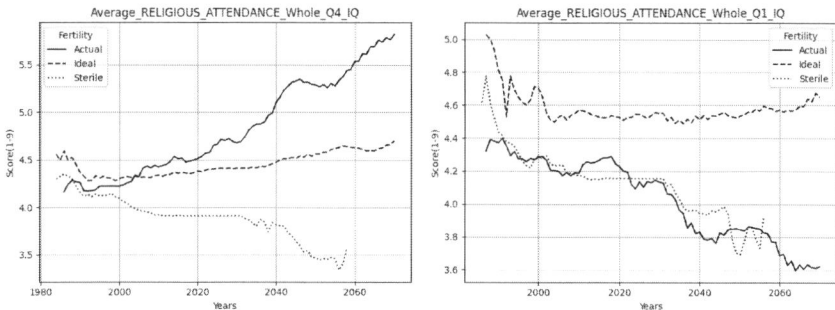

Graph 57 and 58. Average Religious Attendance; Top & Bottom IQ Quartiles.

That said, it is easy enough to see how suppressed political personality traits can still have a direct effect on one's own personal lifestyle and fertility, but when it comes to dormant religiousness, it's hard to see how that can have its full effect, unless it is phenotypically expressed: in church-going, daily rituals, calendar observation, and obedience to religious strictures. This is an important consideration because, as the sterile trend lines show, religiousness has been tapering off, though not quite as much as in the high IQ middle-class population as the low IQ population (Murray, 2012). The religious population in America is, at the moment, in a critical knife-edge battle with the fast Life History population that it will ultimately and decisively lose in America sometime before the middle of this century. As already shown, and as per the graphs (59–64) next, you can see that the irreligious fast Life History strategists have overtaken the black population already, despite the black population having a much higher proportion of religious people to start with. As for the white population, the religious slow LH strategists would still seem to have dominance over those prone to early out-of-wedlock pregnancies; likely in part because, as discussed, of whites of the underclass who are prone to breed with other ethnicities, and thus stop identifying as white after a single generation.

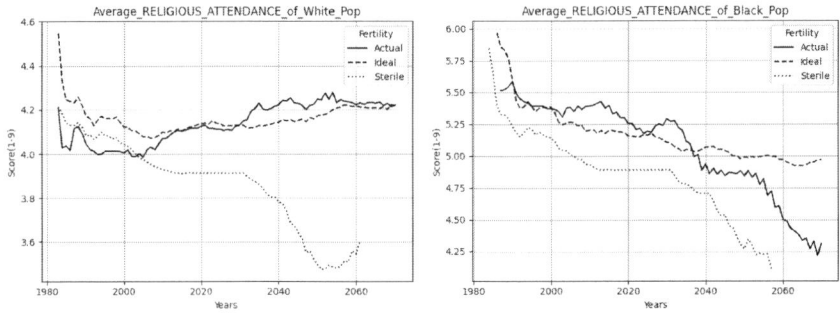

Graph 59 and 60. Average Religious Attendance; White & Black Population.

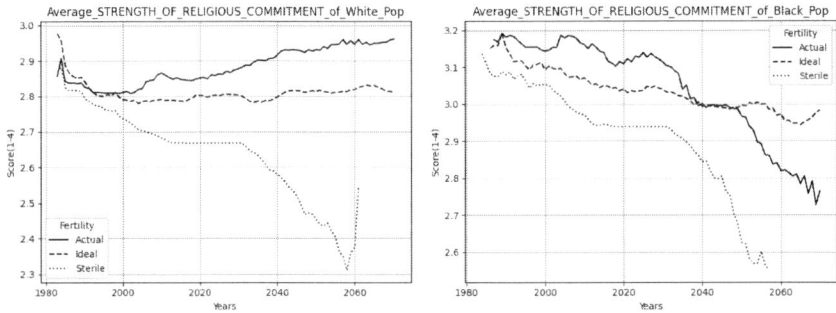

Graph 61 and 62. Average Religious Commitment; White & Black Population.

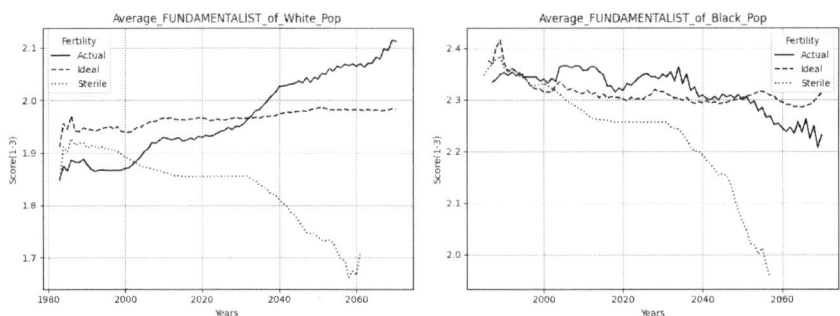

Graph 63 and 64. Average Religious Belief; White & Black Population.

So if the religious population doesn't buck the secularization trend with Generation Z, and regain the ground it has lost in the culture wars soon, these fertility extrapolations will never likely become a reality, to the degree predicted here. And then the r-strategist breeders will be left to consume the whole of the American population, all the sooner. To examine the percentage of the white and black population that are married (graphs 65 and 66), we find a similar dynamic. As mentioned before, marriage has been utterly decimated in the black and other minority ethnic populations, but you can see in the graph that the married section of the Gen X population weren't outbreeding their illegitimately born counterparts; and now marriage has continued to fall out of favour with Millennials. Of course, Millennials haven't completed their fertility yet, but the outcome of the race looks pretty clear.

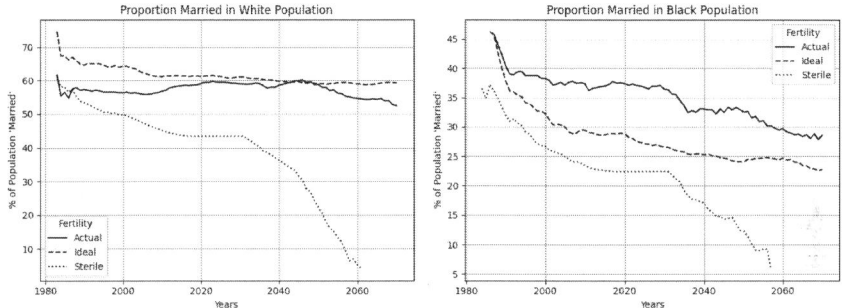

Graph 65 and 66. Proportion Married in the White & Black Populations.

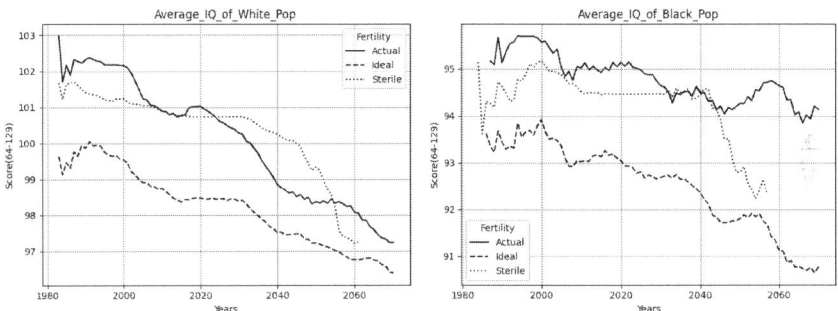

Graph 67 and 68. Average IQ in the White & Black Populations.

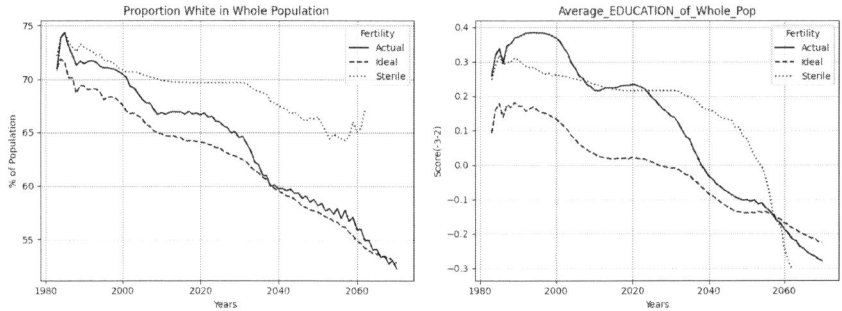

Graph 69 and 70. Percentage of the Population White and the Level of Education.

If we examine the effects on the cognitive capital of the American population (graphs 67 and 68), we can see that the white population is just as deeply stuck in low IQ fertility as the black population, albeit falling from a greater height. Gen Z offers no hope on this front, but IQ decline actually dramatically accelerates with them; likely a result of Negative Flynn Effects setting in from the declining quality of America's public school (state school in British English) system. And as we can see, with the trends in the ethnic proportion of the overall American population (graph 69), whites are set to plummet from three quarters, to just half of the population by the middle of this century; only further dragging down the average IQ.

The Breakdown of the Education System

Lastly, we can take a look at what would be the ultimate culprit underlying all these trends in differential fertility, if they weren't predestined to begin with: the education system. It's pretty clear to see who does all the breeding from the last graph, number 70—the least educated people who drop out of schooling the soonest to have children, and subsist off welfare. When we look underneath the bonnet of these simulations, we find that it's not the *average number of children* parameter the heritability algorithm radically affects—it's the *age at first child* that drops dramatically. That's the major power in fertility over the long term, and today only a small minority of teenage pregnancies are religious conservatives that married very young.

The conclusion is seemingly inescapable. Though the traditionalist conservatives will inevitably win the immediate culture war in America, at least against the feminist and LGBTQ+ wing of Woke politics, at some cultural turning point, and subsequent minority ethnic takeover of the Democratic Party, likely around the mid-2030s, if America is still one nation then, it will be far too late to save the whole of the nation from collapse, when social conservatism is finally restored to power. The underclass cannot be stopped. Racially charged class conflicts will ultimately boil over into civil war, if the United States doesn't break apart in an amicable manner. Though the white-aligned religious conservative cognitive elite would ultimately regain control over the country's private elite institutions, it would be just in time to see itself lose control over the democratic system, forever, by sheer force of numbers; much in the style of post-Apartheid South Africa.

In view of the fact that both the states of California and Texas have been campaigning for separatist movements in America for some time now (Ayres, 2020), we do not see the whole of America coming apart at once in one huge South African 'end-game scenario' later on in this century. Indeed, it has been forcefully argued that even the contemporary wave of black rights activists on the Woke side of politics are campaigning for a black ethno-nationalist separatist outcome; it's just yet to find a way of expressing itself territorially, in secession movements of states like Mississippi — attempted anarchist states in Portland and Seattle notwithstanding (Dattel, 2019).

Regardless of the exact nature in which the political landscape evolves in the United States over the next half a century, one has to consider a much greater and more universal process occurring in the private world of property, labour, and geographic mobility. Cognitive capital will emigrate away from undesirable places to live; brain drain and brain gain; white flight and gentrification. In the last chapter we will examine these socio-economic forces that will control the collapse of the West into crippling third-world poverty and survey the prospect of Western civilization surviving by this, in a few pockets across the globe.

Chapter Seven

The New Byzantiums

'And so it stays just on the edge of vision,
A small unfocused blur, a standing chill
That slows each impulse down to indecision.
Most things may never happen: this one will.'[1]

Most Things May Never Happen...

In his melancholy poem 'Aubade', Philip Larkin wakes up at four o'clock in the morning having previously drunk himself to sleep as usual, and becomes eerily aware of what's 'really always there' in the dark: 'Unresting death, a whole day nearer now.' We are all going to die. It is simply untrue to think that 'things can only get better' and that life progresses in some linear fashion. People reach their prime and, like Larkin, when he wrote his poem, eventually find themselves 'past their prime', becoming increasingly unhealthy and elderly. They can try to stay positive, and put death to the back of their minds; most people do, but there is no getting away from it. As Larkin puts it:

'Being brave
Lets no one off the grave.
Death is no different whined at than withstood.'

As we discussed earlier, the same is true of civilizations. They all appear to undergo cycles. This was noticed in Ancient Greece and Ancient Rome (see McGing, 2010), but it has probably been best articulated by the Islamic philosopher Ibn Khaldun (1332–1406), with his concept of *assabiyah*, which roughly translates as 'social cohesion' or 'social solidarity'; something which religion, as we have discussed, appears to be central to maintaining. Ibn Khaldun noticed that civilizations begin as desert tribesmen—living under harsh and challenging conditions—that are extremely high in social solidarity. As a consequence, they are

---

[1] 'Aubade' (Larkin, 23rd December 1980).

focused, cooperative, and are driven by a sense of their eternal importance. As a result, they dominate other tribes and build up high civilizations marked by cities, in which conditions are relatively luxurious. Eventually, they become individualistic, and decadent; losing their sense of social cohesion. They are invaded by a new set of desert tribesmen—who are motivated and fervent, because they are high in social cohesion. The new desert tribesmen develop cities and high civilization, and the process occurs all over again (see Fromherz, 2010). Interestingly, a recent quantitative study, based on various measures, has shown a clear decrease in *assabiyah* in Western countries between 1800 and the year 2000 (Hertler et al., 2020).

This fundamental idea—that civilizations are built by those who have martial values as a result of surviving brutal conditions, but that luxurious conditions, brought about as a result, lead to decadence and the decline of civilization—has led various philosophers to note that civilizations appear to go through something akin to seasons. As German thinker Oswald Spengler (1991) discussed in his 1918 book *The Decline of the West*: in the spring, civilizations are born and begin to develop. At this stage, they are extremely religious and very high in social solidarity, as in the Dark Ages and Early Medieval Europe. In the summer, they are marked by youthful vigour, often engaging in serious risks via exploration, as we see in Europe in the sixteenth and seventeenth centuries, and they are still deeply religious. In the autumn, the fruits of the civilization are harvested. We see incredible inventiveness and scientific originality, but, as conditions are now relatively luxurious, people start to become less religious, more individualistic, and they start to question the martial values of the civilization, and especially the religion which promotes these. As Roman historian Tacitus (56 AD–120 AD) (Tacitus, 2014, p. 135) noted: 'The parents themselves are the first to give their children the worst examples of vice and luxury. The stripling consequently loses all sense of shame, and soon forgets the respect he owes to others as well as to himself.'

With greater luxury, there is less of a check on individualism, and as there is increasing dysphoria in the cities—as we live in an evolutionary mismatch of strangers, and even foreigners. This is what we begin to see in nineteenth-century Europe, or around the time of Socrates, if we look at Ancient Greek civilization. By the time we move to the end of autumn, and the beginning of winter, all of the old values are subject to question, the society has lost a sense of its own eternal importance, and it is strongly individualist. No longer seeing itself as superior, and lacking religiously-upheld ethnocentrism, it permits immigration from poorer societies, which leads to Balkanization and ethnic conflict (Glubb, 1976).

As discussed above, patriarchy is understood as a system whereby males control females and, in particular, regulate female sexuality and reproduction, in favour of males who invest time and resources in the females. It has been argued that patriarchy is adaptive because, if males control females, their paternity anxiety is reduced, as is inter-male conflict over this issue. This helps to create a more harmonious and group-selected society (Grant & Montrose, 2018). But no longer believing in its religion, which tended to uphold traditional ideas, including patriarchy, there is increasing female influence in the winter of civilization; with women becoming increasingly independent and strident. This was observed during the decline of Greece, of Rome (where questions were asked of Emperor Augustus about how to reverse the process), and even during the decline of Baghdad, where there were female imams and lawyers (Glubb, 1976, p. 16). According to Spengler, it is in the autumn that there appears a Socrates, or a Rousseau, who questions everything. And we enter an age of rationalism, in which technological progress goes hand-in-hand with scepticism about religion, about aristocratic rule, about tradition, and about everything that has held society together. At first this creates optimism about a better future, in which standards of living are much improved. But there is also a decline in religious certainty; with everything focused around material wealth, and an increasing sense of dysphoria, as the conditions we are evolved to live under fall apart, along with the traditions that provide us with comfort and structure.

This process of rationalization continues, argues Spengler, and every idea is questioned, then everything is rationalized down to money (even having children); all of the old ways are heavily criticized, and there is no longer any optimism, or soul, holding society together, as people are enveloped by a sense of doom. Society is strongly individualist, and so we enter the winter of civilization—although individualists may club together into weakly bonded coalitions in order to defend themselves, and provide their lives with some sense of meaning. It might even be suggested that, as such, people are then likely to be high in mental instability, and anxiety, and they would deal with this through over-compensation: creating groups based around strongly black-and-white and dogmatic thinking, as we have already explored. Extreme nihilism, which at least makes sense of their lives, combined with a stress on individualizing values, would be the result. This constant critique, and artificial attempts to create meaning, leads to a nihilistic, pessimistic world. And a gulf of mutual enmity between the money-focused elite and the masses opens up, in part because there is no longer any religious belief that the position of the elite is somehow deserved—and, for this, the elite abdicate their aristocratic offices, and dis-identify themselves with their society. Thus the elite also become extreme individualists; with the easy conditions that civilization has created permitting runaway individualism, and having no interest in the group. All of this can be seen with the predatory capitalists of today, and the huge and growing gap between the rich and the poor. Society becomes fragmented, democracy and order break down, and demagogues take over by leading an increasingly alienated mass. This, according to Spengler, is the Age of Emperors. These Emperors are given extraordinary powers to sort out the mess of conflict that society has degenerated into, including problems of external invaders.

The despair which people feel is lifted by vague religious yearnings. As society becomes yet more chaotic, we see the development of a 'Second Religiousness', which is an anti-intellectual and rehashed version of the religion on which the society was founded. So, in Rome, argues Spengler, we see the rise of the Cult of the Emperor, and, in particular, the Mystery Cults, where members were initiated into secret practices and worshipped specific gods. Spengler insisted that, when he was writing, the West's Second Religiousness remained a number of generations in the future. During this period, society becomes so badly weakened that it is often taken over by other societies, which are more youthful, or it descends back into a Dark Age, to be reborn anew.

Autumnal Societies and Intelligence

It was noted in these autumnal societies of the past that the people of the higher social classes, and thus those who, on average, were more intelligent, appeared to stop having children. This occurred both in civilizations that had developed effective contraception, as well as in those that had not. This is crucial because all aspects of civilization have been shown to be associated with intelligence. We have national IQ scores for many countries, and these have been shown to be highly reliable, because they strongly correlate with other intuitive markers of intelligence at a national level, such as the performance of countries in international assessments of educational attainment (Lynn & Becker, 2019). As discussed earlier, it has been found that there is a strong association between average national IQ and all aspects of civilization, including education, wealth, earnings, democracy, lack of corruption, health, the ability to access clean water and maintain sanitation, law and order, liberal values, and lack of religious dogmatism (Lynn & Vanhanen, 2012). Accordingly, it always appears to be the case that intelligence is selected for, resulting in the rise of civilizations, but that aspects of these civilizations result in a negative association between intelligence and fertility, with the consequence that the civilization collapses. Then people with relatively low intelligence find themselves under intense selection for intelligence—due to the harsh conditions in which they find themselves—and the process begins all over again. In a number of these Classical civilizations, per capita major innovations can be charted across time, and, as in our case, they reach a peak, and then go into decline; this is consistent with an intelligence peak and subsequent decline, as wealthier, and so more intelligent, people reduce their fertility (Huebner, 2005b). We have already seen this in Figure 1.1.

It is unclear quite why other civilizations reached a negative association between intelligence and fertility, just before reaching an industrial revolution, but our civilization did so *after* achieving the Industrial Revolution. One possibility is that, for various reasons, in this round of civilization environmental conditions were extremely harsh—for example, we experienced the Maunder Minimum in the late seventeenth century, when it was intensely cold—and this very strongly selected for religiousness. With this, there was very intense group selection. This resulted in extremely strong selection for pro-social, cooperative traits, which are themselves associated with religiosity, as well as a nationalist religiosity, as a means of elevating ethnocentrism.

It has also been shown that we became more religious across the Middle Ages, during which time Europeans were executing about 2% of young men per generation; something which would be expected to elevate pro-social traits and religiousness, which it appears to have done (Dutton & Madison, 2018). The Black Death, in killing as much as half of the European population, would have selected for health—which is associated with religiousness—as well as Conscientiousness; the ability to follow rules and execute plans. It also disproportionately wiped out the poor, who tend to be lower in traits associated with religiousness, such as Agreeableness and Conscientiousness. These traits would have aided survival, as they are also associated with religiosity. And, further, Christianity had inherited a Jewish taboo on contraception, and we have noted that reliable contraception is a significant factor in bringing about the negative association between fertility and intelligence (Meisenberg, 2007). Thus, with their intense religiosity, the Europeans needed to reach a higher level of luxury before they started losing their religiosity, and before they started employing contraception. This propelled them beyond the Industrial Revolution, before they went into intelligence decline.

How Roman Civilization Held On

There are two previous civilization collapses that we understand in some detail and which we can, thus, employ to give us some understanding of how the collapse of our own civilization might proceed. Most recently, there has been the Classical Collapse; the collapse of Roman civilization. As already discussed, this was seemingly set off by a sequence of interrelated events including growing infertility among the higher classes, leading to intelligence decline and all of its correlates; by warmer conditions that permitted greater general mutation, and the rise of individualism and the collapse of religiosity, resulting in feminism, multiculturalism, nihilism, further individualism, and a further erosion of trust and, thus, an erosion of positive and negative ethnocentrism. And then, in sixth century, this already declining and war-ridden population was hit by harsher conditions which themselves contributed to the Justinian Plague and the death of about 60% of the population. Accordingly, most of the Roman Empire regressed in socio-economic terms. With there no longer being the previous 'excess', towns and cities collapsed and were depopulated as people scrambled for land which they could farm, with a population collapse leading to empty land. People living in colder areas made their way south in search of land to farm, resulting in conflict but also in fundamental changes in who populated which areas, as is most obvious with regard to what happened to England. The education system and literacy collapsed, as more intelligent people had been ceasing to breed, and also because people had more immediate survival concerns. Less intelligent as populations were becoming, buildings became smaller and simpler. Huge amounts of Roman knowledge were gradually forgotten. Even the animals were becoming smaller, as Roman agricultural innovations, such as to do with breeding, were not passed on by people because they were living in an unstable environment that was increasingly short-term focused (see Lacey & Danziger, 1999, p. 134). Scientific knowledge, much of it thanks to the Ancient Greeks, was also lost to the West due to a combination of it being incomprehensible to such a low IQ population (see Dutton & Van der Linden, 2017) and due to the anti-intellectual nature of early Christianity, which put belief in certain dogmas, including the Bible as 'the Word of God', above rational or empirical truth. Indeed, it even regarded rationality as part of the culture of the pagans, preferring divine revelation and authority (De Benoist, 2004).

However, many people seem to forget that the Roman Empire never completely collapsed; it retreated. With the collapse of Rome, civilization was preserved in Byzantium, and specifically in the city of Constantinople, now Istanbul. It managed to keep going until 1453, when it finally fell to the Turks. By this time the, albeit less developed, Western Europe was into its summer, its Renaissance, anyway, and this was boosted by the flood of learning, preserved old texts full of innovation that had died out in the West, and intelligence that duly fled to Western Europe in the form of Greek scholars (Schaff, 1891, Ch. XI). However, hundreds of years earlier, this same process had happened in reverse. Intelligent people in the West gravitated towards Constantinople, because they wanted to be in a place of relative order and comfort, surrounded by other intelligent people, something which was possible due to educated people knowing Latin. This is a somewhat forgotten aspect of Western history and, if anything, this continuous influx of intelligence would have aided the survival of Byzantium.

The Roman Empire split in two, remaining split from 395 onwards. The Western Empire, eventually directed from Ravenna in Italy, collapsed in about 476, breaking up into assorted independent regions, no longer under the control of any recognized emperor. But 'Rome' continued in the Greek-speaking East which eventually adopted Orthodox Christianity in the Great Schism of the eleventh century (Moorhead, 2013). Such a place was attractive to people who liked civilization and thus to intelligent people, who would also be more likely to have the means and planning ability to get there. In about 1071 (sources vary with regard to the precise year), in the wake of the Norman Conquest of England, a large group of Anglo-Saxon notables emigrated in about 300 ships. They arrived in Constantinople some years later. Some of them remained in Constantinople, in the service of the emperor (Nicol, 1974). The wealthy and educated migrated to Byzantium if they could, and so desired, and there were other migrations from England to Byzantium in the Middle Ages (Lindsay, 1952, p. 294). This is what we would expect to happen anew: refuges of civilization, that are both intelligent and religious, holding out. These may possibly set off a process of group selection, before a full collapse back into Darwinian conditions.

Our Classical Collapse

If we compare ourselves to this Classical situation, there are certainly many points of comparison. We can conceive of two stages to this collapse: the early stage, in which there is the beginnings of a right-wing backlash and some 'coming apart', and a later stage of more pronounced collapse and the development of conservative 'refuges' of civilization. We will begin by looking at the first stage.

Every demographic indicator would imply that we should be on the cusp of a period of dramatic change. At the genetic level, we would expect the West to be gradually sliding into a world that will break apart into the r-strategists on the one hand—as we breed for low intelligence, low impulse control, and selfishness—and K-strategists on the other hand, as we breed for traditional religiousness, conservatism, agreeableness, and other traits that make people desire to nurture, which is why some K-

traits predict fertility in modern societies with reliable contraception (Richardson et al., 2017).

While the processes we have already outlined — of the individualizers, and their spreading of fitness-damaging ideologies, collapsing mortality salience making people less religious and more individualistic, and the general way that the left is able to manipulate the right into ceding ground — have long pushed society leftwards, beneath the surface, since at least the 1960s, fertility has been associated with the highly heritable traits of extreme religiousness, and being extremely right-wing, and it has been weakly negatively associated with low IQ, which correlates with both traits, since around 1900. Thus, as the traditional separation between slow and fast Life History traits is coming apart, this Brave New World, where the only real obstacle to having children (apart from infertility) is that you have been successfully inculcated with Woke ideas, or that the evolutionary mismatch that Wokeness has created, has caused you sufficient dysphoria that you don't want children. If you want children even in spite of these — because you're religious, group-oriented, nurturing, or you're unintelligent, impulsive, or self-important ('you just *want* them') — then you can have them. And this is precisely what has been happening.

On this basis, we would expect a particular scenario to play out, and it appears that this is roughly the scenario which has occurred. Although there would be minor political cycles — whereby we oscillated between periods of being more or less left-wing — overall, society would move in a generally more and more left-wing direction. At the turning point of the 1960s, this would begin to speed up dramatically, presumably because at that point approximately 20% of the society espoused individualist values, leading, as we have discussed, to a relatively sudden shift in opinion, as people begin to defect to what they regard as the 'winning team'. It may even be, in Britain at least, that 1997, and the election of Tony Blair's New Labour government, constituted a further dramatic turning point, as the generation born before World War II were mainly retired by this time. At this point, the left had been pursuing a long 'March Through the Institutions', but this was accelerated by the Blair government — which was dominated by 'Boomers', including Tony Blair himself — such that the last few areas that had not yet been taken over by the left, such as the police and the army, fell to the left, and almost absolute dominance could be cemented of those institutions that had already substantially fallen, such as the universities. A dramatic shift began to take place whereby all organs of society became politicized in a left-wing fashion, and were increasingly obliged, in many cases by law, to promote left-wing values of 'equality and diversity' above all else (see Gabb, 2007). This is strikingly similar to the way in which, until 1871,

English universities were under the control of the Church of England, and the promotion of Anglicanism was more important than any academic ideals such as the fearless pursuit of truth, meaning that serious research took place outside the universities among gentleman scholars such as Sir Francis Galton, whom we met earlier. You could not be a long-term fellow at Oxford or Cambridge unless you were ordained, and you could not study at Oxford, Cambridge, or Durham unless you were Anglican (Dutton, 2019b, pp. 64–65).

In summer 2020, this process of politicization of societal institutions had become so extreme that Premier League footballers were obliged to wear badges promoting the 'Black Lives Matter' movement on their shirts, despite its association with mob terror and violence (Draper, 29th August 2020). Companies competed to signal how in favour of the 'Black Lives Matter' movement they were, with tea companies PG Tips and Yorkshire Tea telling critics of Black Lives Matter, such as Laura Towler of nationalist group Patriotic Alternative, not to buy their tea (Tweedy, 9th June 2020). When Conservative Chancellor of the Exchequer Rishi Sunak was pictured drinking Yorkshire Tea, the company felt the need to emphasize, under pressure from a left-wing Twitter mob, that it did not support Conservative politics (*BBC News*, 9th June 2020). In other words, the left have, effectively, complete control over all aspects of cultural life.

The people may elect right-wing governments—and vote for overtly right-wing policies in referenda, such as Brexit—but it is the left who are effectively in charge, backed up by left-wing mobs who will intimidate dissenters into conformity, or do all that they can to ensure that dissenters are crushed, through pressuring to get them fired, or otherwise financially damaged; as has happened with many dissident academics. Most prominently, as discussed above, in 2018, Cambridge University sociologist Noah Carl was fired from his university because he had conducted empirically accurate research on race differences, to which the left-wing mob objected, and because he had associated with academics who were even more 'controversial' than himself. But there have been many other cases (see Carl & Woodley of Menie, 2019).

By summer 2020, with the rise of the Black Lives Matter movement, the mob was successfully pressuring academic journals to officially withdraw scientific studies which had passed peer-review, which presented facts, or reasoned interpretations, which the leftist mob disliked and regarded, for example, as 'racist' (e.g. *Retraction Watch,* 31st July 2020). 'Truth' is not especially important to those who are obsessed with power; hence they may aver that, if facts may be used by groups they dislike, they must *not* be facts. No greater testimony to their power-hungry Machiavellianism can be seen than in the way that, if activists in such groups die, fellow activists do not wish them to 'Rest in Peace' but rather to 'Rest in Power' (Hampton, 30th September 2019), because 'power' for these people is, ultimately, the only point of life. The violence and fanaticism of such groups has been demonstrated in considerable depth in an exploration of 'Antifa' by American journalist Andy Ngo (2021), a book which Antifa members successfully intimidated one bookshop into not selling (*AP News*, 14th January 2021).

The Right-Wing Backlash

The rise of multiculturalism can perhaps be compared to the rise of Christianity during the Classical Collapse, insomuch as you have middle-class people, which Early Christians certainly were, as has been documented (Stark, 2020), playing for status in a context of peace, warmth, and weakened group selection by employing individualizing foundations. The difference is that, though they prized celibacy, they actually combined these foundations with pro-natalism, causing them to have large numbers of children; more than the pagans. We differ from the Classical Collapse in that the Second Religiousness will not take over in this way. This is because our conditions are so easy, and group selection is so weak, that runaway individualism has led to the Second Religiousness being Gnostic-like, and thus associated with anti-natalism. So, if we are comparing ourselves to the Early Classical Collapse, then it would be like seeing a 'Pagan Revival' in which the ideas of Emperor Julian the Apostate (331–363, r. 361–363), who tried to revive paganism, triumphed (Bowersock, 1997).

Based on the breeding patterns previously discussed, while this process of left-wing empowerment was occurring, the percentage of society who were, for mainly genetic reasons, completely resistant to it, and totally rejected it, would be growing. Indeed, they would be worse than completely resistant to it. They would actively favour, or at least be open to, views which, even for mainstream society, would seem amazingly regressive. Just as leftists 'virtue-signal' to showcase their commitment to the cause, these people would 'purity-signal' in much the same way. Accordingly, they would be increasingly opposed to all of the accepted dogmas of mainstream society. They would be positively and negatively ethnocentric, and specifically ethno-nationalist, they (including their female members) would be opposed to feminism and would espouse traditional sex roles. They would be opposed to homosexuality, at least its identity-politics form; they would regard transsexuals as suffering from a series of mental disorders, just as the empirical evidence indicates is generally the case (Dutton & Madison, 2020b). And they would be uninterested, even relative to the mainstream, in 'harm avoidance' and 'equality'. Indeed, they might even regard 'harm avoidance' as a decadent sign of weakness, with hurting people sometimes being necessary to socialize them, to put the good of the group first; just as was believed in Victorian public schools (particularly prestigious private schools where pupils usually board), with their ubiquitous use of flogging (Dutton, 2019b). They would regard the promotion of 'equality' as ludicrous, believing that it is for the good of their ethnic group that the 'best people' are encouraged to rise to the top. The internet would allow these kinds of people to easily find each other and to not feel isolated, meaning that some of them would increasingly possess the confidence and bravery to challenge the mainstream. These people would be gradually increasing, alongside a decline in intelligence, whereby low IQ people would also be attracted to many of their ideas, due to the fact that those with low IQ are more in touch with their instincts, with adaptive psychological biases; and ideas of these extreme conservatives are adaptive in an evolutionary sense. Crucially, however, people like this would be a growing presence among the elite, and highly intelligent in society, as intelligent leftists would fail to reproduce. And, as discussed, they would be a more prominent presence among Generation Z, because its intelligent elite would, anyway, be less intelligent than the previous generation's, and, thus, more inclined to ignore the dominant ideology.

McCarthyism in Reverse

If this process was occurring, and such a faction was growing, then we would expect to see increasing discussion, and condemnation, of relatively young 'far right' people and groups, as the relatively young would be increasingly polarized between intelligent r-strategists (products of selfish people and deviations from traditional religiosity) and K-strategists (the religious and the conservative). Consistent with this, there is undoubtedly increasing mainstream discussion of these kinds of groups. Entire academic tomes have been dedicated to exploring the 'identitarian movement', for example (Zúquete, 2018), which is anti-globalization, anti-Islam, and pro-ethno-nationalism. We would expect the left to sniff the air, and to, on some level, be aware that this process was taking place, which would result in a sustained attempt to crush the opposition, by very strongly restricting them. It can be argued that this has been particularly noticeable since the shock election of Donald Trump as American President in 2016. In its wake, 'Big Tech'—such as Google, PayPal, and YouTube—have evolved from being relatively neutral platforms to platforms which appear to be actively assisting the left. Dissident conservatives are thrown off Twitter and YouTube due to violations of increasingly stringent speech codes, or simply at the whim of leftists who work for these organizations to enforce such codes. In January 2021, even a mainstream, though moderately conservative, British radio station was removed from YouTube, though this was reversed under pressure (Kelion, 5th January 2021). Their ability to make money, through advertising, from their videos is stopped due to policies branding them 'controversial' or they are simply banned from all advertising. Or they are 'shadow banned', meaning their videos become difficult to find, or are suppressed by the 'algorithm', causing them to reach a much smaller audience. Often, YouTube directs their viewers towards videos by Canadian psychologist Jordan Peterson, who appears to just about have mainstream acceptability, rendering Peterson 'controlled opposition' (Day, 2018). Sometimes, their books and other products are banned from Amazon, which has a monumental share of the book-selling market.

This kind of reaction is not unique to the left by any means, and it tends to occur when a system is on the brink of undergoing radical change. It can even be said to parallel Rome's extreme persecution of Christians—'the Great Persecution'—in the early fourth century, right before the subsequent emperor, Constantine the Great, converted (Shin, 2018). When the conservative system was in the process of collapse, by the 1950s, there was a similar strong clampdown on activities which were perceived as undermining it, and which had previously been tolerated. In the United States, this is most obvious in the campaign by Senator Joseph McCarthy (1908–1957) to create a 'Red Scare' and drive left-wing people, and thus their ideas, out of Hollywood, off the television, out of academia, and, essentially, out of public discourse, in the guise of the fight against the Soviet Union (see Herman, 2000). It was against this background that James Flynn, whose 'Flynn Effect' we examined earlier, who had been fired from a number of academic posts in America, left for a university post in New Zealand, realizing he was effectively unemployable in academia in his home country (Dutton, 2021a). Thus, cancel culture has been referred to, by American satirist Bill Maher, as 'McCarthyism in reverse' (*TMZ*, 27th February 2021).

In the 1950s in America, and particularly in Britain, homosexuality was clamped down on with increasing severity, accompanied by a fervent media campaign against it, and increasing prosecutions for homosexual offences, to which the state had previously turned a blind eye. In America, gays were purged from government circles, with the justification that they were 'mentally unstable' and a security risk because they could be blackmailed over their sexuality. In the early 1950s, two British homosexuals had been revealed to be Soviet spies. They defected to the Soviet Union, setting off a 'veritable moral crusade' against homosexuals by the Home Secretary Sir David Maxwell-Fyfe (1900–1967). Prosecutions were ramped up, and even the famous actor John Gielgud (1904–2000) was not spared, being fined £10 in 1953 for 'persistently importuning for immoral purposes'. In 1952, *The Sunday Pictorial* had condemned homosexuals as 'Evil Men'. In 1954, there was a public scandal, when a peer of the realm, the 3rd Baron Montagu of Beaulieu (1926–2015), was found guilty of homosexual offences and sentenced to 12 months in prison (Dockray & Sutton, 2017). In many ways, the 1950s was the swan song of the traditional society and, as a consequence, it strongly increased its antipathy to the nascent liberal society. But power of numbers meant that it was on borrowed time. Eventually, so many people had defected towards liberal attitudes that, in 1967, homosexuality was legalized in Britain. The traditionalists, even if they were outbreeding liberals by this stage, simply couldn't replenish themselves fast enough to stop the tide of increasingly liberal people, who increasingly replaced them in all of society's institutions, until a point was reached where they completely controlled them, and the 'radicals' of the 1960s and 1970s were the 'Establishment'. In Britain, this seemed to occur around the year 1997.

Further, if this process were occurring, then it would evidence in society being extremely polarized, just as it was in the 1960s when the last great switch took place. In general, when societies become this polarized, then those who have, up until that point, been dissidents—persecuted, ridiculed, and ostracized—begin to become the Establishment, as they reach sufficient strength in numbers to persuade increasing numbers of people that they, brimming with youthful confidence, are the future, and the current Establishment is moribund. According to the research by Peter Turchin (2016) on cycles of polarization, which we explored earlier, Western society is increasingly unstable due to declining population, relative well-being (especially huge wealth inequality), popular discontent (as evidenced in votes against ruling class dogma, and votes for radical parties), elite over-production (as seen in the unsustainably high levels of university participation, resulting in many graduates being little more than glorified secretaries), and thus intra-elite competition (leading to aspirant elites attempting to topple the elite, angrily feeling entitled to be part of it). This leads to counter-elites, or surplus-elites, who will challenge the current elite, possibly even by violent means. In the past, societies with these precise conditions—Turchin has traced them throughout history—are subject to outbreaks of political violence, revolutions, and civil wars. According to Turchin, on this basis, the 2020s should constitute a peak of instability, marked by precisely these eventualities. These events tend to be followed by fundamental changes in the nature of society. According to many of Turchin's markers of polarization, such as levels of political violence, the 2020s will be at least as polarized as the

1960s were; these having been a tumultuous decade in Western countries. Based on other indicators, Turchin finds that America is as polarized—in terms of its level of political stress—as it was in the period immediately prior to the American Civil War, though he emphasizes that:

> '...we are rapidly approaching a historical cusp at which American society will be particularly vulnerable to violent upheaval. However, a disaster similar in magnitude to the American Civil War is not foreordained. On the contrary, we may be the first society that is capable of perceiving, if dimly, the deep structural forces pushing us to the brink. This means that we are uniquely equipped to take policy measures that will prevent our falling over it.'

The invasion of the American Capitol by furious Trump supporters in January 2021, supposedly to stop legislators from declaring Joe Biden the official winner of the disputed November 2020 election, is a clear sign of extreme polarization in American politics; a sign that something is shifting. The result was that the left, with clear hyperbole, declared the riot a 'coup attempt' and an 'insurrection' (Hill, 11th January 2021).

Interestingly, since 2015, the percentage of Britons who think that homosexuality is wrong has slowly started to increase, which may partly be as a result of the growth of the Muslim population (Booth, 11th July 2019). Certainly, following the *British Social Attitudes Survey*, Britons who feel that premarital sex is 'mostly or always wrong' fell from 30% in 1983 to 10% in 2007, and hardly moved since then; fractionally rising between 2015 and 2018. Those believing homosexuality is 'mostly or always wrong' has fallen from 70% in 1985 to 30% in 2010 and, again, appears to have plateaued, but then slightly risen between 2015 and 2018. Belief that people who want children ought to get married has fallen across time since 1983 in all cohorts, except the most recent (those born in the 1980s), where it has plateaued at 30%. The proportion of this cohort stating that premarital sex is wrong increased from 10% to 15% between 2007 and 2012. By the 2030s, such people would be expected to be roughly 25% of the population, and they should be starting to shift attitudes in their direction. A study on national populism, by British researchers Roger Eatwell and Matthew Goodwin, has tracked identification as conservative among British 18-year-olds across time. It is clearly increasing, consistent with our evidence from the GSS in America. Among Baby Boomers (born in the 1940s, 1950s, and early 1960s), 17% identified as conservative. Among Generation X (roughly 1965–1980), this was 22%. For Millennials (early 1980s to mid-1990s), it was 23%, while for Generation Z it was 30% (Eatwell & Goodwin, 2018).

Analysis of Britain's large-scale YouGov polls by Eric Kaufmann (8th July 2020) has found that, as a rule, the younger people are, the more liberal they tend to be. However, this is not the case with those aged 18, when interviewed in 2020. This cohort is as liberal as people who are 40 years old. Conservatism tends to increase with age, due to people becoming more Conscientious (rule-following, high in impulse control), less open to new experiences, and less tolerant of ambiguity (Cornelis et al., 2008). Thus, a change is happening among the very young. According to YouGov, identification as 'right-wing' falls to 27% among 26-year-olds and then rises to 40% among 40-year-olds. This cannot be because 18-year-olds have not been to university yet, a process which might inculcate them with liberal ideas. This is because the same data find that the age of peak liberal identification is becoming older, when you compare YouGov surveys conducted in different years. So, there seems to be a fundamental shift occurring, consistent with the long-term breeding model for right-wing traits, finally beginning to bear fruit among the 'Zoomer' generation (those born in the later 1990s and early 2000s).

Further consistent with increasing conservatism, those who are referred to as part of i-Gen, Generation Z, or Zoomers — born in the mid-1990s onwards, and thus never having known a world without the internet — lose their virginity later, leave home later, start dating later, are less sexually promiscuous, and have less sexual intercourse than was the case with the previous generation. We have found evidence of their growing conservatism in the GSS, but other research had pointed to similar trends. They are also more likely to simply never have sexual intercourse at all. According to American psychologist Jennifer Twenge (2017), Americans born in the 1980s and early 1990s (known as Millennials and i-Gen), were more likely to report having no sexual partners since the age of 18 (implying they were virgins), compared to GenXers born in the 1960s and 1970s, in the General Social Survey. Among those aged 20–24, more than twice as many Millennials born in the 1990s (15%) were virgins, compared to GenXers born in the 1960s at the same age (6%). All kinds of environmental factors could be behind these changes, such as children no longer being optimally socialized to be adults, and thus taking longer to grow up, the increased presence of internet pornography interfering with the desire for sexual intercourse (Gobry, 15th December 2019), or mutation accumulation increasingly interfering with the optimum development of human sexuality (Charlton, 20th July 2015). However, a reduction in promiscuity would be consistent with a religiously-driven rise in conservative attitudes playing a part in what is happening.

All of this is consistent with the prediction that society is going to move in a more conservative direction, as our data prognosticate. In this regard, it might be argued that it is Black Lives Matter protestors, and their ilk, who are aspirant elites, and they are attempting to push society in an even more left-wing direction. However, it can be countered that they are more akin to the anti-homosexuality and anti-Communist campaigners of the 1950s and 1960s in Britain and America. It is those who are, effectively, in cultural power (not dissidents) that are promoting ever-more extreme manifestations of Political Correctness, possibly because they fear that they are losing their grip on power. The BLM mob, to the extent that it is composed of aspirant elites, is attempting to signal their extreme adherence to the current cultural regime, as a means of elevating their status within it. They cannot be said to be challenging it. They are merely encouraging it to be even more extreme, partly as a means of leveraging individual status for themselves. Congruous with this, BLM is promoted by the mainstream, including Big Tech, and other companies, which we might otherwise expect 'anarchists' to despise.

Now is the Summer of Love Made Glorious Winter by Our Discontent

The 'Summer of Love', in 1967, involved about 100,000 hippies and other leftists converging on a district in San Francisco for a festival of free-love, drug-taking, music, and the exchange of leftist ideas. It can be seen to symbolize the fundamental shift to individualizing foundations — 'the 1960s cultural revolution' — that the West was undergoing (McWilliams, 2000).

The real challenge comes from those who are agitating for fundamental change, and, in a society that is so dominated by the Woke agenda, this can only realistically be what has long been called the 'far right', and the 'religious right' — the very people who are growing demographically, compared to all other political perspectives, and who are, seemingly for genetic reasons, constitutionally resistant to the evolutionary mismatch which the Woke society has brought about. What we would predict is that, through pure pressure of numbers, it will eventually become inevitable that such people breach the dams of the institutions of culture, such as the universities, and this will occur even if the Woke Establishment attempt to obviate this problem, by contracting the size of higher education. The result will be a reverse Gramscian 'March Through the Institutions' (see Gabb, 2007),[2] as these extreme conservatives permeate upwards into them, and then begin to gradually change their culture, just as once happened in reverse.

---

[2] This kind of 'cultural revolution' or 'takeover from beneath' via a 'March Through the Institutions' was famously proposed by the Italian Marxist philosopher Antonio Gramsci (1891–1937) (see Gabb, 2007).

The Woke takeover of universities altered university culture, such that the emphasis moved away from the uninhibited examination of ideas, in pursuit of the truth, with the assumption that truth is amoral, and that people being offended by subjectively unpleasant truths is a price worth paying, because the pursuit of truth is, in effect, religiously important. Indeed, it has been argued that this way of thinking stemmed from the formerly Christian nature of universities, whereby scientists believed that they were uncovering the nature of God's revelation; meaning that to lie would be blasphemous. Even as scientists stopped being traditionally religious, this transcendental belief in the truth remained, possibly because they had been raised in a religious society themselves, and possibly because academics were a tiny elite, with outlier high intelligence (Dutton & Charlton, 2015). Outlier high intelligence has been shown to be associated with autistic traits, and thus with an obsession with systematizing, and thus with the truth (Karpinski et al., 2018). As noted above, this is likely because an obsession with systematizing allows them to solve ever-more difficult problems. It may also be because autistics, being intensely sensitive to stimuli, take in more information, and more subtle information, allowing them to better solve problems.

As the universities expanded, they would have taken in more and more academics of lower and lower intelligence, though still with high IQ within the normal range; we might call them 'Mid-Wits'. This is evidenced in Danish data on the decline in IQ of the average holder of a PhD between 1995 and 2010 (Akcigit et al., 2020). These people would be attracted to university careers due to the social prestige that they accord, not due to an interest in the truth. Normal range IQ is associated *not* with autistic traits but, conversely, with empathy, altruism, social conformity, and other traits which would make them seemingly better potential colleagues, though also less interested in the truth, or in certain kinds of truth. Such people would seem to make better colleagues than high-functioning autistics, meaning they would be employed, and promoted over them, permitting the universities to become decreasingly interested in the importance of the truth as the fundamental value and increasingly interested in cooperation and social conformity.

Similarly, it has been argued that the rise of females in academia will have similar consequences. The female average IQ differs little from the male IQ, except that the male range is wider. But females are higher in Conscientiousness, which is the other crucial predictor of educational attainment (Nettle, 2007; Dutton, 2017; Almlund et al., 2011). The result is the rise of what Bruce Charlton (25th July 2013) has called 'Head Girls' in academia. The 'Head Girl'—the chief prefect at British girls' schools—combines normal range high intelligence with high Conscientiousness, high Agreeableness and the higher social conformity, and concern with empathy over systematizing that, on average, distinguishes stereotypical females from stereotypical males. Clearly, the Head Girl, charming and ambitious towards socially approved goals, will be appointed ahead of the autistic, socially inept, obsessive, laughably dressed, potential genius, removing him from the one 'safe space' for his genius work which society previously permitted him (see Dutton & Charlton, 2015; Dutton, 2021b). Eventually, therefore, individualizing foundations would be put above the pursuit of truth, just as Christian dogmas were once put above the pursuit of truth. This would drive out the genius-types, as already discussed. Universities would, thus, become extensions of the New Church, just as universities were once an extension of the Christian Church. As such, they would provide useful knowledge to a lesser extent and they would go into decline, as happened before, as we will see below. This ironically would mean that they would ultimately become less attractive to status-seeking Mid-Wits. In order to avoid collapse, there would need to be a 'backlash' such that the university once again focused on useful knowledge and truth, forcing it to be open to geniuses once again; something rendered easier by the substantial exodus of Mid-Wits, completing 'The Priestly Cycle of Universities'.

Anyway, we would expect this leftist takeover to go into reverse. Just as, in the sixteenth century, those at the bottom of society did not replace themselves, leading to downward social mobility, liberal academics will not replace themselves, leading to upward social mobility by fertile religious-conservative types. They will change the culture of academia, such that it is not interested in 'equality' and 'care' but instead focused on what is good for the ethnic group, as well as on loyalty to this group, and on maintenance of the sacred. In other words, it will revert to something more along the lines of Victorian academia, wherein English literature was promoted as a form of replacement religiosity to hold society together (Scruton, 2000). Anthropology was promoted as a means of aiding imperial expansion (by better understanding subject peoples), and better comprehending the evolution of humanity, and why Europeans had ended up at humanity's apex. Alternatively, it was a means of better understanding the 'peasant culture', which was the purest, and least polluted, manifestation of the national essence (see Dutton, 2013b). We would suspect that the assorted examples of 'grievance studies', as well as any research with an 'equality' or otherwise unscholarly agenda, will simply be defunded. Liberal elites could attempt to prevent this process, by contracting academia and shutting down universities, and other organs of culture, but this seems improbable because, at the beginning of the process of reversal, these would still be the sources of their power and of their livelihoods.

Accordingly, we would start to see the increasing percolation upwards of what we might call Nick Fuentes-types or, at least, slightly more cerebral incarnations of him. Fuentes, who was born in 1998 in Illinois, is a prominent podcaster, who was banned from YouTube in 2020 under their increasing regime of censoring and shutting down dissident right-wing channels (Oster, 18th February 2020). Fuentes is a committed Catholic who opposes immigration and feminism and wants to keep the United States predominantly European (Green, 18th November 2019). He is vocally critical of the LGBT movement, and has argued that 'globalists', including those who run the broadcaster CNN, should be arrested and deported from America or simply executed as traitors (Media Matters Staff, 24th April 2017). He is also noticeably high in Extraversion—a personality trait defined by feeling positive feelings strongly, taking risks, and being generally gregarious (Nettle, 2007). Extraversion is associated with fertility, for multiple possible reasons, including extraverts being more confident with the opposite sex, and more likely to take risks in pursuit of pleasure, resulting in accidental pregnancy (Alvergne et al., 2010). Consequently, we would actually expect future generations to be subtly higher in Extraversion than past generations, with somebody such as Fuentes being an example of how this process plays out. As already discussed, these people would be youthful, energetic, and brimming with missionary zeal in a society that would increasingly be chaotic and perceived as having 'run out of steam'. Such a worldview would also be more attractive to many young people used to extreme Wokeness; the way that you rebel, the way that you genuinely cause offence to the current system, is by being 'far right'. Fuentes, for example, is notorious for being deliberately and provocatively offensive to the multiculturalist Establishment; to the Church of Multiculturalism. Consistent with this, it has been found that the most offensive words are no longer the kinds of sexual terms that caused offence in a religious society, in which sexuality was controlled and taboo. The most offensive terms are now words that are considered 'racist' (see Dutton, 2007). As the culture shifts, as noted earlier, 'intelligence' will start to become further associated with 'conservatism' as intelligent people, who had previously suppressed their binding-values, suddenly persuade themselves of the correctness of the current dispensation; Vicar of Bray-like.³ This, of course, will result in a middle-class arms race of increasing conservatism.

As people move the culture in a more conservative direction, as earlier noted, it will be manifestations of runaway individualism that will come under the most severe attack. One of the most pronounced examples of individualism, we would aver, is the transgender movement, whereby it is proposed that objective truth is so strongly secondary to the 'feelings' of an individual that an individual may assert something that is, biologically, empirically inaccurate—that they are 'woman' even though they are biologically male, or vice versa—and this must be accepted by the population. In other words, the level of individualism is so extreme that reality itself is subject to it, and if reality offends or upsets an individual, then the way in which reality is publicly described must be changed, to avoid offending the sensitivities of the individual. Moreover, there must be social, and even legal, penalties for those who refuse to accept this new world in which, in essence, an individual's delusion is 'truth' because for it not to be 'truth' is hurtful to the feelings of that individual. In a sense, this worldview turns individuals into gods who each have 'their truth', define themselves, and must be worshipped as gods by other gods. Those who fail to accept them as gods—those who assert that there is objective truth, which they do merely to empower themselves over marginalized gods—are thus evil gods and there is an eternal Gnostic-like battle between these 'good' and 'evil' gods, with each of us being 'gods'. It is, after all, only God who defines Himself: 'God said to Moses, "I am who I am"' (Exodus, 3:14). 'And the Lord God said, "The man has now become like one of us, knowing good and evil"' (Genesis, 3:22). Interestingly, many Gnostic sects espoused the idea that each of us contains a 'divine spark', implying that, in a sense, we are God incarnate (Logan, 1996, p. 169).

Furthermore, such transgender individuals have the right to tell people which 'personal pronoun' they wish to be used in reference to them, and they will pressure for social and even legal penalties to be imposed upon those who fail to show them proper deference, by not employing their desired personal pronoun. This can be seen, we would suggest, as the ultimate manifestation of a society focused on the individualizing values of harm avoidance and equality; wherein those who

---

3   For non-British readers, the Vicar of Bray was supposedly a parish priest who continuously changed his religious views in order to stay in office during the religious upheavals of the seventeenth and eighteenth centuries. He was the subject of a popular eighteenth-century song (Timbs, 1862, p. 173).

deviate from societal norms, to such an extreme degree, must be rendered 'equal' by the alteration of fundamental concepts—such as 'male' and 'female'—in order to accommodate them. Traditionally, of course, it is the monarch who tells you how he should be addressed. In the reign of Henry VIII (1491-1547, r. 1509-1547) it became treason, a capital offence, 'maliciously' to 'deny any of the king's titles' (Ridley, 1986, p. 247).

The rising conservative society would regard the entire transgender debate as morally repellent. And they would likely regard individuals who are transgender as repellent as well, as people spreading a sense of confusion, disgust, and social discord, which is bad for the coherence of the society. In this regard, it has been demonstrated that transsexuals have highly elevated levels of physical and mental illness, as well as elevated personality disorders, such as Narcissistic Personality Disorder and Psychopathic Personality Disorder (Dhejne et al., 2016). One study found that, of a male and female sample of people suffering from gender dysphoria, 57% fitted the criteria for Narcissistic Personality Disorder, and 81% fitted the criteria for some kind of personality disorder, mainly Borderline Personality Disorder—which is marked by a highly unstable sense of self, due to a fundamental fear of abandonment. Sufferers have a chronic sense of emptiness, and, not knowing who they are, causing perpetual experimentation with multiple identities; and they experience intense negative moods very easily (Jolfei et al., 2014). A review has found other studies that have highlighted this relationship between transsexuality and Narcissistic Personality Disorder, including Narcissistic Rage.

It seems that transsexuals, with their borderline personalities, make sense of the void by changing their gender identity (Lawrence, 2008) and, being high in autistic traits, are aroused by objects or parts of anatomy, such as breasts, and prone to fetishes. These issues come together, in their being aroused by the idea of themselves as another gender. They are high in Dark Triad traits, which would predict a ruthlessly individualistic and self-deluded orientation. This is likely because transgenderism is associated with developmental instability, and thus with mutational load. It reflects the fact that something has gone awry in development, due to genetic or environmental factors, or due to a combination of these. Accordingly, it is associated with left-handedness—which implies the brain having developed asymmetrically, when optimum development is symmetrical—and many markers of poor genetic health (Blanchard, 2008). These even include elevated levels of hearing problems (Reisner et al., 2016), which can hardly be regarded as a product of discrimination, or some other environmental variable, precipitated by being transgender. This would be precisely the kind of individualism that would be clamped down on. It may even be that, in the future, there are serious legal consequences for doctors who now allow young children to overtly alter their gender, especially when we consider the evidence of transsexuals, who reach middle adulthood, and increasingly wish to revert back to their originally assigned gender (see Dutton & Madison, 2020b).

The Concurrent Decline of Western Civilization

As discussed, we would expect this shift to the right to take place alongside a more general decline in civilization; the beginnings of 'winter', due to declining IQ. The bitter fruits of this will be harvested at the time that the West starts to become more conservative. What would this look like?

This is, seemingly, already with us. It will mean the growth of the culture of the 'third world', and the shrinking of the global area that we would regard as 'first world'. We note, before exploring this further, that this was symbolically captured on 6th January 2021 when the US Capitol was stormed by an angry pro-Trump mob. Violent and disputed elections — and, of course, this has been preceded by BLM and Antifa violence — a total lack of trust between the two sides (trust being a correlate of intelligence), and the mob-storming parliaments and presidential palaces are the markers of elections in third world countries. In this sense, in 2021, it might be argued that American IQ had fallen so low, along with its levels of trust, partly due to ethnic and genetic diversity, that it became, in this crucial symbolic sense, third world. Former presidents, indeed, piquantly referred to what happened as 'worthy of a third-world banana republic' (*RT*, 7th January 2021). Democracy requires high levels of trust, and diversity militates against trust, as does low IQ (see Vanhanen, 2012).

But, let us look at such a society in more detail. It is widely agreed by scholars of societal cycles that there are eight key markers of civilizational decline, at least some of which may be with us already:

1. A decrease in stratification, and differentiation, in terms of the kinds of work pursued.
2. A decline in how economically specific the society is. Could this already be with us in the form of people increasingly switching jobs or juggling multiple part-time jobs?
3. A weaker relationship between the political class and the economic class, which implies lack of state control. Could this already be with us, in the rise of Big Tech?
4. A fall in the resources invested in culture and arts. Could this already be with us, in the growing attitude that the purpose of higher education is simply to make money?

5. Restriction in exchange of ideas between individuals. Could this already be with us, with the rise of Big Tech censorship? On the other hand, this situation is artificially created by individualist ideologues.
6. Decrease in opportunities for trade and the distribution of resources. Do we see this in the partial breakdown of free trade blocs, such as the European Union? However, this breakdown is, again, voluntary.
7. A loss of coordination; society being decreasingly well organized. Could this already be with us such as in the sluggish response to the beginnings of Covid-19 in March 2020?
8. Breakaway states and smaller polities. This can be seen in Britain splitting from the European Union, as well as in powerful separatist movements in Scotland, Flanders, and Catalonia (Piris, 2017).

The lack of unity that precedes this is caused by political factionalism, regional separatism, religious conflict, and military coups or attempted coups (Hertler et al., 2020). It can be argued that we may have *all* of these, at least if we count January 2021 as an attempted coup, though this may be stretching it.

We have already observed the correlates of societal low IQ. The education system falls apart, which can be seen in the way that universities increasingly teach ideological subjects, such as Gender Studies, and that even scientific subjects are under ideological control with individualist dogmas of 'equality' having replaced the Christian, binding dogmas that were dominant until 1871 when all students had to be Anglican and fellows had to be ordained and unmarried (Dutton, 2019b). This may eventually lead to people losing faith in the entire higher education system, at least in countries where Wokeness has taken over higher education, and ceasing to bother with it, as employers decreasingly regard it as teaching anything useful. It would be noticed that genuine innovation occurred among independent researchers, people affiliated to more open-minded institutions, or at certain foreign universities where Wokeness was less dominant. In addition, with universities no longer being as much a marker of prestige, those of very high status would look to distinguish themselves from the university-educated rabble either by attending less Woke foreign universities or by bypassing university in favour of something else, which would then become prestigious.

This has happened before. Oxford and Cambridge Universities were effectively in decline from the early sixteenth century to the late nineteenth century, considered to be little more than expensive finishing schools that were dominated by the Church. Their curriculums were out of date, teaching little of use or interest to intelligent middle-class people, let alone teaching science (Stone, 2019), meaning they became dominated by the aristocracy. Teaching standards, in fact, were so poor that undergraduates were forced to hire private tutors if they hoped to obtain an honours degree (Leader et al., 1988, p. 62). In other words, such universities ceased to be an indicator of intelligence and useful knowledge. They merely indicated that your parents were wealthy. Science was taught at Dutch and German universities, with many intellectual Englishmen in the eighteenth and early nineteenth centuries preferring to attend these (Brickman, 1960, p. 100), especially Leiden University (Davids, 2014, p. 245). They signalled not just wealth but intelligence and useful knowledge. Well into the nineteenth century, the Scottish universities also had a superior academic reputation. They taught the latest science, while Oxford and Cambridge were finishing schools for 'the idle and the rich', offering 'little that was new for the well-prepared student' in contrast to the Scottish universities which thus attracted the 'serious student' (Horner, 1993, p. 171). Sometimes, during this period, wealthy young men simply eschewed university altogether, completing their education with the 'Grand Tour' of Europe, often accompanied by a personal tutor (Fyson, 1977, p. 22), though this might sometimes involve spending a little time at, for example, a German university (Le Faye, 1998, p. 29). Only when Oxford and Cambridge reformed, in the 1870s, to imitate these foreign universities and so teach more science and be less dominated by the Church did their reputations start to grow and did attendance figures rise (Stone, 2019).

People will also become less interested in ideals, such as education, as a good in itself and will reduce everything down to money; something inherent, we might suggest, in the introduction of university tuition fees by Tony Blair's New Labour government in 1998. The health system will start to become less reliable, as will public amenities. The correlation between illegitimacy and low IQ reflects the more sexually impulsive nature of low IQ people, so we will see the breakdown of the family, and a society obsessed with sex which, interestingly, was far less taboo and far less regulated in Medieval England than in subsequent eras, due to the society combining religiosity with relatively low IQ. This is why Chaucer and even Shakespeare had to be censored for nineteenth-century audiences. Shakespeare plays were 'Bowdlerized', a term derived from the name of their censor. The English writer Thomas Bowdler (1754–1825)

(Schramm, 2019, pp. 52–53) produced editions of Shakespeare plays, and of works by other writers, expurgated such that they were supposedly more suitable for women and children (e.g. Bowdler, 1818).

Most significantly, there will be a clear rise in corruption, and all manner of other crime and disorder, and the societal infrastructure will lack the organization, or even the will, to control the situation. This occurred during the Black Lives Matter riots of 2020 when the police had been ordered not to respond to complaints in some areas, such as central Seattle, of rioting, looting, intimidation, and even the establishment of an 'autonomous zone', because of an anti-police moral panic in the wake of the death of black criminal George Floyd (1973–2020) while resisting arrest in Minneapolis (Bowles, 7th August 2020). In other words, the way of life of the developing world will spread into what is now the developed world, and ethnic diversity will only make this worse, because it will lead to ethnic conflict, social distrust, and further strife.

These growing regions of third world chaos will be conservative, ethnocentric, and religious, but you would not wish to live there, other than in certain safer areas, much like developing countries today. In fact, as noted, they may actually be less conservative and religious than the better-off areas, precisely because they are less intelligent; so there will not be runaway conservatism. In developing countries today, the more intelligent tend to wish to leave, with migration being a consistent correlate of IQ. For reasons that must be obvious by now, we would not expect these low IQ areas to be genuinely democratic. As this collapse occurs, the more intelligent people, the wealthier people, and perhaps also the more religious people will wish to leave these areas, and will be able to do so due to greater resources, higher future orientation, and a superior ability to solve problems. Indeed, it can already be observed as certain areas 'gentrify' and other areas depopulate, decline, and become home mainly to those who are too poor, or too lacking in future-orientation, to leave, such as Detroit. This process will intensify, until some areas are clearly 'civilization', populated by conservatives, and others are 'diverse', populated by ethnic minorities and whites of low IQ, and despised white liberals, increasingly of low IQ, and gradually ceasing to exist. We would expect the United States to gradually disunite, large parts of Europe to be Arabian, and for the more intelligent of these to, of course, defect to various Byzantine retreats. They will establish multiple refuges in which 'civilization' will be maintained, even if it does not actually progress, or even if it only mildly regresses. This breakdown of national bonds is to be predicted by the earlier breakdown in group selection, as well as by the distrust wrought by ethnic diversity (Putnam, 2007) and genetic diversity (Rushton, 2005) already noted.

Where are we now, if we were about during the decline of Roman civilization? If we base it on per capita major innovations, then we reached a peak in about 1870, of 16 major innovations per 10 million of population per year. We are now at one third of peak inventiveness, at approximately 5 such innovations; which is back where we were in 1600 (Huebner, 2005a), a time when, interestingly, the best writers tended to simply imitate the Golden Age (Mahajan, 1966, p. 48), just as we see increasing 'remakes' today. If we compare this to Rome, peak macro-innovation levels were in 50 AD when they reached 3 per 10 million of population. Precise comparisons, obviously, cannot be made, but a third of peak would be somewhere between 250 AD and 450 AD, which is, indeed, the period of Rome's decline.

Problems with the Classical Comparison

But this kind of comparison is problematic for a number of reasons. Firstly, although the rise and fall of civilizations seems to involve clear points of commonality each time, each civilization is also very different in how it develops, making it difficult to make precise comparisons of this kind. For example, Ancient Greeks may have got to about the level of early eighteenth-century England, in some respects, but they never invented printing. Secondly, our civilization is fundamentally different from all previous civilizations, in that it was much more innovative. Even if we compare it to Classical Greece, which was in many ways more innovative than Classical Rome, they only accomplished about 5 major innovations per 10 million, in about 450 BC. In fact, it could be argued that Europe was in decline from 450 BC until about 950 AD, with a long period, between 250 AD and 950 AD, of one or two innovations. So, Rome was part of a period of overall decline, and we are in fact in about the year 50 BC (this being one third of Classical civilization peak), which, fascinatingly, is roughly when evidence of proto-feminism begins to be noticed (see Glubb, 1976). American theologian Frank Viola notes that in around 44 BC, 'a "new" type of woman emerged in Rome'. By the first century, they had spread throughout the Roman Empire. They were 'liberated married women who pursued their social lives at the expense of their families and who defied previously accepted norms of marriage fidelity and chastity'. Not only did they refuse to wear a veil in public (as had been the custom for married women), but they were also 'sexually promiscuous and dressed in a seductive manner' (Viola, 2005, p. 37, footnote 40).

And thirdly, and most importantly, we have never before developed a civilization composed of such a large percentage of people, who were so physically and mentally unhealthy, that most will not be able to survive the decline of civilization, let alone our equivalent of the Justinian Plague. To put it another way, we have never had a civilization in which Darwinian pressures are as lax as they are now, and consequently, we have never had a civilization before composed of so many people who are reliant on the maintenance of that civilization in order to survive. As we have discussed, child mortality, on average, was 50% in 1800 in Western Europe. Now, child mortality is less than 1%, and national populations are ten times, or more, what they were in 1800, when they were at the maximum that could be sustained, by a pre-industrial society. This implies that approximately 90% of Western people would soon die, if modern civilization, and its associated medical innovations, collapsed, and this number would be higher if civilization continued developing for a while, which we would predict that it will, if sluggishly, for a few more decades yet. As we have explored, mental and physical health—as well as fertility, and other indicators of being adapted to survive and flourish—are robustly associated with being religious, and being right-wing; whereas poor mental health and poor physical health correlate with being irreligious and left-wing. This, among issues we have examined, implies that those who are irreligious and left-wing are high in mutational load, and are the very people who wouldn't have survived childhood under pre-industrial conditions. To varying degrees, they have instincts which would have washed out under those conditions, such as to not have children or to favour other ethnic groups over your own, or to believe that life has no eternal significance.

But these people never became especially significant, under previous societal cycles, because industrialization never occurred, and so, with their high mutational load, they simply died as children, without the possibility of influencing the society with their fitness-damaging ways of thinking. Now, of course, they have managed to do so, and to a very significant degree. This is a key reason why our civilization cannot be compared to previous civilizations that enter their winter. We have come so much further than those civilizations, but we have, for that reason, undergone a process of 'dysgenics' to a far greater extent. It is not just that child mortality has collapsed either. The rise of in vitro fertilization means that people who are, directly or indirectly, too genetically unhealthy to have children at all are able to artificially have children. And these children have elevated poor physical health precisely because, under natural conditions, the sperm from which they come would not fertilize an egg, or the egg would be un-fertilizable, due to problems with the female, or a combination of these factors. For all of these reasons, we have what has been termed a 'crumbling genome', to an extent that was not true of previous civilizations at this stage (Kondrashov, 2017).

Consequently, it is not absolutely certain, even if it is likely, that civilization will regress, in precisely the same way, to more harsh conditions of Darwinian selection; as has occurred in previous cycles. In effect, the more advanced a civilization is — the weaker the selection pressures imposed on its people are — the sicker and less intelligent those people can become, before the civilization falls. As discussed earlier, such a civilization has built up so much 'capital' that it could keep going for a very long time, before its people start eating into the capital, unable to perform the very simple tasks necessary to operate the super-intelligent machines to whom the running of society has effectively been transferred.

The Late Bronze Age Collapse

In this sense, the coming 'collapse' will be more like the Late Bronze Age Collapse, which occurred in about 1200 BC, than the Classical Collapse. By 1200 BC, there was a relatively advanced civilization in the Mediterranean; perhaps as advanced as that of Classical Greece around 1,000 years later (Castleden, 2002; Harding, 2000). This was composed of a series of trading, though occasionally hostile, societies that were thus intimately interlinked: Minoa and Mycenae in Greece, the Hittite Empire in Anatolia in modern day Turkey, the New Kingdom of Egypt, and various city states around Syria, such as Ugarit. These powerful states were connected through trade and colonization to lesser societies such as Canaan (Collins, 2000, p. 22). This civilization rapidly collapsed in around 1200 BC. This seemingly occurred due to a related sequence of factors including climate cooling and famine (possibly caused by a volcanic eruption in Iceland), disease, revolts, and warfare, set off by a fierce invading group, or confederation of ethnic groups, perhaps fleeing famine, called the Sea Peoples. The Greek states, the Hittite Empire, and Ugarit were completely destroyed; their cities becoming deserted ruins. Egypt and some Syrian states declined into relative poverty (see Cline, 2021, or Drews, 2020).

As a result of the Late Bronze Age Collapse, it has been proposed that some Canaanites ceased to farm and made their way into the hills of Canaan as nomadic pastoralists, eventually turning back to agriculture, with farmland having been freed up by mass starvation. Here, they developed a separate identity as 'Israelites'. It has also been proposed that religious differences caused this separation to take place (Dever, 2006). Greek civilization was so comprehensively destroyed that no cities remained. When it began to revive, around 800 BC, the previous civilization was immortalized in the semi-mythological figures of Homer's works (Cline, 2021). In Dark Age Greece, people had such limited understanding of how large buildings could have been constructed, and had forgotten the past to such an extent, that some people believed that a large wall, for example, had been built by giants (Martin, 2008). Legends in the Middle East tell of how pyramids were built by a race of giants (Walker, 1988, p. 20). Similarly, some Saxons regarded the greatest Roman buildings in Britain as having been the work of giants, unable to comprehend how they might have been erected (Place, 1968, p. 2).

The Late Bronze Age Collapse was devastating because it rendered a huge proportion of the population 'unfit' with extreme rapidity. A population, that was used to relatively easy conditions, and had been able to grow and become genetically diverse accordingly, now very suddenly had nowhere near enough food, nowhere near good enough shelter, and, it being colder, was subject to a host of diseases that bred better in the colder weather, and in the context of only primitive medicine. The result was conflict, displacement, and death on an apocalyptic scale, dwarfing anything that occurred during the Justinian Plague or the Black Death. Lacking any excess resources, people would have turned back to simply obtaining food, meaning that cities—full of people who can do something other than obtain food, due to the excess of food—would have quickly depopulated. Desperate for resources, people would have cannibalized the cities for anything of practical use, and then abandoned them. Mass-migrations would have taken place as people desperately searched for land that they could farm. Lacking sufficient yield from their farms, some people would have gone into the wilderness to hunt for food, returning to an even simpler lifestyle, as seemingly occurred with the Canaanites. Those who lacked the skills to pursue farming or otherwise successfully obtain food—artisans, intellectuals—would have had nothing to offer any more and would likely have perished, although some may have had the intelligence to successfully 'switch careers'. They would suddenly need to spend every waking hour focused on obtaining food, with nobody having the excess resources necessary to pay for anything other than essentials, let alone being taught how to read. Groups of related people would have banded together and fought for the control of agricultural land, massacring their competitors where necessary. Lawlessness would ensue, resulting in a gap in the market for protection rackets and a desire to be taught military skills. People who were more intelligent and strategic, though ruthless, would have been selected for in this environment. Where possible, intelligent people would have used their resources in order to escape the anarchy to the last refuges of civilization.

Now, imagine such a collapse occurring in our own civilization. Unlike the Late Bronze Age Collapse, this would be on a global scale, due to the interconnected nature of the modern world. Only the most primitive and isolated peoples would avoid being impacted by it. How might it transpire? As average intelligence continues to decline, we will produce fewer and fewer per capita innovations and, eventually, rising disorder—due to constant short-term decisions—will make it difficult to sustain innovations that we can currently sustain. Thus, we can imagine international travel being scaled back and airports falling into disrepair. Eventually, the population—of low IQ, genetically sick people—will grow so high, due to indirect selection for fertility, that innovation of techniques to maximize food production will be outpaced by population growth, because we will no longer be sufficiently intelligent to come up with new innovations. By this time, a large percentage of people will have an IQ and personality type that will render them unemployable, these people will have large numbers of children, and they will be chronically genetically sick. There simply won't be the resources, by this stage, to sustain public welfare or the necessary health and emergency services and, due to rising conservatism among the more intelligent, there won't be the desire to do so either, even if the resources were available. This underclass will be violent, impulsive, criminal, and diseased, as their high mutational load will render them unable to fight off diseases, and their impulsivity will likely mean they are high in sexually transmitted diseases and addicted to drugs. Even now, there is an ongoing problem with STDs among this demographic (Anguzu et al., 2019), especially among its younger members, where it is increasing (Shannon & Klausner, 2018). All the while antibiotics are getting weaker as bacteria become increasingly resistant to them (Felter, 15th November 2019).

As was the case in the Victorian era with their concept of the underclass '*residuum*' that might 'contaminate' higher classes, this class will be regarded almost as a separate, and very dangerous, species that you need to stay away from (MacDuffie, 2014, p. 227), meaning there will be little sympathy for them as they scramble for food. In that they will be 'liberal', a belief may develop that this is simply God punishing them, as He did the people of Sodom and Gomorrah. They will likely lack the intelligence or skill to farm or even hunt and they will simply degenerate into violent anarchy, with more intelligent and religious people controlling the available land and keeping the underclass at bay. These conservative people are likely to feel under a constant threat of attack—rather like American pioneers surrounded by native tribes—which will elevate their religiousness, and ethnocentrism, despite their relatively luxurious environment. However, as discussed, they will also simply be more religious, for genetic reasons, than many people are today. This may set off a system of group selection, because of the way in which religiosity is associated with markers of fitness, and due to the runaway conservatism that we would expect to occur. This means that it is possible that civilization will not have to undergo a total devastation, whereby it will have to start from scratch. It will be preserved in these high IQ, conservative, and religious refuges before rising again. All it would take, among this underclass, to cause an unparalleled collapse would be some novel virus. We would be unable to find a cure and there would simply be mass death. But what other processes might set us off, quickly, down the path to a New Dark Age?

Chapter Eight

The Long Slide

'Never such innocence,
Never before or since,
As changed itself to past
Without a word...'[1]

Never Such Innocence

We commenced this exploration with a poem by Philip Larkin, written in 1967, which dealt with the—at that time—still relatively taboo-breaking subject of promiscuous sexual intercourse. The volume of poetry of which that poem was part—*High Windows*—was published in 1974. In many ways, this seems like another world compared to today. Britain, for example, still retained many vestiges of the traditional society, such that Larkin mused with amazement in 'High Windows' on the 'paradise' of sexual freedom, lack of religiosity, and absence of deference to the old social order which appeared to be enveloping England at the time, and did so ever more comprehensively in the coming decades.

These were the 'decades of the self', of the individual, and they were decades in which the rights of the individual, as well as equality of all individuals, and their right to be treated equally, gradually trumped all other considerations, at least in much public discourse. Looking back now, even the 1970s seems like such an 'innocent' time, just as Larkin regarded the year 1914—a sunny, August evening prior to the horrors of the Great War—as poignantly naïve when he looked back on it in 1964: 'Never such innocence again.' These were times of high social trust; when you thought about the group far ahead of yourself. The self-orientation of a century later could hardly have been conceived by most people in 1914.

Of course, there is an extent to which, if you want to have children, you need to think about something beyond the self. You need to have a

---

[1] 'MCMXIV' (Larkin, 1964).

desire to nurture somebody else, and to sacrifice your own selfish desires for the good of somebody else. And what is 'the good' of somebody else? It is often assumed to mean raising them such that they can become successful and contented members of society, which means that they have to learn to be cooperative with other people and, sometimes, to sacrifice their own selfish desires for the collective good. Of course, some children are not raised like this. They are indulged, and raised as individualists, and there is a growing body of evidence that those children experience considerable problems adjusting to being independent adults in comparison to those who are raised in a traditional and group-oriented fashion, when the necessary confounds are controlled for (Dutton & Madison, 2020a).

However, as we have found, all the time that this individualizing process was occurring, and all the time it was increasingly encouraging larger and larger percentages of Western populations to be individualistic and even not to breed, there was a remnant population who were very substantially resistant to this process. Indeed, as we have observed, they were likely resistant for genetic reasons. They were the kind of people who would have survived under the conditions of intense inter-group competition and high child mortality that existed prior to the Industrial Revolution, and its attendant medical and living-standard advances. As such, though they became a smaller and smaller percentage of the population, they maintained evolutionarily adaptive desires, such as the desire to have large families. Once the society switched towards individualizing values, more and more people became individualists, and, eventually, these people were encouraged into, or depressed into, not wanting children, or, at least, they did not want large families. This occurred due to never-before seen conditions of luxury, permitting runaway individualism. As a result, the fertility advantage of those with these group-oriented traits—the traditionally religious, and the far right—grew, and they began to outbreed everybody else. Due to the high heritability of these traits, this meant it was inevitable for genetic reasons that the society would return to a situation in which individualizing values were marginal, just as they had been in 1800, and binding values predominated. This, we have shown, is what is likely going to happen, and there are some indications that this switch is already taking place, though it will take place in a time of growing lawlessness and instability due to declining intelligence and a rising population. Indeed, it will take place during an unparalleled collapse in which conservative and intelligent people struggle to maintain the vestiges of civilization in refuges surrounded by Neo-Darwinian chaos.

Chapter Eight

A Scenario Road Map to the New Dark Age

Timing is always the most difficult aspect in predicting the future and, naturally, it is very difficult to predict the future in any precise detail because there are so many possibilities and contingencies. From our simulation of the United States GSS population, if we really had to, we would predict the middle of this century, thirty years from the time of publication of this book, to be the prophetic 'turning point', when most of the states of America become self-aware that they're facing a crisis of skilled labour emigration and underclass over-population; the horrifying revelation that welfare provisions will soon no longer be tenable as they once were. However, this doesn't necessarily apply well to Europe or East Asia, simply because the numbers are different. Moreover, the process of getting there could be accelerated by further immigration crises between South America and the United States (consider also crises between Africa/Arabia and Europe). Civilizational decline might even be slowed down by some effects of, say, the internet, in reducing the gap in fertility between the middle and underclass population; though we haven't seen any evidence of that—the internet could just as well exacerbate the gap even further.

Then there is the absolute wealth of implications that population evolution will have on the modern world. Let's take a couple of areas for example that you might not have considered so far but would seem to be potentially quite important. What would global decline in intelligence and Conscientiousness do to our ability to manage the current ecological threats or disasters on various continents? Invasive Cane Toads in Australia and Tumble Weed in North America are two better known examples of ecological disturbances (Crosby, 2015, p. xiv). Three more case studies peculiar to Britain might be the growing threats of lethal Asian hornets, disease carrying tiger mosquitoes, and building-destroying Japanese knotweed (Booy et al., 2015). But there are countless potential or actual invasive species all over the world. Most come over as stowaways on global trade vehicles; a few have even escaped from zoos or gardens. In the developed world, border controls, pest control companies, and various environmental organizations work tirelessly to protect against (or mitigate) the damage caused by such pests. If we are to expect the presence and effectiveness of these organizations to taper off over the latter course of this century, an immense amount of damage to agriculture, infrastructure, and public health would naturally ensue.

What about the present arrangements of our global energy infrastructure? Obviously the highly complex nuclear energy sources will be decreasingly viable as countries like France, which are deeply reliant on this kind of power source (*BBC News*, 30th October 2014), haemorrhage cognitive capital. But will market forces and hard-coded industry standards force nuclear power plants to be decommissioned safely, or will they, by force of political will, be kept going with 'Homer Simpson' grade employees, until inevitable Fukushima-type catastrophes unfold? If continuing global energy demands mean we have to move back to simpler energy sources, which ones will present themselves as such? Will oil and gas sources still be viable? When will the complexity of extracting, transporting, refining, and distributing fossil fuels prove too much to cope with? Will wind turbines, solar panels, and hydroelectric generators be maintainable into the future? Or will we suffer ever-more power-cuts—already a constant problem in countries like India (Sharma, 27th February 2020)—until the day comes that national electricity grids can no longer be maintained? If competent engineers are going to become as scarce as they are in most of the Global South today, then energy and numerous other technical industries, from plumbing to biotechnology, will all implode.

And then there are the entire areas of enquiry that operate somewhat independently of the trends we have discussed in this book, and yet may have just as profound effects on the course of the future, such that they might radically interfere with the timing and character of the events we have predicted to unfold. Two such subjects we consider to be of particular importance are the environment and economics.

Environmental Catastrophe

To the environment, it is well known that the mainstream scientific establishment has it that, for the foreseeable future, global average temperatures will continue to rise. However, though it is ever in the interest of the environmentalist left to portray the scientific establishment as having come to some rigid and well-defined Doomsday Consensus, the reality is that there are many competing models on how quick and how severe that rise will be, to what extent the greenhouse effect is responsible for that rise, and what proportion of that greenhouse effect is actually man-made (Lawson, 2008). The fact that careful critics are emotionally condemned as 'climate deniers', implicitly associating them with Holocaust denial, should be regarded as evidence that those who use such terms harbour secret doubts, hence their cognitive dissonance, expressed in emotional outbursts. A similar psychology, of course, may be found in those who angrily dismiss out of hand the very possibility that human activity might be partly responsible for climate change.

Nevertheless, it must be readily admitted that global average temperatures have thus far continued to creep up, though not at the rate as many of the more alarmist models would have predicted. It's fairly safe to say, too, that man has had a significant role in that, through the dynamics of greenhouse gases. The implications of this trend continuing most emphatically does not add up to some kind of apocalyptic, mass extinction event[2] that will wipe out all life on earth forever, as Hollywood alarmism and general mass hysteria of the environmentalist wing of politics might inculcate us into believing. Through the many millions of years of our planet's history, life on earth has thrived during epochs of vastly hotter global average temperatures than what is being anticipated today. For example, it was so hot during the Triassic, the time of the early dinosaurs, that there were no icecaps (Ward, 2006, p. 184). Nevertheless, as far as the implications are for our declining first world civilization, rising temperatures would only further exacerbate the downturn. For instance, certain areas of the globe are going to be more exposed to the risk of flooding; you don't want to be living in the Netherlands when the sea levels are rising. All the while, the infrastructure developed to prevent flooding will be decaying, due to an ever-intensifying dearth of competent engineers. As a general rule, warmer weather makes for further relaxed selection pressures.[3] Consider, for instance, the difficulty of being a homeless and otherwise poorly sheltered person in a colder country versus in a hotter one. Being left out in the cold in the northern parts of Europe or North America becomes an existential threat, whereas living outside in some hotter countries is tantamount to a lifestyle choice. As the developed world transitions into a largely homeless or shantytown urban civilization, due to the underclass population explosion, an increasingly warmer climate would therefore delay the Malthusian collapse of that same population, as they're saved from the difficult and cold Darwinian conditions, traditional to the 'Global North'.

---

[2] It may be reasonable, though some disagree, to conceive that at the present moment our planet is undergoing a man-made extinction event, commonly referred to as the Anthropocene or Holocene Extinction, but this is driven by habit destruction, pollution, and poaching, not global warming, which are altogether readily conflated into one vague and overarching environmental alarmism. Any form of climate change will of course present itself as problematic to many species faced with a changing environment, to which they were, up to that point, well adapted, but 'climate change' only ever amounts to an extinction event in the most extreme cases, where it is induced by a geological catastrophe, such as an erupting super-volcano or an asteroid impact. Otherwise, evolution always finds an elegant way through a changing environment; indeed, evolution has even found its way, more desperately, through the last five mass extinction events of our planet (see Wagler, 2011).

[3] It must of course be admitted that, in conjunction with desertification and drought, an otherwise easy warm climate turns into a place very difficult to inhabit.

That being said, however, the term 'global warming' has been increasingly dropped in favour of 'climate change'; even the term 'global weirding' has been popularized (Clarke-Ezzidio, 20th April 2021). The reason for this is that rising global average temperatures don't simply mean that everywhere gets warmer—earth's climate is a vastly more complex network of natural processes. Melting ice caps would reduce the salinity of the ocean water and thus change the global ocean currents, causing all kinds of unexpected effects. Because there is more latent energy in the atmosphere with rising temperatures, the overall implication is that weather becomes more extreme; or extreme weather events, such as storms and floods, become more frequent. This means that, all the while the environment might be getting easier to live in, in terms of greater amounts of available edible biomass, and decreasing mortality by exposure, it will at the same time be becoming more unstable, as the population has to increasingly deal with ever-more severe weather events. It's not difficult to imagine how that will be increasingly 'problematic' as the population loses its protective first world infrastructure.

It has also been suggested that we may be approaching another 'grand solar minimum' beginning in the 2030s, comparable to the intensely cold Maunder Minimum of the seventeenth and early eighteenth centuries. This is where the sun's activity dips, such that less of its heat reaches earth, possibly causing a 10-degree centigrade or so drop in global average temperatures, otherwise overwhelming the upward trends in global temperatures powered by greenhouse gases for many decades to come (Zharkova, 2020). However, other scientists have suggested the opposite: that this cooling will be less significant than that and more likely will be overwhelmed by man-made processes of global warming than vice versa (Starr, 19th May 2020); so the reality remains uncertain.

It might indeed be regrettable if we don't see a large drop in solar activity in the near future, because another little paid-attention-to finding that's come out in environmental science in recent years is that earth's magnetic field is weakening (Neustaeter, 16th June 2020). This increases our exposure to solar storms. The most dramatic instance in history of a solar storm was the 'Carrington Event' of 1st to 2nd September 1859, named after its observer, amateur astronomer Richard Carrington (1826–1875) (Carrington, 1859). This temporarily wiped out the West's primitive electricity network. It caused paper in telegraph offices to catch fire, telegraph operators to be electrocuted, electric fires on ships, and aurora borealis down to the tropics (Testot, 2020, p. 292). We should generally only expect a Carrington-like solar flare to directly impact earth once a century or so. There have been notable near misses in recent history, such as the close scrape on 23rd July 2012, which would have created a storm comparable to the 1859 Carrington Event (Phillips, 23rd July 2014). If earth's magnetosphere continues to weaken, this means that the smaller solar flares that impact earth more often will be sufficient to cause the same damage as their larger counterparts in the past. This increases the likelihood of a Carrington Event occurring, which in today's world would cripple our electronic infrastructure. Depending on the severity of the storm, the internet and telecommunications (on which global trade and finance depends), the nation's power grids, and most electronic machinery could all fail at once. There is much more the developed world could be doing than it currently is to better protect the nation's electronic infrastructure against dangerous solar flaring, but for the trends discussed in this book, necessary adequate preparation would seem to be decreasingly likely to take place as time goes on, especially if we're not satisfactorily hit by a 'wake-up call' sub-Carrington flare in the near future. And it should also be kept in mind that earth's magnetic field doesn't just shield us from solar flares, but also from cosmic rays, which are a cancer risk (Cucinotta & Cacao, 2017). So just as the depletion of the ozone layer of our planet's stratosphere has increased our exposure to UV radiation, so too will the weakening of our magnetosphere bring similar consequences via cosmic radiation. It remains an open question as to whether earth's magnetic field will continue to deteriorate, even as far as triggering a magnet pole reversal—but these are the risks involved, and they seem to us to be very real and dangerously under-discussed in society; likely being displaced in attention by the more mainstream forms of climate alarmism we looked at first.

Finally, it's worth keeping in mind the threat of volcanic eruptions. These large volcanic eruptions have a track record of destabilizing and finishing off weakened civilizations, and serious thought has been given to the devastating effects a comparable eruption could have on our modern world (Newhall et al., 2018). As noted above, it has been argued that a volcanic eruption in Iceland was the ultimate cause of the Late Bronze Age Collapse (Yurko, 1999). Similarly, the fall in temperature that set off the Justinian Plague, discussed earlier, has been put down to a volcanic eruption (Sivertsen, 2006, p. 86).

Economic Catastrophe: The Break-Up of Nations

Moving on from potentially interfering processes from changes to the natural environment, we come to the subject of economics. Much of what we've been discussing on what you might call the 'downwards evolution of labour markets' across the developed world is solidly grounded in mainstream economic thought. We have predicated much of our vision of the future on the notion that skilled labour, and all forms of capital, will move according to basic push–pull economic incentives and disincentives. People and businesses will prefer to migrate towards states or nations where there are lower taxes, and will be all the more likely to do so if said state or nation is relatively close to where the prospective mover is currently located. This will be increasingly the case if the wave of democratic break-ups of nation states in the developed world is going to occur, as we cautiously predict.

People and businesses also want to buy property where it is increasingly popular, and thus likely to appreciate in value, and sell property where it is decreasingly popular, and thus likely to depreciate in value. It is also basic common sense that areas of expensive real estate can only be afforded by very high-skilled wage-earning individuals, and very profitable businesses, such that unskilled labour and less profitable businesses will have to gravitate towards cheaper areas in order to live and to operate. These self-reinforcing dynamics of economic migration are the basis for many dramatic runaway effects in regional development, such as gentrification, 'brain drain', and much of what might otherwise have been considered a purely social phenomenon: 'white flight' (see Kaufmann, 2019). Regional inequalities within and between countries arise for these reasons, and they're generally only reversed, or otherwise treated, by government intervention; social housing, town or city planning, tax incentives, and subsidies. But with the coming multiplication of the numbers of governments in the world, governments will be decreasingly able to affect these forces for regional inequalities due to being in intense competition with each other.

In this book, we have, for brevity's sake, often referred to the decline 'of the West' or the decline 'of the developed world' as a whole; as if it were going to all at once and everywhere decline into oblivion. But as we've argued in the previous sections concerning Neo-Byzantiums, barring any massive environmental disaster like an extreme solar storm or large volcanic eruption, this isn't actually how it will work in practice. The decline of the first world will actually be a story of winner and loser countries, where in each subsequent round the winning countries will fight over the ever-dwindling amounts of quality human and resource capital. A 'round' might be a decade or so of time, and the countries that lose the round by virtue of seeing mass emigration of skilled labour and capital will see standards of living implode into that of the third world. Whilst this is going on, winner countries will themselves split up, due to the demographic and cultural factors previously discussed, and then intensely compete with each other in succeeding rounds. This game will go on for round after round, until there are only a few dozen or so small 'winner' countries scattered across the world. These will be the only countries that could still be considered to be belonging to the first world, by living standards. These winner countries will be the proto-Neo-Byzantiums, and whichever of them will survive the test of time, and come to flourish, and perhaps even gradually imperialize and dominate the rest of the world, will prove to be the true Neo-Byzantium. That said, we don't necessarily expect there to be just one Neo-Byzantium, but we don't imagine there will be many such countries surviving in the next century either.

If the reader is in search of a method for predicting the future, in order to make wise investments for themselves and their family, we would encourage them to frame the world as it is now, as currently undergoing the game or process we just described. Let's take the United States as an example. Currently, the United States is facing two threats of secession, from Texas and California, each one varying in fervour at any one time, depending on whether the Democratic or Republican Party controls Washington, DC (Robinson, 4th February 2017; Ford, 22nd January 2021). If California voted to secede from the union, this democratic mandate would presumably be honoured by Washington, for although they may not like it, and, as happened with Brexit, opponents may try to make it as difficult and as slow and painful as possible, in a likely vain effort to try to reverse the outcome, nevertheless, it's hard to see how Washington could possibly invent a legitimatizing ideology to stop such a democratic mandate over the long run, especially if, in other places in the world, secession votes had been honoured before, such as between Scotland and the rest of the UK.

In the short run, an independent California would likely do quite well, as it is home to the most successful technology and media entertainment companies in the world. On the other hand, taxes are notoriously steep in California, as it is a particularly left-wing state, by American standards; taxes are needed to fund large amounts of public spending (Birrell, 22nd May 2021). This could prove to be California's undoing over the long run, as its competitor to the south west, Texas, being a conservative state, has very low taxes indeed (DeVore, 1st June 2021). This has recently attracted some major tech companies. Oracle, as well as Tesla and others, have moved from California to Texas, not only to enjoy better taxes themselves, but also to attract 'talent' such as the software engineers, who earn notoriously high salaries; they also increasingly prefer work in cities such as Houston and Dallas for tax reasons. This is part of a more general 'exodus from America's most populous and economically powerful state' which has seen California's population falling (Birrell, 22nd May 2021). It might be noted too that this dynamic already exists with California's northern neighbour, Washington State, where the tax regime is also a significantly better deal for the taxpayer (Pasia, 8th April 2020). You might expect, for this reason, an independent Texas to win in the battle for capital, against an independent California. That may be the end result of the 'first round' so to speak, but both Texas and California continue to see a mass influx of unskilled and often illegal labour across the Mexican border. These immigrants, in most cases, prove to be a net burden on the provision of public services; they remain as members of the underclass (e.g. Martin & Ruark, 2010). Both of these states are ticking demographic time bombs, as they contain a very large proportion of underclass Hispanics, who have much higher and faster levels of fertility than their white middle-class neighbours (Livingston, 8th August 2019). For this reason, we wouldn't expect Texas to win against its other, whiter states to the north. It's much the same story on the west coast between New York and Florida, with large differences in tax, for political reasons, attracting capital and skilled labour from the north to the south. Both states, however, again, have huge exploding underclass demographic issues, and thus we also shouldn't expect either of these states to produce a proto-Neo-Byzantium in the long run.

It might not always be clear what direction a given city or state is heading in, because of conflicting forces. For London, having a left-wing mayoralty, you might have thought that the same trends would apply as they do in New York and Los Angeles. However, the tax arrangement in the very centre of London, referred to as 'The City of London', is different, and gentrification in London, due to rapidly rising housing prices, has, over the previous decade, been very effective in reversing previous racial demographic trends, and pushing unskilled labour into certain outer boroughs (Kaufmann, 2019).

Thus far, London and other North Western European countries, and their cities, have proven to have been the net winners in the latest round of intense competition for labour within Europe. All of the Southern and Eastern European countries face, to varying degrees, existential crises from low birth rates, because of the immense amount of youth emigration that has occurred over the past several decades in search of higher paid jobs (Grant, 3rd October 2019). A smaller labour force at home means less economic growth and a smaller tax base, which, in conjunction with an ageing population that will be placing increasing pressure on its state pensions and healthcare, augers serious problems for many of these countries. The effects of the coronavirus epidemic may have exacerbated this birth rate implosion, especially in areas that depend on tourism such as Italy (*BBC News*, 9th June 2021).

A Rural Renaissance?

It must be remembered that we are living through an increasingly automated age that's hollowing out the demand for unskilled white-collar work in the developed world, driving further inequality within the labour market, between high-paid skilled white- and solid-collar workers, and everyone else, who are increasingly fortunate to even have a job at all (Ford, 2015). The viability of a modern economy is directly contingent upon the provision of skilled labour, which in most instances is associated with STEM higher education and accumulated industry experience. This means that net migration between countries doesn't tell the whole story. If it's mostly the unskilled portion of the labour force that is emigrating out of an economy (which is commonly the case in times of economic crisis), that is of little consequence; indeed, it would provide relief in cases where the emigrant was a net burden on the social services. Another more subtle distinction that is important to make is the fertility of the person emigrating. If the said individual was never going to have any children, then his exit from the economy is just the loss of one individual. But if that same individual has a large family, then the long-term opportunity cost of his exit compounds over generations.

All the while unskilled white-collar work is increasingly disappearing due to automation, advances in technology have also been enabling skilled white-collar work to be increasingly performed remotely—even anywhere in the world. Recent events have only accelerated the speed of this transition to remote working; shifting worker and business attitudes are increasingly discounting the value of paying for premium office space in London. A new report out of the Tony Blair Institute found that one in five jobs in the UK can be classified as 'anywhere jobs' in the sense that they can in theory be done anywhere (Kakkad et al., 2021). These are virtually all high-skilled roles, 'mainly in ICT, financial and professional services in London and the South East'. The report expresses some anxiety concerning this new found revolution in the mobility of skilled labour the coronavirus epidemic has triggered, because of the opportunity it provides for employers to offshore this abroad, and indeed for the workers themselves to move abroad. The report urges policy makers to review infrastructure and incentives, to keep such business in the country; and indeed seize on the opportunity to attract these 'anywhere jobs' from elsewhere into the UK.

It is astute of Tony Blair and his think tank to catch on early to this emerging threat to the UK economy, that has hitherto benefited from siphoning off the working population from struggling Southern and Eastern European economies. London, and the wider South East of England, is one of the most expensive areas in the world to live, meaning that these high-skilled workers have to funnel an unusually large percentage of their income into rental or mortgage payments. If it is not necessary that they need to commute into an office in London on any regular basis, then they have every economic incentive to move further out into the country; the more infrequent the requirement to come in, the further they are able to move away. Indeed, if the work becomes entirely remote, then, barring any issues with time zones, the whole world opens up to them, and indeed so it does for the business seeking to recruit. This is vital to consider because, from what we've discussed in this book, the intelligent religious conservative types, upon whom the burden of renewing the next generation of high-skilled labour is entirely placed, don't want to raise their families in small expensive apartments in the inner city or among the urban sprawl of Greater London, which they will increasingly consider decadent or dangerous places to be. They would, however, be attracted to the countryside in certain other areas of the UK or Europe, where housing is much cheaper, and the culture is more amenable to their character. This would mean for the first time in a long while that Southern and Eastern Europe would have the upper hand over the Northwest, and many a youngster who migrated one way in the past, may now be planning to move back the other way, and bring a few friends with him in the process.

Such a long-term migration of skilled white-collar workers out of the cities would then naturally lower the value of real estate in those same cities and their wider urban sprawl. This has further implications for the equally well-paid skilled blue-collar workers, because their line of work generally takes them where real estate is most valuable. An established downwards trend in the population of cities would cause real estate investors to withdraw and construction projects would be disbanded. Buildings might no longer be profitable to maintain, and they would thus fall into disrepair and have to be demolished. This would mean little to no work for the skilled blue-collar labour market, and they would thus follow their skilled white-collar counterparts into the countryside, or wherever they may go. With an exodus of both skilled blue- and white-collar workers out of the cities, it is difficult to see how any economy could be sustained in these urban places at all; the cities might completely implode in a crisis of unemployment.

Calling in the Debts

Quite apart from the trends discussed in this book, many economists and other commentators do anticipate future pension and debt-inflation crises that will cause harsh reductions in standards of living, ever-increasing wealth inequality, and even the implosion of the middle class (see Kotkin,

2020). With regard to the pensions crisis, this is simply because economists buy the mainstream projections of population demographers that predict birth rates to hereafter persistently decrease and create a 'top-heavy population pyramid', where there simply aren't enough young people around to take care of, and otherwise pay for, the retired and elderly. We of course would modify that prediction, and say that birth rates will reverse and surge across the world again, creating an 'hourglass population pyramid', but that the population will be replenished by people who will more likely be an extra burden on the welfare state, further exacerbating the problem and bringing the crisis forward. Much of the care industry is unskilled work, and thus would likely be somewhat alleviated from a resurgence in birth rates boosting the size of the unskilled labour force, but the provision of modern housing, utilities, and healthcare will not stand to gain from this resurgence.

Of course, this is to frame the subject of pensions crises in terms of a loss of future productive capacity. But pension fund sustainability is more typically discussed monetarily; as a discrepancy between the number of savers paying into the system, and the number of retirees drawing out of the system. For most of the developed world, where a pension fund becomes insolvent, the government will step in to assist the pensioners affected, whether by propping up the fund itself, compensating the pensioners directly, or simply by just providing a state pension, and other forms of welfare, to fall back on. In this way, the approaching pension crisis will ultimately fuse into the larger public debt crisis, in which developed countries continue to borrow and spend ever-greater proportions of their increasingly stagnant GDP, partially because of leftist ideals. This, and indeed all forms of borrowing, directly affects inflation for three separate reasons.

Firstly—and it's perfectly amazing how widely this is not known—borrowing money creates inflation by increasing the money supply (Ryan-Collins et al., 2012). Money, of course, is not food or anything else that has intrinsic value. Coins are tokens of exchange which we employ to the extent that we have confidence that other people will accept them. Money was once linked to gold or silver because of a confidence that these precious metals would maintain their value; even though, in practice, it would be impossible for everyone to redeem all of their money in gold or silver at the same time because there wouldn't be enough gold or silver. This fact further demonstrates that money is simply a matter of confidence.

The benefit of a system of credit, of loans, is that innovative individuals can realize large-scale money-making and otherwise useful projects. Moreover, it's been well argued that credit-based finance, against instantly-settled exchanges of rare metals, was historically instrumental in helping cultivate economic development, and peaceful relations between elites, in historically gold and silver poor North Western Europe (Ferguson, 2008). Also, banking was the most central institution to the development and success of the British, and later American, empires, which even now, because of big finance, continue to exist in a private capacity (Cain & Hopkins 2014). Nevertheless, as we will now explain, with too much lending, you end up with boom and bust economics.

Today, money is no longer linked to gold or silver, but to nothing. And so, in that sense, it is linked simply to confidence in the banks or in the governments that create it, hence the term 'fiat currency', meaning 'currency by decree'. As such, money is 'created' and exists so long as investors have confidence in the 'money temples'. This may seem extraordinary, but this really is the essence of the system (Rayner-Hilles, 2019). If you lend money, more people can buy houses, so there are fewer houses per capita, so house prices increase. This is a key reason why housing across the Western world has been soaring in price since banks and their reserve requirements were deregulated in around the 1980s (Ryan-Collins et al., 2017). Mortgages became mainstream and ordinary middle-class people — who might earlier have purchased a house outright — had to apply for one if they wanted to purchase a home. When a mortgage is taken out, banks literally create new money (technically referred to as M1) to fund the purchase of the home, and this money enters into circulation and causes inflation. In a sense, this very act is stealing from their depositors. It reduces, by inflation, the value of their savings; it is theft by inflation.

Secondly, and counteracting this, debt creates deflation by banks destroying money when the debt is paid back, and also because interest rates on debt withdraw money from circulating in the real economy of goods and services. That latter point is worth emphasizing, because it gets to a wider point about crippling levels of usury that's commonly seen preceding a civilizational collapse and even how it contributes to it. Ancient Greece and Rome were marred by debt crises. For example, in 391 BC the 'demagogues', who ran Rhodes, needed to pay people to attend the assembly, so that they could retain influence over them. They raised this money by not paying naval commanders. The commanders couldn't pay their troops, the troops sued, so the commanders overthrew the government (Graeber, 2014, Ch. 9, 'The Mediterranean').

We have a cultural expectation today that money saved should just accumulate ever-more money indefinitely, like a rolling snowball. But money earned as interest, or rent or profit, has to come from somewhere, and it comes from the real economy; causing deflation. The developed world today has a class of extraordinarily wealthy people, multi-billionaires, sometimes referred to as plutocrats, with snowballs so large that they actually overshadow a lot of small countries. If he wanted to, Elon Musk could buy every loo roll on earth tomorrow. Yet again, it is taken for granted that a snowball is never too large not to be kept rolling for even further increase. Taken together, these two contradictory effects of borrowing money are the ultimate cause of business boom–bust cycles. Debt cycles tend to align, because when times are good, and people feel confident, people want to borrow money to invest and spend now, and pay in the future. This creates rampant spending and inflation to begin with (the boom) and then ultimately crippling deflation as time goes on, crashing the economy at the end (the bust).

You might wonder how such a ridiculous monetary system as this could have remained the basis of the developed world's economies for so long, and indeed have intensified over time. Perhaps it's for a lack of intelligence and political will, but of course, politically, nobody wants the economy to crash, or for there even to be too much inflation. Therefore there has been established a monetary doctrine or paradigm called 'Keynesianism', in which the destabilizing effects of debt-inflation, that ultimately cause economic crashes, are simply 'treated' by massive government intervention, through fiscal expenditure to bail out institutions and people, and central banking, to lower interest rates and buy back debt, when it is causing too much deflation. This is what its founder John Maynard Keynes (1883-1946) prescribed to the British government to bring itself out of the 1930s debt deflation crisis, and this is what was employed again in 2010 after the financial crisis brought about exactly the same conditions on a vastly larger scale (Ireland, 2010). Indeed, we have seen a quiet revolution in central banking since this crisis, as it has become the new tacit norm that central banks will lower interest rates to zero or even negative, and print money to buy off and forgive public and private debts (quantitative easing), and generally do whatever it takes to stop deflation from occurring (Halligan, 11th July 2020).

Many have expressed panic and horror at the central bank's new found enthusiasm for printing money, fearing it will over the long run cause a runaway Weimar Germany type hyperinflation, and they have dumped all their cash savings for gold and other forms of equity (Halligan, 11th July 2020). That perhaps might seem unreasonable, considering the inflation by quantitative easing is created only to directly counteract and neutralize the deflation created by crippling amounts of debt, yet the loss of confidence in fiat currency here is telling, and should not go un-noted. The founder and CEO of the world's largest hedge fund, Ray Dalio (2012), published a white paper on the new super-Keynesian paradigm of central banking, presenting it as the new natural order of things that must be respected. Yet in apparent contradiction to the spirit of that paper, Dalio (15th March 2021) published an article expressing his horror or bemusement as to why anyone would want to buy public debt, when bonds pay little to nothing in terms of interest rates, and you are exposed to the threat of inflation. Dalio has publicly stated that 'cash is trash' and, though it's extremely volatile, he'd even rather own cryptocurrency.

So what's the case here? Does the new trend of monetary expansion and the ever-growing appetite for debt pose an existential threat to the developed world, that would otherwise undercut the crisis we've been predicting on the basis of evolutionary demographics? In the best-case scenario, the current arrangement will not crash the global economy; it will just create extreme, ludicrous levels of wealth inequality. In effect, governments and banks will conspire to print off ever-more money to fund decadent public expenditure, as well as private investors' portfolios, and hand it over to the extremely wealthy, and this will be acceptable because the latter never actually spend their wealth on real goods and services, just on financial assets. This is the ironic nature of usury — the usurer doesn't accumulate the real-world resources that people require to live; only paper assets. So in effect the government and the super-rich will be swapping back and forth ever larger sums of money, and none of it will ever affect anything real. This can continue as long as confidence continues.

It could be argued that, in a sense, not literally of course, we are living through a period of hyperinflation. Property, stocks, and rare metals are skyrocketing in value, not so much because they're increasing in value, so much as because money is decreasing in value. But the price of food, rent, and basic utilities isn't hyperinflating, and will not do so unless there is a fall in our productive capacity, caused by a shortage of competent engineers for example — this is 'cost push' inflation. This is the best-case scenario, however. The fact of the matter is that the new paradigm does potentially pose a massive threat to any individual currency, and we should expect the number of currencies to increase in the first world, as countries come apart. When third world countries try to pull off these types of money printing stunts to pay for public spending this almost always leads to their currency massively devaluing in exchange rate with more reputable currencies, as investors seek to dump the currency, and the country thereafter cannot afford to import anything or sell bonds denoted in its own currency. In extreme cases, such as Zimbabwe or Venezuela, this even causes inflation within the country itself, as citizens want to dump the currency in favour of rare metals, the US dollar

(Haslam & Lamberti, 2014), and perhaps even cryptocurrencies going into the future—though a volatile store of wealth, it is an extremely useful form of wealth for evading seizures by a third world governments and moving wealth beyond their jurisdiction.

Ultimately, with regard to the aforementioned continuing rounds of 'loser countries' we're predicting to fall, as we march into the future decade by decade, we might realistically expect this to be the fate of any monetary system they try to set up in order to pay for unsustainable expenditure. Their currencies will become worth less than the paper they're printed on, trade will occur, even if illegally, in terms of other countries' currencies, rare metals, or cryptocurrencies, and in that sense they will become truly bankrupt and destitute. More Venezuelas and Zimbabwes lie ahead.

Put again simply, there is a real economy, based on production, and a debt economy, based on confidence as well as on having far more resources than a nation needs. As a nation becomes less intelligent, it cannot produce sufficient resources anymore, confidence is lost, the debts are called in, the central banks will create more money, but what happens if confidence is lost even in these major currencies? This would be expected as the governments, reflecting lower intelligence, inspire less confidence. This has the potential to bring even further forward an economic collapse, resulting in the collapse of public services ministering to an increasingly sick and unintelligent population.

These are but a few scenarios of how, in more concrete terms, a collapse might come about. These would act as push factors, compelling even more relatively intelligent conservatives to make the 'Great Escape' to various Neo-Byzantiums.

Paradise

We can imagine a future poet, raised in a highly individualistic society and living in one of the refuges of civilization, penning verses that express the polar opposite of the sentiments in 'High Windows'. He will notice a young couple walking in the park and clearly getting along, though they will be chaperoned, obviously, with the chaperones watching them at a distance to ensure that nothing untoward occurs. They will, however, have no problem discussing issues such as 'race' or even the kinds of genetic, and even theological, factors which have meant that they are in the Neo-Byzantium and others are subject to, as they might put it, 'the full wrath of God'. The elderly poet will 'know' that this is 'paradise' and he will think about how all of those who would have interfered with this— the Social Justice Warriors, the Woke priests of the Church of

Multiculturalism—have 'gone down the long slide', and how you no longer have to 'sweat in the dark', fearing that they might 'cancel' you.

We can imagine that his society will perceive itself in Biblical terms, with God having rescued its people from the diabolical Babylon that surrounds it: 'For all nations have drunk the wine of the passion of her sexual immorality, and the kings of the earth have committed immorality with her, and the merchants of the earth have grown rich from the power of her luxurious living.' God will inspire him, or will have inspired his ancestors, to 'Come out of her, my people, lest you take part in her sins, lest you share in her plagues' (Revelation, 18:3).

But, as with Larkin, though in reverse, this old poet might also find himself nostalgic for a period of sexual freedom in which people could act on their sexual desires for each other with relatively little restraint, and in which everything was done to stop children having 'hurt feelings'—medals for taking part, only the weakest forms of discipline, always trying to 'understand' how people feel rather than judging them, at least within certain limits. You see, all of this will have 'gone down the long slide as well, like free bloody birds'. There'll be a very different kind of 'paradise' for a very different kind of people.

References

Adams, R. (1st May 2019). Cambridge college sacks researcher over links with far right. *The Guardian,* https://www.theguardian.com/education/2019/may/01/cambridge-university-college-dismisses-researcher-far-right-links-noah-carl

Adorno, T.W., Frenkel-Brunswik, E. & Levinson, D. (1950). *The Authoritarian Personality.* New York: Harper.

Aitken, R. (2020). *The Noble Liar: How and Why the BBC Distorts the News to Promote a Liberal Agenda.* London: Biteback.

Akcigit, U., Pearce, J.G. & Prato, M. (2020). *Tapping Into Talent: Coupling Education and Innovation Policies for Economic Growth.* Copenhagen: National Bureau of Economic Research.

Allen, M. & Jones, T. (Eds.). (2016). *Violence and Warfare Among Hunter-Gatherers.* London: Routledge.

Almlund, M., Duckworth, A., Heckman, J. & Kautz, T. (2011). Personality, psychology and economics. In Hanushek, S., Machin, S. & Woesmann, L. (Eds.). *Handbook of the Economics of Education.* Amsterdam: Elsevier.

Alvergne, A., Jokela, M. & Lummaa, V. (2010). Personality and reproductive success in a high-fertility human population. *Proceedings of the National Academy of Science,* 107: 11:745–750.

Amd, M. (2020). Reward omissions variably augment racial bias along political ideology. *PrePrints,* 2020100218, doi: 10.20944/preprints202010.0218.v1.

American Association for the Advancement of Science. (17th August 2008). Biracial Asian Americans and mental health. *EurekAlert!* https://www.eurekalert.org/pub_releases/2008-08/uoc--baa081108.php

Andersson, A.M., Jensen, T.K, Juul, A. et al. (2007). Secular decline in male testosterone and sex hormone binding globulin serum levels in Danish population surveys. *Journal of Clinical Endocrinology and Metabolism,* 92: 4696–4705.

Anguzu, G., Flynn, A., Musaazi, J. et al. (2019). Relationship between socio-economic status and risk of sexually transmitted infections in Uganda:

Multilevel analysis of a nationally representative survey. *International Journal of STD and AIDS,* 30: 284–291.
AP News. (14th January 2021). Powell's books says Andy Ngo's book will not be in store. *AP News.* https://apnews.com/article/portland-3dd2bc3ecc27be60a25c98eec18504fc
Apostolou, M. (2014). *Sexual Selection Under Parental Choice: The Evolution of Human Mating Behaviour.* Hove: Psychology Press.
Argyle, M. (1994). *The Psychology of Social Class.* London: Routledge.
Aschauer, W. & Mayerl, J. (2019). The dynamics of ethnocentrism in Europe. A comparison of enduring and emerging determinants of solidarity towards immigrants. *European Societies,* 21: 5.
Aston, M. (1967). *Thomas Arundel: A Study of Church Life in the Reign of Richard II.* Oxford: Clarendon Press.
Atherstone, A. (2015). *Reformation: A World in Turmoil.* Oxford: Lion Books.
Ayres, S. (31st December 2020). Renewed calls for 'Texit' are growing. Will they go anywhere? *Spectrum News,* https://spectrumlocalnews.com/tx/san-antonio/news/2020/12/31/there-s-talk-about--texit--swirling-again--will-it-go-anywhere-
Badcock, C. (2003). Mentalism and mechanism: Twin modes of human cognition. In Crawford, C. & Salman, C. (Eds). *Human Nature and Social Values: Implications of Evolutionary Psychology for Public Policy.* Mahwah, NJ: Erlbaum.
Banks, G., Batchelor, J. & Mcdaniel, M. (2010). Smarter people are (a bit) more symmetrical: A meta-analysis of the relationship between intelligence and fluctuating asymmetry. *Intelligence,* 38: 393–401.
Baron-Cohen, S. (2002). The extreme male brain theory of autism. *Trends in Cognitive Sciences* 6: 248–254.
Barrett, J. (2004). *Why Would Anyone Believe in God?* Lanham, MD: AltaMira Press.
BBC News. (9th June 2020). PG and Yorkshire Tea tell Black Lives Matter critics 'don't buy our tea'. https://www.bbc.com/news/business-52978990
BBC News. (17th July 2013). Same-sex marriage becomes law in England and Wales. https://www.bbc.com/news/uk-politics-23338279
BBC News. (8th July 2016). Women to serve in close combat roles in the British military. https://www.bbc.com/news/uk-36746917
BBC News. (30th October 2014). EDF France: Inquiry after drones buzz nuclear sites. https://www.bbc.com/news/world-europe-29831897
BBC News. (9th June 2021). Italy's plummeting birth rate worsened by pandemic. https://www.bbc.co.uk/news/world-europe-57396969
Barker, J. (2014). *1381: The Year of the Peasants' Revolt.* Cambridge, MA: Harvard University Press.

Beardmore, J.A. & Karimi-Booshehri, K. (1983). ABO genes are differentially distributed in socio-economic groups in England. *Nature,* 303: 522–524.

Beckett, A. (28th May 2019). 'A Zombie party': The deepening crisis of conservatism. *The Guardian,* https://www.theguardian.com/politics/2019/may/28/a-zombie-party-the-deepening-crisis-of-conservatism

Benedictow, O. (2006). *The Black Death, 1346–1353: The Complete History.* Woodbridge: The Boydell Press.

Benenson, J.F. (2013). The development of human female competition: Allies and adversaries. *Philosophical Transactions of the Royal Society B,* 368: 2013007920130079.

Berggren, N., Jordahl, H. & Poutvaara, P. (2017). The right look: Conservative politicians look better and voters reward it. *Journal of Public Economics,* 146: 79–86.

Bethlehem, R.A., Baron-Cohen, S., Van Honk, J., Auyeung, B., & Bos, P.A. (2014). The oxytocin paradox. *Frontiers in Behavioral Neuroscience,* 8, 48.

Betzig, L.L. (1986). *Despotism and Differential Reproduction: A Darwinian View of History.* London: Aldine Publishing Co.

Bierce, A. (2002). *The Unabridged Devil's Dictionary.* Atlanta, GA: University of Georgia Press.

Birrell, I. (22nd May 2021). California nightmare: How high taxes, rampant crime, suffocating wokery, streets littered with homeless addicts, and years of liberal policies are blamed for ruining the Golden State… as thousands of families flee to Republican Texas and Florida. *Mail Online,* https://www.dailymail.co.uk/news/article-9608111/How-high-taxes-rampant-crime-streets-littered-addicts-blamed-ruining-Golden-State.html

Blanchard, R. (2008). Review and theory of handedness, birth order, and homosexuality in men. *Laterality,* 13: 51–70.

Bloch, M. (1992). *Prey Into Hunter: The Politics of Religious Experience.* Cambridge: Cambridge University Press.

Bloom, N., Jones, C.I., Van Reenen, J. & Webb, M. (2020). Are ideas getting harder to find? *American Economic Review,* 110: 1104–1144.

Blum, D. & Holling, H. (2017). Spearman's law of diminishing returns: A meta-analysis. *Intelligence,* 65: 60–66.

Bobbio, N. (2016). *Left and Right: The Significance of a Political Distinction.* Hoboken, NJ: John Wiley & Sons.

Bongie, L. (1998). *Sade: A Biographical Essay.* Chicago, IL: University of Chicago Press.

Bonnell, V. & Freidin, G. (2015). Introduction. In Bonnell, V., Copper, A. & Freiden, G. (Eds.). *Russia at the Barricades: Eyewitness Accounts of the August 1991 Coup.* London: Routledge.

Booth, R. (11th July 2019). Acceptance of gay sex in decline in UK for first time since AIDS crisis. *The Guardian,* https://www.theguardian.com/society/2019/jul/11/acceptance-gay-sex-decline-uk-first-time-since-aids-crisis

Booy, O., Wade, M. & Roy, H. (2015). *Field Guide to Invasive Plants and Animals in Britain.* London: Bloomsbury.

Bowersock, G.W. (1997). *Julian the Apostate.* Cambridge, MA: Harvard University Press.

Bowlder, T. (1818). *The Family Shakespeare: In Which Nothing Is Added to the Original Text But Those Words and Expressions Are Omitted Which Cannot With Propriety Be Read Aloud In a Family.* London: Longman, Hurst, Rees, Orme, and Brown.

Bowles, N. (7th August 2020). Abolish the police? Those who survived the chaos in Seattle aren't so sure. *Chicago Tribune,* https://www.chicagotribune.com/nation-world/ct-nw-nyt-defund-the-police-seattle-20200807-ydg6r5gwwzgoble7xd5bld5yoq-story.html

Boycott, R. (10th March 2002). One man's war against his demons. *The Guardian,* https://www.theguardian.com/uk/2002/mar/10/politics.race

Boyer, P. (2001). *Religion Explained: The Human Instincts That Fashion Gods, Spirits and Ancestors.* London: Heinnemann.

Bradshaw, M. & Ellison, C. (2008). Do genetic factors influence religious life? Findings from a behavior genetic analysis of twin siblings. *Journal for the Scientific Study of Religion,* 47: 529–544.

Brant, A., Munakata, Y., Boomsma, D., et al. (2013). The nature and nurture of high IQ: An extended sensitive period for intellectual development. *Psychological Science,* 24: 1487–1495.

Bratter, J. & King, R. (2008). 'But will it last?' Marital instability among interracial and same-race couples. *Family Relations,* 67: 160–171.

Brickman, W. (1960). *Introduction to the History of International Relations in Higher Education.* New York: New York University.

Brown, C. (2001). *The Death of Christian Britain: Understanding Secularisation, 1800–2000.* London: Routledge.

Bruce, S. (2002). *God is Dead: Secularisation in the West.* Oxford: Blackwell.

Bruce, S. (2001). Christianity in Britain: RIP. *Sociology of Religion,* 62: 191–203.

Buchanan, P. (2010). *Playing with Fire: The Controversial Career of Hans J. Eysenck.* Oxford: Oxford University Press.

Burger, O. & DeLong, J.P. (2016). What if fertility decline is not permanent? The need for an evolutionarily informed approach to understanding low fertility. *Philosophical Transactions of the Royal Society B: Biological Sciences,* 371(1692): 20150157.

Buss, D. (1989). *The Evolution of Desire: Strategies of Human Mating.* New York: Basic Books.

Cain, P.J. & Hopkins, A.G. (2014). *British Imperialism: 1688–2000*. London: Routledge.

Camden, L. & Gaetz Duarte, S. (2006). *Mennonites in Texas: The Quiet in the Land*. College Station, TX: Texas A & M University.

Campbell, J. (1991). The lost centuries: 400–600. In Campbell, J. (Ed.). *The Anglo-Saxons*. London: Penguin.

Carl, N. (22nd July 2021). Wokeness as a bootlegger-baptist coalition. *Noah's Newsletter,* https://noahcarl.substack.com/p/wokeness-as-a-bootlegger-baptist

Carl, N. (2017). Lackademia: Why do Academics lean left? *Square Space*. London: Adam Smith Institute.

Carl, N. & Woodley of Menie, M.A. (2019). A scientometric analysis of controversies in the field of intelligence research. *Intelligence, 77*: 101397.

Carl, N. & Billari, F. (2014). Generalized trust and intelligence in the United States. *PLOS One, 9*(3): e91786.

Carrington, R.C. (1859). Description of a singular appearance seen in the Sun on September 1, 1859. *Monthly Notices of the Royal Astronomical Society, 20*: 13–15.

Casey, T. (2002). *The Social Context of Economic Change in Britain: Between Policy and Performance*. Manchester: Manchester University Press.

Castleden, R. (2002). *Minoans: Life in Bronze Age Crete*. London: Routledge.

Cattell, R. (1938). Some changes in social life in a community with a falling intelligence quotient. *British Journal of Psychology, 28*: 330–450.

Centola, D., Becker, J., Brackbill, D. & Baronchelli, A. (2018). Experimental evidence for tipping points in social convention. *Science, 360*: 1116–1119.

Chagnon, N. (1968). *Yanomamö: The Fierce People*. New York: Holt, Rinehart and Winston.

Charlton, B.G. (20th July 2015). Mutation accumulation and modern Western sexuality. *Intelligence, Personality and Genius,* https://iqpersonalitygenius.blogspot.com/2015/07/mutation-accumulation-and-modern.html

Charlton, B.G. (25th July 2013). The Head Girl Syndrome—the opposite of creative genius. *Intelligence, Personality and Genius,* http://iqpersonalitygenius.blogspot.com/2013/07/the-head-girl-syndrome-opposite-of.html

Charlton, B.G. (2009). Clever sillies: Why high IQ people tend to be deficient in common sense. *Medical Hypotheses, 73*: 867–870.

Chowdry, H., Crawford, C., Dearden, L., Goodman, A. & Vignoles., A. (2010). *Widening Participation in Higher Education*. London: ESRC.

Cinar, Y. (2018). *From Conflict to Peace. Rehabilitation Process in the Phase of Transforming Conflict: The Case of Northern Ireland*. Hamburg: Anchor Academic Publishing.

Clark, G. (2014). *The Son Also Rises: Surnames and the History of Social Mobility.* Princeton, NJ: Princeton University Press.

Clark, G. (2007). *A Farewell to Alms: A Brief Economic History of the World.* Princeton, NJ: Princeton University Press.

Clark, P. (2008). *The Chinese Cultural Revolution: A History.* Cambridge: Cambridge University Press.

Clark, V. & Tuffin, K. (2015). Choosing housemates and justifying age, gender and ethnic discrimination. *Australian Journal of Psychology,* 67: 20–28.

Clarke-Ezzidio, H. (20th April 2021). Why we need to talk about 'global weirding'. *The New Statesman,* https://www.newstatesman.com/politics/environment/2021/04/why-we-need-talk-about-global-weirding

Cline, E. (2021). *1177 B.C: The Year Civilization Collapsed.* Princeton, NJ: Princeton University Press.

CNN Business. (15th July 2021). Minimum wage workers can't afford rent anywhere in America. https://edition.cnn.com/2021/07/15/homes/rent-affordability-minimum-wage/index.html

Cochran, G. & Harpending, H. (2009). *The 10,000 Year Explosion: How Civilization Accelerated Evolution.* New York: Basic Books.

Coffey, J. (2014). *Persecution and Toleration in Protestant England 1558–1689.* London: Routledge.

Coleman, V. (1996). *Adela Pankhurst: The Wayward Suffragette 1885–1961.* Melbourne: Melbourne University Press.

Collins, P. (2000). *From Egypt to Babylon: The International Age 1550–500 BC.* Cambridge, MA: Harvard University Press.

Collins, J. & Page, L. (2019). The heritability of fertility makes world population stabilization unlikely in the foreseeable future. *Evolution and Human Behavior,* 40: 105–111.

Committee on Finance. (1996). *Welfare Reform Wrap-up: Hearing Before the Committee on Finance, United States Senate, One Hundred Fourth Congress, First Session, April 27, 1995.* Washington, DC: United States Printing Office.

Conway, L., Gornick, L., Houck, S. et al. (2015). Are conservatives really more simple-minded than liberals? The domain specificity of complex thinking. *Political Psychology,* https://doi.org/10.1111/pops.12304

Cornelis, I., Van Hiel, A., Roets, A. & Kossowska, M. (2008). Age differences in conservatism: Evidence on the mediating effects of personality and cognitive style. *Journal of Personality,* 77: 51–58.

Costello, T., Bowes, S., Stevens, S. et al. (2021). Clarifying the structure and nature of left-wing authoritarianism. *Journal of Personality and Social Psychology,* doi: 10.1037/pspp0000341.

Crosby, A. (2015). *Germs, Seeds and Animals: Studies in Ecological History.* London: Routledge.

Cucinotta, F. & Cacao, E. (2017). Non-targeted effects models predict significantly higher mars mission cancer risk than targeted effects models. *Scientific Reports*, 7: 1832.

Dagnall, N., Drinkwater, K., Parker, A. et al. (2015). Conspiracy theory and cognitive style: A worldview. *Frontiers in Psychology*, 6: 206.

Dalio, R. (2012). How the economic machine works. *Economic Principles*. https://economicprinciples.org/

Dalio, R. (15th March 2021). Why in the world would you own dollar debt. *LinkedIn*, https://www.linkedin.com/pulse/why-world-would-you-own-bonds-when-ray-dalio/

Daly, M. & Wilson, M. (1988). *Homicide*. New Brunswick, NJ: Transaction Publishers.

Dattel, G. (2019). Separatism vs. integration: Can separate ever be equal? *Academic Questions*: 476–486.

Davids, K. (2014). The scholarly Atlantic: Circuits of knowledge between Britain, the Dutch Republic and the Americas in the eighteenth century. In Oostindie, G. & Roitman, J. (Eds.). *Dutch Atlantic Connections, 1680–1800*. Leiden: BRILL.

Day, J. (2015). Bertrand Russell on Eugenics. *Mankind Quarterly*, 55: 254–267.

Day, V. (2018). *Jordanetics: A Journey into the Mind of Humanity's Greatest Thinker*. Lugano, Switzerland: Castalia House.

De Benoist, A. (2004). *On Being a Pagan*. Atlanta, GA: Ultra (Trans. Graham, J.).

De Castella, T. (23rd February 2011). Council cuts: Just what is a 'non-job'? *BBC News*, https://www.bbc.com/news/magazine-12549785

Deary, I., Harris, S. & Hill, W.D. (2019). What genome-wide association studies reveal about the association between intelligence and physical health, illness, and mortality. *Current Opinion in Psychology*, 27: 6–12.

deHaven-Smith, L. (2013). *Conspiracy Theory in America*. Austin, TX: University of Texas Press.

Demeneix, B. (2014). *Losing Our Minds: How Environmental Pollution Impairs Human Intelligence and Mental Health*. Oxford: Oxford University Press.

Desilver, D. (7th August 2018). For most U.S. workers, real wages have barely budged in decades. *Pew Research Center*, https://www.pewresearch.org/fact-tank/2018/08/07/for-most-us-workers-real-wages-have-barely-budged-for-decades/

Dever, W. (2006). *Who Were the Early Israelites and Where Did They Come From?* Grand Rapids, MI: Wm. B. Eerdmans Publishing.

DeVore, C. (1st June 2021). New poll finds all those people moving to Texas aren't going to be voting for Democrats. *The Federalist*, https://thefederalist.com/2021/06/01/new-poll-finds-all-those-people-moving-to-texas-arent-going-to-be-voting-for-democrats/

Dhar, S. (1st May 2021). 'Apocalyptic' second wave of COVID-19 in India leaves families hunting for oxygen. *USA Today,* https://eu.usatoday.com/in-depth/news/world/2021/04/30/india-covid-19-crisis-oxygen-scarce-bodies-burning-through-night/7410583002/

Dhejne, C., Van Vlerken, R., Heylens, G. & Arcelus, J. (2016). Mental health and gender dysphoria: A review of the literature. *International Review of Psychiatry,* 28: 44–57.

DiAngelo, R. (2018). *White Fragility: Why It's So Hard for White People to Talk About Racism.* Boston, MA: Beacon Press.

Dockray, K. & Sutton, A. (2017). *Politics, Society and Homosexuality in Post-War Britain: The Sexual Offences Act of 1967 and Its Significance.* Stroud: Fonthill Media.

Dodds, B. (2008) Patterns of decline: Arable production in England, France and Castile, 1370–1450. In Dodds, B. & Britnell, R. (Eds.). *Agriculture and Rural Society After the Black Death: Common Themes and Regional Variations.* Hatfield: University of Hertfordshire Press.

Doebler, S. (2015). Relationships between religion and two forms of homonegativity in Europe: A multilevel analysis of effects of believing, belonging and religious practice. *PLOS ONE,* 10(8): e0133538.

Dolezal, R. (2017). *In Full Color: Finding My Place in a Black and White World.* Dallas, TX: BenBella Books.

Dorril, S. (2006). *Black Shirt: Sir Oswald Mosley and British Fascism.* London: Viking.

Doyle, A. (17th December 2020). University 'safe spaces'? They're a danger to us all: As a study reveals freedom of speech is under dire threat, ANDREW DOYLE, who has faced 'woke' disdain, blasts back. *Mail Online,* https://www.dailymail.co.uk/news/article-9065713/ANDREW-DOYLE-University-safe-spaces-theyre-danger-all.html

Doyle, A. (24th January 2019). We need a new alternative-comedy movement: Today's woke comics pose as edgy and anti-establishment. They're neither. *Spiked,* https://www.spiked-online.com/2019/01/24/we-need-a-new-alternative-comedy-movement/?fbclid=IwAR1DsDikvgHrEv6xDjwAc2FSDO-8VDNRNv6raFS7iRw9Td9Hnf4catrVf04

Doyle, J. (2nd August 2019). I want criminals to be terrified, says Priti Patel. *Mail Online,* https://www.dailymail.co.uk/news/article-7316055/I-want-criminals-terrified-says-Priti-Patel-Home-Secretary-restore-confidence-Britain.html

Draper, R. (29th August 2020). Premier League set to speak to club captains about keeping the Black Lives Matter slogan on players' shirts amid increased scrutiny of the movement. *Mail Online,* https://www.dailymail.co.uk/sport/football/article-8677473/Premier-League-speak-captains-keeping-Black-Lives-Matter-slogan-shirts-season.html

Drews, R. (2020). *The End of the Bronze Age: Changes in Warfare and the Catastrophe ca. 1200 B.C.* Princeton, NJ: Princeton University Press.

Dutton, E. (2021a). Obituary: James Robert Flynn. *Mankind Quarterly,* 61: 773–779.

Dutton, E. (2021b). *Witches, Feminism and the Fall of the West.* Whitefish, MT: Radix.

Dutton, E. (2020a). *Making Sense of Race.* Whitefish, MT: Washington Summit Publishing.

Dutton, E. (2020b). The next great awakening. *National Policy Institute,* https://nationalpolicy.institute/2020/06/27/the-next-great-awakening/

Dutton, E. (2019a). *Race Differences in Ethnocentrism.* London: Arktos.

Dutton, E. (2019b). *Churchill's Headmaster: The 'Sadist' Who Nearly Saved the British Empire.* Melbourne: Manticore Press.

Dutton, E. (2017). The male brain, testosterone and sex differences in professional achievement. *Mankind Quarterly,* 58: 93–100.

Dutton, E. (2014). *Religion and Intelligence: An Evolutionary Analysis.* London: Ulster Institute for Social Research.

Dutton, E. (2013a). The cultural mediation hypothesis: A critical examination. *Intelligence,* 41: 321–327.

Dutton, E. (2013b). The philosophy of anthropology. *Internet Encyclopedia of Philosophy,* https://iep.utm.edu/anthropo/

Dutton, E. (2008a). Death metaphors in the secularisation debate: Towards criteria for successful social scientific analogies. *Sociological Research,* 6: 8.

Dutton, E. (2008b). *Meeting Jesus at University: Rites of Passage and Student Evangelicals.* Aldershot: Ashgate.

Dutton, E. & Madison, G. (2020a). Spare the rod and spoil the group's cultural fitness? Conditions under which corporal punishment leads to detrimental and beneficial outcomes. *Medical Hypotheses,* 145: 110334.

Dutton, E. & Madison, G. (2020b). Gender dysphoria and transgender identity is associated with physiological and psychological masculinization: A theoretical integration of findings, supported by systematic reviews. *Sexuality Research and Social Policy,* https://doi.org/10.1007/s13178-020-00489-z

Dutton, E. & Madison, G. (2018). Execution, violent punishment and selection for religiousness in Medieval England. *Evolutionary Psychological Science,* 4: 83–89.

Dutton, E. & Woodley of Menie, M. A. (2018). *At Our Wits' End: Why We're Becoming Less Intelligent and What It Means for the Future.* Exeter: Imprint Academic.

Dutton, E., Madison, G. & Dunkel, C. (2018). The mutant says in his heart, 'There is no God': The rejection of collective religiosity centred around the worship of moral gods is associated with high mutational load. *Evolutionary Psychological Science,* 4: 233–244.

Dutton, E. & Van der Linden, D. (2017). Why is intelligence negatively associated with religiousness *Evolutionary Psychological Science,* 3: 392–403.

Dutton, E., Van der Linden, D. & Lynn, R. (2016). The Negative Flynn Effect: A systematic literature review *Intelligence,* 59: 163–169.

Dutton, E. & Van der Linden, D. (2015). Who are the 'clever sillies'? The intelligence, personality, and motives of clever silly originators and those who follow them. *Intelligence,* 49: 57–65.

Dutton, E. & Charlton, B.G. (2015). *The Genius Famine.* Buckingham: University of Buckingham Press.

Eatwell, R. & Goodwin, M. (2018). *National Populism and the Revolt Against Liberal Democracy.* London: Penguin.

Eliade, M. (1957). *The Sacred and the Profane: The Nature of Religion.* London: Routledge.

Eliot, T.S. (1957). *On Poetry and Poets.* London: Faber and Faber.

Ellis, F. (2004). *Political Correctness and the Theoretical Struggle: From Lenin and Mao to Marcus and Foucault.* Auckland: Maxim Institute.

Eysenck, H.J. (1954). *The Psychology of Politics.* London: Routledge.

Eysenck, H.J. (1981). Left-wing authoritarianism: Myth or reality? *Political Psychology,* 3: 234–238.

Fain, E. & Weatherford, C. (2016). Comparative study of millennials' (age 20-34 years) grip and lateral pinch with the norms. *Journal of Hand Therapy,* 29: 483–488.

Felter, C. (15th November 2019). The end of antibiotics. *Council of Foreign Relations,* https://www.cfr.org/backgrounder/end-antibiotics

Ferguson, N. (2008). *The Ascent of Money: A Financial History of the World.* London: Penguin.

Fernandez-Pujals, A., Adams, M., Thomson, P. et al. (2015). Epidemiology and heritability of major depressive disorder, stratified by age of onset, sex, and illness course in generation Scotland: Scottish family health study (GS:SFHS). *PLOS ONE,* 10(11): e0142197.

Fernandes, H., Lynn, R. & Hertler, S. (2018). Race differences in anxiety disorders, worry and social anxiety: An examination of the Differential-K Theory in social psychology. *Mankind Quarterly,* 58: 466–500.

Festinger, L. (1957). *A Theory of Cognitive Dissonance.* Evanston, IN: Rowe and Peterson.

Fieder, M. & Huber, S. (2018). Political attitude and fertility: Is there a selection for the political extreme? *Frontiers in Psychology,* https://doi.org/10.3389/fpsyg.2018.02343

Fienup-Riordan, A. (1990). *Eskimo Essays: Yup'ik Lives and How We See Them.* New Brunswick, NJ: Rutgers University Press.

Figueredo, A.J., Andrzejczak, D., Jones, D., Smith-Castro, V. & Montero, E. (2011). Reproductive strategy and ethnic conflict: Slow Life History as a protective factor against negative ethnocentrism in two contemporary societies. *Journal of Social, Evolutionary and Cultural Psychology*, 5: 14–31.

Fitzgerald, J. (22nd March 2019). Technical change has probably meant loss of more unskilled jobs than globalisation. *The Irish Times*, https://www.irishtimes.com/business/economy/technical-change-has-probably-meant-loss-of-more-unskilled-jobs-than-globalisation-1.3834224

Flaherty, C. (29th August 2018). 'TERF' war. *Inside Higher Ed*, https://www.insidehighered.com/news/2018/08/29/philosophers-object-journals-publication-terf-reference-some-feminists-it-really

Flynn, J.R. (2016). *Does Your Family Make You Smarter? Nature, Nurture and Human Autonomy*. Cambridge: Cambridge University Press.

Flynn, J.R. (2012). *Are We Getting Smarter? Rising IQ in the Twenty-First Century*. Cambridge: Cambridge University Press.

Flynn, J.R. & Shayer, M. (2018). IQ decline and Piaget: Does the rot start at the top? *Intelligence*, 66: 112–121.

Ford, M. (2015). *Rise of the Robots: Technology and the Threat of a Jobless Future*. New York: Basic Books.

Ford, M. (22nd January 2021). We regret to inform you that Republicans are talking about secession again. *The New Republic*, https://newrepublic.com/article/161023/republicans-secede-texas-wyoming-brexit

Fox, D. (2020). *Antisocial, Narcissistic, and Borderline Personality Disorders: A New Conceptualization of Development, Reinforcement, Expression, and Treatment*. London: Routledge.

Fox, K. (2004). *Watching the English: The Hidden Rules of English Behaviour*. London: Routledge.

Friedersdorf, C. (26th May 2016). The perils of writing a provocative email at Yale. *The Atlantic*, https://www.theatlantic.com/politics/archive/2016/05/the-peril-of-writing-a-provocative-email-at-yale/484418/

Fromherz, A. (2010). *Ibn Khaldun, Life and Times*. Edinburgh: Edinburgh University Press.

Funk, C., Tyson, A., Kennedy, B. & Johnson, C. (10th December 2020). Biotechnology research viewed with caution globally, but most support gene editing for babies to treat disease. *Pew Research Center*, https://www.pewresearch.org/science/2020/12/10/biotechnology-research-viewed-with-caution-globally-but-most-support-gene-editing-for-babies-to-treat-disease/

Fyson, N. (1977). *Growing Up in the Eighteenth Century*. London: Batsford.

Gabb, S. (2009). Democratic art: The non-poetry of Carol Ann Duffy. *Free Life Commentary*, 186.

Gabb, S. (2007). *Culture Revolution, Culture War: How the Conservatives Lost England and How to Get It Back.* London: Hampden Press.

Galton, F. (1904). Eugenics: Its definition, scope and aims. *American Journal of Sociology,* 10: 1.

Galton, F. (1869). *Hereditary Genius.* London: Macmillan.

Galton, F. (1865). Hereditary talent and character. *MacMillan's Magazine,* 12. (June–August).

Ganley, C., Mingle, L., Ryan, A. et al. (2013). An examination of stereotype threat effects on girls' mathematics performance. *Developmental Psychology,* 49: 1886–1897.

Garcia, G., Hedwig, T., Hanson, B. et al. (2019). The relationship between mixed race/ethnicity, developmental assets, and mental health among youth. *Journal of Racial and Ethnic Health Disparities,* 6: 77–85.

Gardner, H. (1983). *Frames of Mind: The Theory of Multiple Intelligences.* New York: Basic Books.

Gebauer, J., Bleidorn, W., Gosling, S. et al. (2014). Cross-cultural variations in Big Five relationships with religiosity: A sociocultural motives perspective. *Journal of Personality and Social Psychology,* 107: 1064–1091.

Geher, G. & Wedberg, N. (2019). *Positive Evolutionary Psychology: Darwin's Guide to Living a Richer Life.* Oxford: Oxford University Press.

Gladden, P. & Cleator, A. (2018). Slow Life History predicts six moral foundations. *EvoS Journal,* SEEPS II: 43–63.

Glenn, N. (1974). Aging and conservatism. *Annals of the American Academy of Political and Social Science,* 415: 176–186.

Glubb, J.B. (1976). *The Fate of Empires and the Search for Survival.* Edinburgh: William Blackwood & Sons.

Goad, J. (2017). *The New Church Ladies: The Extremely Uptight World of Social Justice.* Stone Mountain, GA: Obnoxious Books.

Gobry, P.E. (15th December 2019). A science-based case for ending the porn epidemic. *American Greatness,* https://eppc.org/publications/a-science-based-case-for-ending-the-porn-epidemic/

Goodhart, D. (2017). *The Road to Somewhere: The New Tribes Shaping British Politics.* London: Penguin.

Gottfried, P. (2004). *Multiculturalism and the Politics of Guilt: Towards a Secular Theocracy.* Columbia, MO: University of Missouri Press.

Graeber, D. (2014). *Debt: The First 5000 Years.* New York: Melville House.

Graham, J., Haidt, J. & Nosek, B. (2012). The moral stereotypes of liberals and conservatives: Exaggeration of differences across the political spectrum. *PLOS ONE,* https://doi.org/10.1371/journal.pone.0050092

Graham, J., Haidt, J. & Nosek, B. (2009). Liberals and conservatives rely on different sets of moral foundations. *Personality Processes and Individual Differences,* 96: 1029–1046.

Grant, D. (13th October 2019). Population decline in Central and Eastern Europe. *Global Risk Insights.* https://globalriskinsights.com/2019/10/population-decline-in-central-and-eastern-europe/

Grant, R. & Montrose, V.T. (2018). It's a man's world: Mate guarding and the evolution of patriarchy. *Mankind Quarterly,* 58: 384–418.

Green, D. (18th November 2019). The Groypers are American Fascists. *The Spectator,* https://spectator.us/groypers-american-fascists/

Grzanka, P., Frantwell, K. & Fassinger, R. (2019). The White Racial Affect Scale (WRAS): A measure of white guilt, shame, and negation. *The Counselling Psychologist,* 48: 47–77.

Gutiérrez, F., Gárriz, M., Peri, J. et al. (2013). Fitness costs and benefits of personality disorder traits. *Evolution and Human Behavior,* 34: 41–48.

Hackett Fischer, D. (1996). *The Great Wave: Price Revolutions and the Rhythm of History.* Oxford: Oxford University Press.

Hackett Fischer, D. (1989). *Albion's Seed: Four British Folkways in America.* Oxford: Oxford University Press.

Hackett Fischer, D. (1970). *Toward a Logic of Historical Thought.* New York: Harper Row.

Haddock, V. (17th September 2006). Republicans' fertile future: Through the past three decades, conservatives have been procreating more than liberals. *SF Gate,* https://www.sfgate.com/opinion/article/Republicans-fertile-future-Through-the-past-2488626.php

Haidt, J. (2012). *The Righteous Mind: Why Good People Are Divided By Politics and Religion.* London: Penguin.

Halligan, L. (11th July 2020). Quantitative easing is a dangerous addiction. *The Spectator.*

Hamilton, W.D. (1996). *The Narrow Roads of Gene Land.* Oxford: Oxford University Press.

Hamilton, W.D. (1964). The genetical evolution of social behaviour: I and II. *Journal of Theoretical Biology,* 7: 1–52.

Hammond, R. & Axelrod, R. (2006). The evolution of ethnocentric behavior. *Journal of Conflict Resolution,* 50: 1–11.

Hampton, R. (30th September 2019). How 'Rest in Power' went from radical eulogy to kitschy Twitter meme. *Slate,* https://slate.com/culture/2019/09/rest-in-power-phrase-history-appropriation-black-activists.html

Harbison, E.H. (2013). *The Age of Reformation.* Ithaca, NY: Cornell University Press.

Harding, A.F. (2000). *European Societies in the Bronze Age.* Cambridge: Cambridge University Press.

Hare, R. (2011). *Without Conscience: The Disturbing World of Psychopaths Among Us.* New York: The Guildford Press.

Harman, H. (2017). *A Woman's Work.* London: Penguin.

Haslam, P. & Lamberti, R. (2014). *When Money Destroys Nations*. London: Penguin.

Hatemi, P. & McDermott, R. (2012). The genetics of politics: Discovery, challenges, and progress. *Trends in Genetics,* 28: 525–533.

Hatemi, P., Medland, S., Klemmensen, R. et al. (2014). Genetic influences on political ideologies: Twin analyses of 19 measures of political ideologies from five democracies and genome-wide findings from three populations. *Behavioral Genetics,* 44: 282–294.

Hawrylycz, J.M., Lein, E.S., Guillozet-Bongaarts, A.L., Shen, E.H., Ng, L., Miller, J.A. & Jones, A.R. (2012). An anatomically comprehensive atlas of the adult human brain transcriptome. *Nature,* 489: 391–399.

Hayford, S. & Morgan, S.P. (2008). Religiosity and fertility in the United States: The role of fertility intentions. *Social Forces,* 86: 1163–1188.

Heath, J.M. (2017). *Warfare in Neolithic Europe: An Archaeological and Anthropological Analysis*. Barnsley: Pen and Sword.

Helgason, A., Palsson, S., Gudbjartsson, D. et al. (2008). An association between the kinship and fertility of human couples. *Science,* 319: 813–816.

Herman, E. & Chomsky, N. (1988). *Manufacturing Consent: The Political Economy of the Mass Media,* New York: Pantheon Books.

Herman, A. (2000). *Joseph McCarthy: Reexamining the Life and Legacy of America's Most Hated Senator*. New York: Simon & Schuster.

Herrnstein, R. & Murray, C. (1994). *The Bell Curve: Intelligence and Class Structure in American Life*. New York: Free Press.

Hertler, S.C., Figueredo, A.J. & Peñaherrera Aguirre, M. (2020). *Multilevel Selection: Theoretical Foundations, Historical Examples, and Empirical Evidence*. New York: Palgrave Macmillan.

Hey, V. (2002). Be(long)ing: New Labour, New Britain and the 'Dianaization' of politics. In Kear, A. & Steinberg, D. (Eds.). *Mourning Diana: Nation, Culture and the Performance of Grief*. London: Routledge.

Hicks, S.R.C. (2004). *Explaining Postmodernism: Skepticism and Socialism from Rousseau to Foucault*. Tempe, AZ: Scholargy Publishing, Inc.

Hill, F. (11th January 2021). Yes, it was a coup attempt. Here's why. *Politico,* https://www.politico.com/news/magazine/2021/01/11/capitol-riot-self-coup-trump-fiona-hill-457549

Hills, P., Francis, L., Argyle, M. & Jackson, C. (2004). Primary personality trait correlates of religious practice and orientation. *Personality and Individual Differences,* 36: 61–73.

Hitsch, G., Hortacsu, A. & Ariely, D. (2010). What makes you click?—Mate preferences in online dating. *Quantitative Marketing and Economics*, 8: 393–427.

Holbrook, C., Izuma, K., Deblieck, C., Fessler, D. & Iacoboni, M. (2016). Neuromodulation of group prejudice and religious belief. *Social Cognitive and Affective Neuroscience*, 11: 387–394.

Holden, M. (4th May 2016). Jewish leaders call for UK's Labour Party to act on anti-Semitism 'cancer.' *Reuters*, https://www.reuters.com/article/us-britain-politics-antisemitism-idUSKCN0XV1NY

Holmes, A. (2016). *The Church of England and Divorce in the Twentieth Century: Legalism and Grace*. London: Routledge.

Horner, W. (1993). *Nineteenth-century Scottish Rhetoric: The American Connection*. Carbondale, IL: Southern Illinois University Press.

Huebner, J. (2005a). A possible declining trend for worldwide innovation. *Technological Forecasting and Social Change*, 72: 980–986.

Huebner, J. (2005b). Response by Jonathan Huebner. *Technological Forecasting and Social Change*, 72: 980–986.

Hugh-Jones, D. & Abdellaoui, A. (2021). *Natural Selection in Contemporary Humans is Linked to Income and Substitution Effects* (No. 2021-02). School of Economics, University of East Anglia.

Hui, C.H., Cheung, S.-H., Lam, J., Lau, E.Y.Y., Cheung, S.-F. & Yuliawati, L. (2018). Psychological changes during faith exit: A three-year prospective study. *Psychology of Religion and Spirituality*, 10: 103–118.

Hunt, E. (12th March 2019). BirthStrikers: meet the women who refuse to have children until climate change ends. *The Guardian*, https://www.theguardian.com/lifeandstyle/2019/mar/12/birthstrikers-meet-the-women-who-refuse-to-have-children-until-climate-change-ends

Ireland, P. (2010). A new Keynesian perspective on the great recession. *National Bureau of Economic Research*, doi:10.3386/w16420.

Iyer, R., Koleva, S., Graham, J. Ditto, P. & Haidt, J. (2012) Understanding libertarian morality: The Psychological dispositions of self-identified libertarians. *PLOS ONE*, 7(8): e42366.

Jacobsen, R., Møller, H., & Mouritsen, A. (1999). Natural variation in the human sex ratio. *Human Reproduction*, 14: 3120–3125.

Jacobson, G. (2019). *Presidents and Parties in the Public Mind*. Chicago, IL: University of Chicago Press.

Jack, A., Friedman, J., Boyatzis, R. & Taylor, S. (2016). Why do you believe in God? Relationships between religious belief, analytic thinking, mentalizing and moral concern. *PLOS ONE*, 11: e0155283.

Jenkins, S. (2006). *Thatcher and Sons: A Revolution in Three Acts*. London: Penguin.

Jensen, A.R. (1998). *The g Factor: The Science of Mental Ability*. Westport, CT: Praeger.

Jensen, A.R. (1972). *Genetics and Education*. London: Methuen.

Joiner, T.E. (1994). Contagious depression: Existence, specificity to depressed symptoms, and the role of reassurance seeking. *Journal of Personal and Social Psychology,* 67: 287–296.

Jokela, M. (2012). Birth-cohort effects in the association between personality and fertility. *Psychological Science,* 23: 835–841.

Jolfei, A., Meybodi, A. & Hajebi, A. (2014). The frequency of personality disorders in patients with gender identity disorder. *Medical Journal of the Islamic Republic of Iran,* 28: 90.

Jones, C. (2019). *Fighting With Pride: LGBTQ in the Armed Forces.* Barnsley: Pen & Sword Books.

Jones, T., Yeager, R., Fletcher, A., Dor, J. & Dolan, T. (2004). *Who Murdered Geoffrey Chaucer? A Medieval Mystery.* London: Methuen.

Justice, S. (1996). *Writing and Rebellion: England in 1381.* Los Angeles, CA: University of California Press.

Kakkad, J., Palmou, C., Britto, D. & Browne, J. (2021). *Anywhere Jobs: Reshaping the Geography of Work.* London: Tony Blair Institute for Global Change.

Kanazawa, S. (2014). Intelligence and childlessness. *Social Science Research,* 48: 157–170.

Kanazawa, S. (2012). *The Intelligence Paradox: Why the Intelligent Choice Isn't Always the Smart One.* Hoboken, NJ: John Wiley & Sons.

Karpinski, R., Kolbe, A., Tetreault, N. & Borowski, T. (2018). High intelligence: A risk factor for psychological and physiological overexcitabilities. *Intelligence,* 66: 8–23.

Kaufman, S., DeYoung, C., Reiss, D. & Gray, J. (2011). General intelligence predicts reasoning ability for evolutionarily familiar content. *Intelligence,* 39: 311–322.

Kaufmann, E. (8th July 2020). Are young people turning to the right? *UnHerd,* https://unherd.com/2020/07/are-the-jordan-peterson-generation-of-zoomers-turning-right/

Kaufmann, E. (22nd June 2020). The great awokening and the second American Revolution. *Quillette,* https://quillette.com/2020/06/22/toward-a-new-cultural-nationalism/

Kaufmann, E. (2019). *Whiteshift: Populism, Immigration and the Future of White Majorities.* London: Penguin.

Kaufmann, E. (2010). *Shall the Religious Inherit the Earth? Demography and Politics in the Twenty-First Century.* London: Profile Books.

Kelion, J. (5th January 2021). TalkRadio: YouTube reverses decision to ban channel. *BBC News.* https://www.bbc.com/news/technology-55544205

Kerry, N. & Murray, D. (2018). Conservative parenting: Investigating the relationships between parenthood, moral judgment, and social conservatism. *Personality and Individual Differences,* 134: 88–96.

Kiernan, B. (2008). *Blood and Soil: A World History of Genocide and Extermination from Sparta to Darfur*. New Haven, CT: Yale University Press.

Kilkelly, U. (2017). *The Child and the European Convention on Human Rights*. London: Routledge.

Kirkegaard, E. (2020). Mental illness and the left. *Mankind Quarterly*, 60: 487–510.

Kirkegaard, E. (2013). Predicting immigrant IQ from their countries of origin and Lynn's National IQs: A case study from Denmark. *Mankind Quarterly*, 54: 151–167.

Koenig, H. (2012). Religion, spirituality, and health: The research and clinical implications. *ISRN Psychiatry*, http://dx.doi.org/10.5402/2012/278730

Kolk, M., Cownden, D. & Enquist, M. (2014). Correlations in fertility across generations: can low fertility persist? *Proceedings of the Royal Society B: Biological Sciences*, 281(1779): 20132561.

Kondrashov, A. (2017). *Crumbling Genome: The Impact of Deleterious Mutations on Humans*. Hoboken, NJ: John Wiley & Sons.

Kong, A., Frigge, M., Thorleifsson, G. et al. (2017). Selection against variants in the genome associated with educational attainment. *PNAS*, 114: 727–732.

Koole, S., McCullough, M., Kuhl, J. et al. (2010). Why religion's burdens are light: From religiosity to implicit self-regulation. *Personality and Psychology Review*, 14: 95–107.

Kuzawa, C. & Bragg, J. (2012). Plasticity in Human Life History Strategy: Implications for contemporary human variation and the evolution of genus *Homo*. *Current Anthropology*, 53: 369–383.

Lacey, R. & Danziger, D. (1999). *The Year 1000: What Life Was Like at the Turn of the First Millennium*. London: Little, Brown and Company.

Lahey, S.E. (2008). *John Wyclif*. Oxford: Oxford University Press.

Landry, A., Ihm, E., Kwit, S. & Schooler, J. (2021). Metadehumanization erodes democratic norms during the 2020 presidential election. *Analyses of Social Issues and Public Policy*, https://doi.org/10.1111/asap.12253

Larkin, P. (23rd December 1980). Aubade. *Times Literary Supplement*.

Larkin, P. (1974). *High Windows*. London: Faber & Faber.

Larkin, P. (1964). *The Whitsun Weddings*. London: Faber & Faber.

Larkin, P. (1955). *The Less Deceived*. London: The Marvell Press.

Lawrence, A. (2008). Shame and narcissistic rage in autogynephilic transsexualism. *Archives of Sexual Behavior*, 37: 457–461.

Lawrence, D.H. (1960). *Lady Chatterley's Lover*. London: Penguin.

Lawson, N. (2008). *An Appeal to Reason: A Cool Look at Global Warming*. London: Overlook Duckworth.

Leader, D., Morgan, V. & Searby, P. (1988). *A History of the University of Cambridge: Volume 3, 1750–1870*. Cambridge: Cambridge University Press.

Leaders. (14th November 2014). The right to fright. *The Economist*, https://www.economist.com/leaders/2015/11/14/the-right-to-fright

Le Faye, D. (1998). *Jane Austen*. London: British Library.

Leeuwen, F., Dukes, A., Tybur, J. & Park, J. (2017). Disgust sensitivity relates to moral foundations independent of political ideology. *Evolutionary Behavioral Sciences,* 11: 92–98.

Leonard, V. (3rd April 2018). Northern Ireland Labour veteran says Corbyn fell short over anti-Semitism. *Belfast Telegraph*, https://www.belfasttelegraph.co.uk/news/northern-ireland/northern-ireland-labour-veteran-says-corbyn-fell-short-over-anti-semitism-36766907.html

Lester, J. (2nd June 2020). 'RIDICULOUS': Anne Boleyn viewers gobsmacked as pregnant queen locks lips with future wife of Henry VIII. *The Sun*, https://www.thesun.co.uk/tv/15137319/anne-boleyn-viewers-shocked-queen-kiss-henry-jane/

Levine, H., Jørgensen, N., Martino-Andrade, A. et al. (2017). Temporal trends in sperm count: A systematic review and meta-regression analysis. *Human Reproduction Update*, 23: 646–659.

Lindsay, J. (1952). *Byzantium into Europe: The Story of Byzantium as the First Europe (326–1204 A.D.) and Its Further Contribution Till 1453 A.D.* London: The Bodley Head.

Lin, C. & Bates, T.C. (2021). Each is to count for one and none for more than one: Predictors of support for economic redistribution. https://doi.org/10.31234/osf.io/3jq4c

Lippold, S., Xu, H., Ko, A. et al. (2014). Human paternal and maternal demographic histories: insights from high-resolution Y chromosome and mtDNA sequences. *Investigative Genetics*, 5: 13.

Livingston, G. (8th August 2019). Hispanic women no longer account for the majority of immigrant births in the U.S. *Pew Research Center*, https://www.pewresearch.org/fact-tank/2019/08/08/hispanic-women-no-longer-account-for-the-majority-of-immigrant-births-in-the-u-s/

Livingston, G. & Brown, A. (18th May 2017). Intermarriage in the U.S. 50 years after Loving v. Virginia. *Pew Research*, https://www.pewresearch.org/social-trends/2017/05/18/intermarriage-in-the-u-s-50-years-after-loving-v-virginia/

Logan, A.H.B. (1996). *Gnostic Truth and Christian Heresy: A Study in the History of Gnosticism*. London: A. & C. Black.

Lynn, R. (2020). *Memoirs of a Dissident Psychologist*. London: Ulster Institute for Social Research.

Lynn, R. (2013). Who discovered the Flynn effect? A review of early studies of the secular increase of intelligence. *Intelligence,* 4: 765–769.

Lynn, R. (2011). *Dysgenics: Genetic Deterioration in Modern Populations*. London: Ulster Institute for Social Research.

Lynn, R. (2001). *Eugenics: A Reassessment.* Westport, CT: Praeger.

Lynn, R. & Becker, D. (2019). *The Intelligence of Nations.* London: Ulster Institute for Social Research.

Lynn, R. & Vanhanen, T. (2012). *Intelligence: A Unifying Construct for the Social Sciences.* London: Ulster Institute for Social Research.

MacDonald, K. (2019). *Individualism and the Western Liberal Tradition: Evolutionary Origins, History, and Prospects for the Future.* Amazon KDP.

MacDonald, K. (2008). Effortful control, explicit processing, and the regulation of human evolved predispositions. *Psychological Review,* 115: 1012–1031.

MacDuffie, A. (2014). *Victorian Literature, Energy, and the Ecological Imagination.* Cambridge: Cambridge University Press.

Mahajan, V.D. (1966). *England Under the Tudors and Stuarts.* New Delhi: S. Chand. & Co.

Malthus, T. (1798). *An Essay on the Principle of Population.* London: J. Johnson.

Martin, J.A., Hamilton, B.E., Osterman, M.J. & Driscoll, A.K. (2019). Births: Final data for 2018. *National Vital Statistics Reports,* 68: 1–47.

Martin, T. (2008). *Ancient Greece: From Prehistoric to Hellenistic Times.* New Haven, CT: Yale University Press.

Martin, J. & Ruark, E. (2010). *The Fiscal Burden of Illegal Immigration on United States Taxpayers.* Washington, DC: Federation for American Immigration Reform.

Mayes, J. & Wheeler, D. (2002). *Regional Climates of the British Isles.* London: Routledge.

McEnery, T. (2004). *Swearing in English: Bad Language, Purity and Power from 1586 to the Present.* London: Routledge.

McGing, B. (2010). *Polybius's Histories.* Oxford: Oxford University Press.

McPherson, M., Smith-Lovin, L. & Cook, J. (2001). Birds of a feather: Homophily in social networks. *Annual Review of Sociology,* 27: 415–444.

McWilliams, J. (2000). *The 1960s Cultural Revolution.* Boulder, CO: Greenwood Publishing.

Media Matters Staff. (24th April 2017). Right Side Broadcasting, the 'unofficial version of Trump TV,' Forced to apologize for contributor's call to 'kill the globalists' at CNN. *Media Matters for America.* https://www.mediamatters.org/cnn/right-side-broadcasting-unofficial-version-trump-tv-forced-apologize-contributors-call-kill

Meisenberg, G. (2019). Social and reproductive success in the United States: The role of income, education and cognition. *Mankind Quarterly,* 59: 357–393.

Meisenberg, G. (2010). The reproduction of intelligence. *Intelligence,* 38: 220–230.

Meisenberg, G. (2007). *In God's Image: The Natural History of Intelligence and Ethics*. Kibworth: Book Guild Publishing.

Mews, S. (2012). The trials of *Lady Chatterley*, the modernist bishop and the Victorian archbishop: Clashes of class, culture and generations. *Studies in Church History*, 48: 449–464.

Mian, E. (4th May 2016). Sadiq Khan keeps his Muslim beliefs close to his chest — but he has no choice. *iNews,* https://inews.co.uk/opinion/comment/sadiq-khan-keeps-muslim-beliefs-close-chest-no-choice-5316

Miller, G. (2000). Mental traits as fitness indicators: expanding evolutionary psychology's adaptationism. *Annals of the New York Academy of Sciences*, 907: 62–125.

Miller, G. (2019). *Virtue Signaling: Essays on Darwinian Politics and Free Speech*. Cambrian Moon.

Mills, T. (2016). *The BBC: The Myth of Public Service*. London: Verso.

Moberg, M. (2018). *Engaging Anthropological Theory: A Social and Political History*. London: Routledge.

Moorhead, J. (2013). *The Roman Empire Divided: 400–700 AD*. London: Routledge.

Mordechai, L., Eisenberg, M., Newfield, T. et al. (2019). The Justinianic Plague: An inconsequential pandemic? *Proceedings of the National Academy of Sciences*, 116: 25546–25554.

Moritz, S., Göritz, A., McLean, B. et al. (2017). Do depressive symptoms predict paranoia or vice versa? *Journal of Behavior Therapy and Experimental Psychiatry*, 56: 113–121.

Morris, I. (2014). *War! What Is It Good For? Conflict and the Progress of Civilization from Primates to Robots*. New York: Farrar, Straus and Giroux.

Moss, J. & O'Connor, P. (2020). The Dark Triad traits predict authoritarian political correctness and alt-right attitudes. *Heliyon*, 6: e04453.

Mozafari, M., Farahbakhsh, R. & Crespi, N. (2020). Hate speech detection and racial bias mitigation in social media based on BERT model. *PLOS ONE*, 15(8): e0237861.

Mudde, C. (2000). *The Ideology of the Extreme Right*. Manchester: Manchester University Press.

Mulholland, C. (30th December 2005). Unmarried and same-sex couples free to adopt. *The Guardian,* https://www.theguardian.com/society/2005/dec/30/adoptionandfostering.childrensservices

Mullins, N., Ingason, A., Porter, H. et al. (2017). Reproductive fitness and genetic risk of psychiatric disorders in the general population. *Nature Communications*, 8: 1–6.

Murdock, G.P. & Provost, C. (1973). Measurement of cultural complexity. *Ethnology*, 12: 379–392.

Murray, C. (2012). *Coming Apart: The State of White America, 1960–2010.* New York: Crown Forum.

Naím, M. (2014). *The End of Power: From Boardrooms to Battlefields and Churches to States, Why Being in Charge Isn't What It Used to Be.* New York: Basic Books.

Nagesh, A. (22nd November 2020). US election 2020: Why Trump gained support among minorities. *BBC News,* https://www.bbc.com/news/world-us-canada-54972389

Navrady, I.B., Ritchie, S.J., Chan, S.W.Y. et al. (2017). Intelligence and neuroticism in relation to depression and psychological distress: Evidence from two large population cohorts. *European Psychiatry,* 43: 58–65.

Nettle, D. (2007). *Personality: What Makes You Who You Are.* Oxford: Oxford University Press.

Nettle, D. & Pollett, T. (2008). Natural selection on male wealth in humans. *American Naturalist,* 172: 658–666.

Neustaeter, B. (16th June 2020). The Earth's magnetic field is weakening and scientists don't know why. *CTV News,* https://www.ctvnews.ca/sci-tech/the-earth-s-magnetic-field-is-weakening-and-scientists-don-t-know-why-1.4986480

Newhall, C., Self, S., & Robock, A. (2018). Anticipating future Volcanic Explosivity Index (VEI) 7 eruptions and their chilling impacts. *Geosphere,* 14(2), 572–603.

Ngeleja, R., Luboobi, L. & Nkansah-Gyekye, Y. (2017). The effect of seasonal weather variation on the dynamics of the plague disease. *International Journal of Mathematics and Mathematical Sciences,* Article ID 5058085.

Ngo, A. (2021). *Unmasked: Inside Antifa's Radical Plan to Destroy Democracy.* New York: Center Street.

Nicol, D.M. (1974). Byzantium and England. *Balkan Studies,* 15: 173–203.

Norenzayan, A. (2013). *Big Gods: How Religion Transformed Cooperation and Conflict.* Princeton, NJ: Princeton University Press.

Norenzayan, A. & Shariff, A. (2008). The origin and evolution of religious prosociality. *Science,* 322: 58–62.

Nunn, P. (2007). *Climate, Environment, and Society in the Pacific During the Last Millennium.* Amsterdam: Elsevier.

Nyborg, H. (2012). The decay of Western civilization: Double relaxed Darwinian selection. *Personality and Individual Differences,* 53: 118–125.

O'Handley, B., Blair, K. & Hoskin, R. (2017). What do two men kissing and a bucket of maggots have in common? Heterosexual men's indistinguishable salivary α-amylase responses to photos of two men kissing and disgusting images. *Psychology and Sexuality,* 8: 171–188.

Oesterdiekhoff, G. & Vonderach, G. (2021). World history and societal evolution: Historical periods and psychological stages. *Mankind Quarterly,* 61: 820–853.

Ok, E., Qian, Y, Strejcek, B. & Aquino, K. (2020). Signaling virtuous victimhood as indicators of Dark Triad personalities. *Journal of Personality and Social Psychology,* https://doi.org/10.1037/pspp0000329

Oster, M. (18th February 2020). White nationalist Nick Fuentes' YouTube channel is banned for hate speech. *The Jerusalem Post,* https://www.jpost.com/diaspora/antisemitism/white-nationalist-nick-fuentes-youtube-channel-is-banned-for-hate-speech-617916

Ovid. (2016). Nux. *Loeb Classical Library,* http://www.loebclassics.com/view/ovid-walnut_tree/1929/pb_LCL232.295.xml?result=9&rskey=VaAITF

Paprota, M. (2020). *Constructing the Welfare State in the British Press: Boundaries and Metaphors in Political Discourse.* London: Bloomsbury Publishing.

Park, A., Bryson, C., Clery, E., Curtice, J. & Phillips, M. (Eds.) (2013). *British Social Attitudes: the 30th Report.* London: NatCen Social Research.

Pasia, N. (8th April 2020). How Washington survives without a state income tax. *SeattleMet,* https://www.seattlemet.com/news-and-city-life/2020/04/how-washington-survives-without-a-state-income-tax

Perkins, A. (2016). *The Welfare Trait: How State Benefits Affect Personality.* London: Palgrave Macmillan.

Perry, S. & Scheifer, C. (2019). Are the faithful becoming less fruitful? The decline of conservative protestant fertility and the growing importance of religious practice and belief in childbearing in the US. *Social Science Research,* 78: 137–155.

Peterson, R. & Palmer, C. (2017). Effects of physical attractiveness on political beliefs. *Politics and Life Sciences,* 36: 3–16.

Pew Research Center. (2016). 2016 campaign: Strong interest, widespread dissatisfaction. https://www.pewresearch.org/politics/2016/07/07/2016-campaign-strong-interest-widespread-dissatisfaction/

Pew Research Center. (2020). Religious landscape study: Liberals. https://www.pewforum.org/religious-landscape-study/political-ideology/liberal/

Phillips, T. (23rd July 2014) Near miss: The solar superstorm of July 2012. *NASA Science* https://science.nasa.gov/science-news/science-at-nasa/2014/23jul_superstorm

Piffer, D. (2018). Correlation between PGS and environmental variables. *RPubs,* https://rpubs.com/Daxide/377423

Pinker, S. (18th June 2012). The false allure of group selection. *The Edge,* https://www.edge.org/conversation/the-false-allure-of-group-selection

Piris, J.-C. (2017). Political and legal aspects of secessionism. In Closa, C. (Ed.). *Secession from a Member State and Withdrawal from the European Union: Troubled Membership.* Cambridge: Cambridge University Press.

Place, R. (1968). *Introduction to Archaeology.* New York: Philosophical Library.

Post, F. (1994). Creativity and psychopathology. *British Journal of Psychiatry,* 165: 22–34.

Pound, L.F. (1972). An Elizabethan census of the poor. *University of Birmingham Historical Journal,* 7: 142–160.

Purchase, S. (2006). *Key Concepts in Victorian Literature.* Basingstoke: Palgrave Macmillan.

Putnam, R. (2007). *E Pluribus Unum*: Diversity and community in the twenty-first century. The 2006 Johan Skytte Prize lecture. *Scandinavian Political Studies,* 30: 137–174.

Rector, R.E., Johnson, K.A., Noyes, L.R. & Martin, S. (2003). *The Harmful Effects of Early Sexual Activity and Multiple Sexual Partners Among Women: A Book of Charts.* Washington, DC: The Heritage Foundation.

Raley, R.K., Sweeney, M.M. & Wondra, D. (2015). The growing racial and ethnic divide in US marriage patterns. *The Future of Children,* 25: 89–109.

Ralph, P. & Coop, G. (2013). The geography of recent genetic ancestry across Europe. *PLOS Biology,* 11(5): e1001555.

Rathje, S., Van Bavel, J. & Van der Linden, S. (2021). Out-group animosity drives engagement on social media. *PNAS,* 118: e2024292118.

Ratner, P. (26th April 2018). 7 bizarre conspiracy theories that are actually true. *Big Think,* https://bigthink.com/paul-ratner/7-conspiracy-theories-that-are-actually-true

Rayner-Hilles, J.O.A. (2020). *GSS Simulator – Python.* https://github.com/occultus73/GSS-simulator-python/

Rayner-Hilles, J.O.A. (2019). *Public-Private Currencies.* Unpublished BSc dissertation: Faculty of Engineering and Science, University of Greenwich, London.

Reeve, C.L., Heeney, M.D. & Woodley of Menie, M.A. (2018). A systematic review of the state of the literature relating parental general cognitive ability and number of offspring. *Personality and Individual Differences,* 134: 107–118.

Reisner, S., Poteat, T., Keatley, J., Cabral, M. et al. (2016). Global health burden and needs of transgender populations: A review. *Lancet,* 388: 412–436.

Retraction Watch. (31st July 2020). Springer Nature retracts paper that hundreds called 'overtly racist.' https://retractionwatch.com/2020/07/31/springer-nature-retracts-paper-that-hundreds-called-overtly-racist/

Richardson, G.B., Sanning, B.K., Lai, M.H., Copping, L.T., Hardesty, P.H. & Kruger, D.J. (2017). On the psychometric study of human life history strategies. *Evolutionary Psychology,* 15(1): 1474704916666840.

Richerson, P., Baldini, R., Bell, A. & Demps, K. (2016). Cultural group selection plays an essential role in explaining human cooperation: A sketch of the evidence. *Brain and Behavioral Sciences,* 39: e30.

Ridley, J. (1988). *The Tudor Age.* London: Constable.

Ridley, J. (1986). *Henry VIII.* New York: Fromm International Publishing Corporation.

Rindermann, H. (2018). *Cognitive Capitalism: Human Capital and the Wellbeing of Nations.* Cambridge: Cambridge University Press.

Rindermann, H. & Becker, D. (2018). FLynn-effect and economic growth: Do national increases in intelligence lead to increases in GDP? *Intelligence,* 69: 87–93.

Ritter, R. & Preston, J. (2011). Gross gods and icky atheism: Disgust responses to rejected religious beliefs. *Journal of Experimental Psychology,* 47: 1225–1230.

Robinson, J.A.T. (1963). *Honest to God.* London: SCM Press.

Robinson, M. (4th February 2017). It would be incredibly difficult for California to pull off a 'Calexit' and secede from the US. *Insider,* https://www.businessinsider.com/calexit-california-versus-texas-texit-2017-2?r=US&IR=T

Rodger, H. & Grant, A. (4th May 2021). Anas Sarwar already recognised far more than Labour predecessor Richard Leonard. *Herald,* https://www.heraldscotland.com/news/19276690.anas-sarwar-recognised-far-labour-predecessor-richard-leonard/

Roes, F. & Raymond, M. (2003). Belief in moralizing gods. *Evolution and Human Behavior,* 24: 126–135.

Rossen, J. (1989). *Philip Larkin: His Life's Work.* Iowa City, IA: University of Iowa Press.

RT. (7th January 2021). Clinton, Obama and Bush ashamed of '3rd world banana republic' DC riot as Dems seek to impeach Trump for inciting 'insurrection'. https://www.rt.com/usa/511753-obama-bush-trump-capitol-impeach/

RT. (30th October 2020). 'What next, a white Rosa Parks?' Internet clashes over black model cast to play English Queen Anne Boleyn. https://www.rt.com/uk/505085-anne-boleyn-black-actress/

Ruder A. (1985). Paternal-age and birth-order effect on the human secondary sex ratio. *American Journal of Human Genetics,* 37: 362–372.

Rushton, A. (2008). *Royal Maladies: Inherited Diseases in the Ruling House of Europe.* Victoria, BC: Trafford Publishing.

Rushton, J.P. (2005). Ethic nationalism: Evolutionary psychology and genetic similarity theory. *Nations and Nationalism,* 11: 489–507.

Rushton, J.P. (1995). *Race, Evolution and Behavior: A Life History Perspective.* New Brunswick, NJ: Transaction.

Russell, B. (1916). *Principles of Social Reconstruction*. London: George Allen & Unwin.

Ryabinin, Y. (2017). The basic causes of the contemporary separatism. *Journal of Geography, Politics and Society*, 7: 5–9.

Ryan-Collins, J., Greenham, T., Werner, R. & Jackson, A. (2012). *Where Does Money Come From?* London: New Economics Foundation.

Ryan-Collins, J., Lloyd, T. & Macfarlane, L. (2017). *Rethinking the Economics of Land and Housing*. London: Zed Books Ltd.

Salway, P. (2001). *A History of Roman Britain*. Oxford: Oxford University Press.

Salter, F. (2007). *On Genetic Interests: Family, Ethnicity and Humanity in an Age of Mass Migration*. New Brunswick, NJ: Transaction Publishers.

Saroglou, V., Karim, M. & Day, J. (2020). Personality and values of deconverts: a function of current non-belief or prior religious socialisation? *Mental Health, Religion and Culture*, 23: 139–152.

Sarraf, M., Woodley of Menie, M.A. & Feltham, C. (2019). *Modernity and Cultural Decline: A Biobehavioral Perspective*. Basingstoke: Palgrave Macmillan.

Saunders, B. (18th March 1994). 'Warmly welcomed.' 32 new priests emerge at Bristol and 25 at Sheffield. *The Church Times*.

Schaff, P. (1891). *The Renaissance: The Revival of Learning and Art in the Fourteenth and Fifteenth Centuries*. London: G.P. Putnam's Sons.

Schenkler, B., Chambers, J. & Le Bon, B. (2012). Conservatives are happier than liberals, but why? Political ideology, personality, and life satisfaction. *Journal of Research in Personality*, 46: 127–146.

Schramm, J.-M. (2019). *Censorship and the Representation of the Sacred in Nineteenth-Century England*. Oxford: Oxford University Press.

Schulting, R.J. & Fibiger, L. (Eds.). (2012). *Sticks, Stones, and Broken Bones: Neolithic Violence in a European Perspective*. Oxford: Oxford University Press.

Schwabe, I., Jonker, W. & Van den Berg, S. (2016). Genes, culture and conservatism: A psychometric-genetic approach. *Behavior Genetics*, 46: 516–528.

Schönegger, P. (2021). What's up with anti-natalists? An observational study on the relationship between dark triad personality traits and anti-natalist views. *Philosophical Psychology*, doi: 10.1080/09515089.2021.1946026.

Scruton, R. (2014). *Our Church: A Personal History of the Church of England*. London: Atlantic Books.

Scruton, R. (2007). *A Political Philosophy: Arguments for Conservatism*. London: Bloomsbury.

Scruton, R. (2002). *The Meaning of Conservatism*. South Bend, IN: St. Augustine's Press.

Scruton, R. (2000). *Modern Culture*. London: Continuum.

Sear, R., Lawson, D.W., Kaplan, H. & Shenk, M.K. (2016). Understanding variation in human fertility: What can we learn from evolutionary demography? *Philosophical Transactions of the Royal Society B: Biological Sciences,* 371(1692): 20150144.

Sela, Y., Shackelford, T. & Liddle, J. (2015). When religion makes it worse: Religiously motivated violence as a sexual selection weapon. In Sloane, D. & Van Slyke, J. (Eds). *The Attraction of Religion: A New Evolutionary Psychology of Religion.* London: Bloomsbury.

Settembrini, D. (1976). Mussolini and the legacy of revolutionary socialism. *Journal of Contemporary History,* 11: 239–268.

Seymour-Ure, C. (2008). *Prime Ministers and the Media: Issues of Power and Control.* Oxford: Blackwell.

Shachtman, T. (2007). *Rumspringa: To Be Or Not To Be Amish.* New York: Farrar, Strauss & Giroux.

Shannon, C. & Klausner, J. (2018). The growing epidemic of sexually transmitted infections in adolescents: A neglected population. *Current Opinion in Pediatrics,* 30: 137–143.

Sharma, S. (27th February 2020). Why are there so many power cuts in India? Large amount of electricity produced is simply wasted. *Financial Express,* https://www.financialexpress.com/industry/why-are-there-so-many-power-cuts-in-india-large-amount-of-electricity-produced-is-simply-wasted/1882746/

Shaw, D. & Petrocik, J. (2020). *The Turnout Myth: Voting Rates and Partisan Outcomes in American National Elections.* Oxford: Oxford University Press.

Shepherd, R. (1996). *Enoch Powell.* London: Hutchinson.

Shields, J. (Fall 2018). The disappearing conservative professor. *National Affairs,* https://www.nationalaffairs.com/publications/detail/the-disappearing-conservative-professor

Shin, M.-S. (2018). *The Great Persecution: A Historical Re-examination.* Turnhout, Belgium: Brepols.

Simmel, G. (1957). Fashion. *American Journal of Sociology,* 62: 541–558.

Sivertsen, B. (2006). *The Parting of the Sea: How Volcanoes, Earthquakes, and Plagues Shaped the Story of Exodus.* Princeton, NJ: Princeton University Press.

Skirbekk, V. (2008). Fertility trends by social status. *Demographic Research,* 18: 145–180.

Soisalon-Soininen, J. (27th February 2017). Ex-natsi Holapan ehdokkuus vihreiden listalla sytytti sanasodan – 'Minä en lähtisi kyseenalaistamaan.' *Ilta Sanomat,* https://www.is.fi/kotimaa/art-2000005106718.html

Soto, C., John, O., Gosling, S. & Potter, J. (2011). Age differences in personality traits from 10 to 65: Big Five domains and facets in a large cross-sectional sample. *Journal of Personality and Social Psychology,* 100: 330–348.

Spengler, O. (1991). *The Decline of the West*. Oxford: Oxford University Press (Trans. Charles Francis Atkinson).

Stark, R. (2020). *The Rise of Christianity: A Sociologist Reconsiders History*. Princeton, NJ: Princeton University Press.

Starr, M. (19th May 2020). Yes, a solar minimum is coming. No, it's not going to mess up the world. *Science Alert*, https://www.sciencealert.com/we-re-about-to-experience-solar-minimum-here-s-what-that-really-means

Stein, S. (1992). *The Shaker Experience in America: A History of the United Society of Believers*. New Haven, CT: Yale University Press.

Stone, L. (18th November 2020). The conservative fertility advantage. *Institute of Family Studies*, https://ifstudies.org/blog/the-conservative-fertility-advantage

Stone, L. (2019). The size and composition of the Oxford student body, 1580–1909. In Stone, L. (Ed.). *The University in Society, Volume I: Oxford and Cambridge from the 14th to the Early 19th Century*. Princeton, NJ: Princeton University Press.

Swami, V., Voracek, M., Stieger, S., Tran, U.S. & Furnham, A. (2014). Analytic thinking reduces belief in conspiracy theories. *Cognition*, 133: 572–585.

Tacitus, P.C. (2014). Dialogue on oratory. *Delphi Complete Works of Tacitus*. Delphi Ancient Classics, Book 24.

Taleb, N.N. (2018). *Skin in the Game: Hidden Asymmetries in Daily Life*. New York: Random House.

Testot, L. (2020). *Cataclysms: An Environmental History of Humanity*. Chicago, IL: University of Chicago Press.

Timbs, J. (1862). *Curiosities of History: With New Lights: A Book for Old and Young*. London: C. Lockwood and Company.

TMZ. (27th February 2021). Bill Maher: Cancel culture is destroying America. https://www.tmz.com/2021/02/27/bill-maher-says-cancel-culture-destroying-america-bachelor/

Todd, M. (1977). *Famosa Pestis* and Britain in the fifth century. *Britannia*, 8: 319–325.

Torr, M. (11th November 2014). Not bad for a ginger kid! *Oldham Evening Chronicle*, https://www.oldham-chronicle.co.uk/news-features/101/features/88867/not-bad-for-a-ginger-kid

Tozer, J. (19th May 2009). Police replace Union Flag with gay rights banner to mark action day against homophobia. *Mail Online*, https://www.dailymail.co.uk/news/article-1184327/Police-replace-Union-Flag-gay-rights-banner-mark-action-day-homophobia.html

Trzaskowski, M., Haarlar, N., Arden, R. et al. (2014). Genetic influence on family socioeconomic status and children's intelligence. *Intelligence*, 42: 83–88.

Turchin, P. (2016). *Ages of Discord: A Structural-Demographic Analysis of American History*. Mansfield, CT: Beresta Books.

Turley, S. (2019). *The Return of Christendom: Demography, Politics, and the Coming Christian Majority*. Turley Talks.

Tweedy, J. (9th June 2020). Yorkshire Tea hits back at far-right YouTuber who praised the brand for not tweeting about Black Lives Matter—telling her 'please don't buy our tea again.' *Mail Online*, https://www.dailymail.co.uk/femail/article-8401949/Yorkshire-Tea-hits-far-right-YouTuber-anti-Black-Lives-Matter-tweet.html

Twenge, J. (2017). *iGen: Why Today's Super-Connected Kids Are Growing Up Less Rebellious, More Tolerant, Less Happy and Completely Unprepared for Adulthood and What That Means for the Rest of Us*. New York: Atria Books.

Udry, J.R., Li, R.M. & Hendrickson-Smith, J. (2003). Health and behavior risks of adolescents with mixed-race identity. *American Journal of Public Health*, 93: 1865–1870.

Vaas, R. (2009). God, gains and genes. In Voland, E. & Schiefenhövel, W. (Eds.). *The Biological Evolution of Religious Mind and Behavior*. New York: Springer.

Van Prooijen, J.-W. (2017). Why education predicts decreased belief in conspiracy theories. *Applied Cognitive Psychology*, 31: 50–58.

Vanhanen, T. (2012). *Ethnic Conflicts: The Biological Roots of Ethnic Nepotism*. London: Ulster Institute for Social Research.

Verhulst, B., Hatemi, P. & Martin, N. (2016). Corrigendum to 'The nature of the relationship between personality traits and political attitudes' [Personal. Individ. Differ. 49 (2010): 306–316]. *Personality and Individual Differences*, 99: 378–379.

Verhulst, B., Hatemi, P. & Martin, N. (2010). The nature of the relationship between personality traits and political attitudes. *Personality and Individual Differences*, 49: 306–316.

Vincent, J. (2016). *LGBT People and the UK Cultural Sector: The Response of Libraries, Museums, Archives and Heritage Since 1950*. London: Routledge.

Viola, F. (2005). *The Untold Story of the New Testament Church*. Shippensburg, PA: Destiny Image Publishing.

Volk, T. & Atkinson, J. (2008). Is child death the crucible of human evolution? *Journal of Social, Evolutionary, and Cultural Psychology*, 2: 103–116.

Wagler, R. (2011). The anthropocene mass extinction: An emerging curriculum theme for science educators. *The American Biology Teacher*, 73: 78–83.

Walker, C. (1988). *Wonders of the Ancient World*. Macdonald's Popular Press.

Walker, M. (1977). *The National Front*. London: Fontana/Collins.

Walsham, A. (1999). *Church Papists: Catholicism, Conformity, and Confessional Polemic in Early Modern England*. Woodbridge: The Boydell Press.

Wang, M., Fuerst, J. & Ren, J. (2016). Evidence of dysgenic fertility in China. *Intelligence,* 57: 15-24.

Ward, P. (2006). *Out of Thin Air: Dinosaurs, Birds, and Earth's Ancient Atmosphere.* Washington, DC: Joseph Henry Press.

Waris, O. (19th September 2016). Suomen vastarintaliikkeen ex-johtaja Iltalehdelle: Pahin pelkoni toteutui. *Ilta-Lehti,* https://www.iltalehti.fi/uutiset/a/2016091922341291

Warner, P. (1972). *British Battlefields: The Midlands.* Oxford: Osprey Publishing.

Waytz, A., Iyer, R., Young, L., Haidt, J. & Graham, J. (2019). Ideological differences in the expanse of the moral circle. *Nature Communications,* 10: 1-12.

Webb, S. (2020). *Suffragette Fascists: Emmeline Pankhurst and Her Right-Wing Followers.* Barnsley: Pen & Sword.

West, B. & Scafetta, N. (2010). *Disrupted Networks: From Physics to Climate Change.* London: World Scientific.

West, E. (19th June 2021). The self-loathing of Britain's elites. *UnHerd,* https://unherd.com/2021/06/the-self-loathing-of-britains-elites/

West, R., Meserve, R. & Stanovich, K. (2012). Cognitive sophistication does not attenuate the bias blind spot. *Journal of Personality and Social Psychology,* 103: 506-519.

White, E. (1888). *The Great Controversy Between Christ and Satan During the Christian Dispensation.* New York: Pacific Press Publishing.

Whitehouse, H., Francois, P., Savage, E. et al. (2019). Complex societies precede moralizing gods throughout world history. *Nature,* 568: 226-229.

Williams, J. (2016). *Academic Freedom in an Age of Conformity: Confronting the Fear of Knowledge.* Basingstoke: Palgrave Macmillan.

Wilson, D.S. (2002). *Darwin's Cathedral: Evolution, Religion, and the Nature of Society.* Chicago, IL: University of Chicago Press.

Wilson, E.O. (2012). *The Social Conquest of Earth.* New York: W.W. Norton.

Wilson, E.O. (1998). *Consilience: Towards the Unity of Knowledge.* New York: Alfred A. Knopf.

Wilson, G. (2013). *The Psychology of Conservatism.* London: Routledge.

Wolfinger, N.H. (2018). *Promiscuous America: Smart, Secular, and Somewhat Less Happy.* Charlottesville, VA: Institute for Family Studies. https://ifstudies.org/blog/promiscuous-america-smart-secular-and-somewhat-less-happy

Wood, R., Hood, P. & Spilka, B. (2009). *The Psychology of Religion: An Empirical Approach.* London: Guildford Press.

Woodley of Menie, M.A., Sarraf, M.A., Peñaherrera-Aguirre, M., Fernandes, H.B.F. & Becker, D. (2018). What caused over a century of decline in general intelligence? Testing predictions from the genetic selection and neurotoxin hypotheses. *Evolutionary Psychological Science,* 4:3, 272-284.

Woodley of Menie, M.A., Sarraf, M., Pestow, R. & Fernandes, H. (2017). Social epistasis amplifies the fitness costs of deleterious mutations, engendering rapid fitness decline among modernized populations. *Evolutionary Psychological Science,* 3: 181–191.

Woodley of Menie, M.A. & Dunkel, C. (2015). Beyond the cultural mediation hypothesis: A reply to Dutton (2013). *Intelligence,* 49: 186–191.

Woodley of Menie, M.A. & Fernandes, H.B.F. (2015). Showing their true colours: Secular declines and a Jensen effect on colour acuity — more evidence for the weaker variant of Spearman's other hypothesis. *Personality and Individual Differences,* 88: 280–284.

Woodley of Menie, M.A., Fernandes, H., Figueredo, A.J. & Meisenberg, G. (2015). By their words ye shall know them: Evidence of genetic selection against general intelligence and concurrent environmental enrichment in vocabulary usage since the mid-19th century. *Frontiers in Psychology,* 6: 361. https://doi.org/10.3389/fpsyg.2015.00361

Woodley, M.A. & Figueredo, A.J. (2013). *Historical Variability in Heritable General Intelligence: Its Evolutionary Origins and Socio-Cultural Consequences.* Buckingham: University of Buckingham Press.

Wu, S. & Resnick, P. (2021). Cross-partisan discussions on YouTube: Conservatives talk to liberals but liberals don't talk to conservatives. *arXiv*: 2104.05365.

Yilmaz, O., Harma, M., Bahcekapili, H. & Cesur, S. (2016). Validation of the Moral Foundations Questionnaire in Turkey and its relation to cultural schemas of individualism and collectivism. *Personality and Individual Differences,* 99: 149–154.

You, W. & Henneberg, M. (2016). Type 1 diabetes prevalence increasing globally and regionally: The role of natural selection and life expectancy at birth. *BMJ Open Diabetes Research and Care,* 4: e000161.

You, W. & Henneberg, M. (2017). Cancer incidence increasing globally: The role of relaxed natural selection. *Evolutionary Applications,* 11: 140–152.

You, W. & Henneberg, M. (2018). Relaxed natural selection contributes to global obesity increase more in males than in females due to more environmental modifications in female body mass. *PLOS ONE,* 13: e0199594.

Yu, R. (2016). Stress potentiates decision biases: A stress induced deliberation-to-intuition (SIDI) model. *Neurobiology of Stress,* 3: 83–95.

Yurco, F.J. (1999). End of the late Bronze Age and other crisis periods: A volcanic cause. In Teeter, E. & Larsen J.A. (Eds). *Gold of Praise: Studies on Ancient Egypt in Honor of Edward F. Wente.* Chicago, IL: The Oriental Institute of the University of Chicago.

Zhang, D.D., Lee, H.F., Wang, C. et al. (2011). The causality analysis of climate change and large-scale human crises. *Proceedings of the National Academy of Sciences,* 108: 17296–17301.

Zharkova, V. (2020). Modern grand solar minimum will lead to terrestrial cooling. *Temperature,* 7: 217–222.

Ziegler, P. (1969). *The Black Death.* London: Collins.

Zimmerman, C. (2014). *Family and Civilization.* New York: Open Road Media.

Zuckerman, P. (2011). *Faith No More: Why People Reject Religion.* Oxford: Oxford University Press.

Zúquete, J.P. (2018). *The Identitarians: The Movement Against Globalism and Islam in Europe.* Notre Dame, IN: University of Notre Dame Press.

About the Authors

Edward Dutton is a researcher based in Oulu in northern Finland. Born in London in 1980, Dutton read Theology at Durham University before completing a PhD in Religious Studies at Aberdeen University in 2006. This was developed into his first book: *Meeting Jesus at University: Rites of Passage and Student Evangelicals* (2008). He was made 'Docent' (Adjunct Reader) of the Anthropology of Religion and Finnish Culture at Oulu University in 2011. In 2012, however, Dutton made the move to evolutionary psychology. Since then, Dutton has published in leading psychology journals including *Intelligence* and *Personality and Individual Differences*. He has been a guest researcher in the Psychology Department at Umeå University in Sweden and is academic consultant to a research group in the Special Education Department at King Saud University in Riyadh. In 2020, he was appointed Professor of Evolutionary Psychology at Asbiro University, a business-focused university of applied sciences in Łódź, Poland. Dutton's research has been reported worldwide. He runs a popular internet channel, *The Jolly Heretic,* in which he explores daring scientific research. Dutton is the author of many books, most recently, *Witches, Feminism, and the Fall of the West* (2021), *Islam: An Evolutionary Perspective* (2020), and *Churchill's Headmaster: The 'Sadist' Who Nearly Saved the British Empire* (2019).

J.O.A. Rayner-Hilles is an independent researcher and software engineer based in Caterham in Surrey. He was born there in 1995 and has a degree in Information Technology from Greenwich University in London. Rayner-Hilles is an Associate Member of the British Computer Society. He is the author of the GSS Python Simulator used to make the predictions in this book. He works with Dutton behind the scenes on his internet channel *The Jolly Heretic. The Past is a Future Country* is his first book.